REA's Test Prep Books Are The Best!
(a sample of the hundreds of letters REA receives each year)

" I studied this guide exclusively and passed the [CLEP Introductory Sociology] test with 12 points to spare. "
Student, Dallas, TX

" This [REA] book was much better than reading a college textbook. Get it, it's worth it! By the way, I passed [the CLEP test] with flying colors!!! "
Student, Washington, DC

" Your book was such a better value and was so much more complete than anything your competition has produced — and I have them all! "
Teacher, Virginia Beach, VA

" Compared to the other books that my fellow students had, your book was the most useful in helping me get a great score. "
Student, North Hollywood, CA

" Your book was responsible for my success on the exam, which helped me get into the college of my choice... I will look for REA the next time I need help. "
Student, Chesterfield, MO

" Just a short note to say thanks for the great support your book gave me in helping me pass the test... I'm on my way to a B.S. degree because of you! "
Student, Orlando, FL

(more on next page)

(continued from front page)

" I just wanted to thank you for helping me get a great score
on the AP U.S. History exam... Thank you for making great test preps! "
Student, Los Angeles, CA

" Your *Fundamentals of Engineering Exam* book was the absolute best
preparation I could have had for the exam, and it is one of the major
reasons I did so well and passed the FE on my first try. "
Student, Sweetwater, TN

" I used your book to prepare for the test and found that the advice and the
sample tests were highly relevant... Without using any other material, I earned
very high scores and will be going to the graduate school of my choice. "
Student, New Orleans, LA

" What I found in your book was a wealth of information sufficient to shore up
my basic skills in math and verbal... The section on analytical ability was
excellent. The practice tests were challenging and the answer explanations most
helpful. It certainly is the *Best Test Prep for the GRE!* "
Student, Pullman, WA

" I really appreciate the help from your excellent book. Please keep up
the great work. "
Student, Albuquerque, NM

" I am writing to thank you for your test preparation... your book helped me
immeasurably and I have nothing but praise for your *GRE* preparation."
Student, Benton Harbor, MI

THE BEST TEST PREPARATION FOR THE

CLEP

Financial Accounting

Donald P. Balla, CPA
John Brown University
Siloam Springs, Arkansas

Research & Education Association
Visit our website at:
www.rea.com

Research & Education Association
61 Ethel Road West
Piscataway, New Jersey 08854
E-mail: info@rea.com

The Best Test Preparation for the
CLEP FINANCIAL ACCOUNTING EXAM

Printed in the United States of America

Library of Congress Control Number 2007927668

ISBN 13: 978-0-7386-0313-1
ISBN 10: 0-7386-0313-9

REA® is a registered trademark of
Research & Education Association, Inc.

About Our Author

Donald P. Balla has taught at John Brown University in Arkansas since 1985, although not all of his classes have been within the Business Division. He has taught regular day students and degree completion (advanced) students. He is a self-described educational experimenter and divergent thinker who was recognized as an outstanding teacher of the year in 2005.

Mr. Balla is also a licensed attorney, certified public accountant, and an accomplished musician. "I started out as a musician," he says. "Trying to make a living as a musician turned me into an accountant." Today, most of his legal work is pro bono for the area's expanding Hispanic population.

In a diverse career that spans more than 30 years, he has taught a variety of courses under the subjects of accounting, law, taxes, business, economics, computer programs, music, and art. His unusual Basic Economics class has received national attention among Christian business faculty. "One semester," he says, "a class ran a deficit, extravagantly increased their own grades, and then left the deficit for an honors class to pay off."

Mr. Balla received a master's degree in Music and Composition from Florida State University, an M.S in Financial Services from American College in Pennsylvania, and a Juris Doctor from the University of Arkansas.

Classical guitarist, novelist, electrician, public speaker, and Vietnam veteran, Mr. Balla lives with his wife of 37 years, Judy, within strolling distance of the campus.

About Research & Education Association

Founded in 1959, Research & Education Association (REA) is dedicated to publishing the finest and most effective educational materials—including software, study guides, and test preps—for students in middle school, high school, college, graduate school, and beyond.

REA's test preparation series includes books and software for all academic levels in almost all disciplines. REA publishes test preps for students who have not yet entered high school, as well as high school students preparing to enter college. Students from countries around the world seeking to attend college in the United States will find the assistance they need in REA's publications. For college students seeking advanced degrees, REA publishes test preps for many major graduate school admission examinations in a wide variety of disciplines, including engineering, law, and medicine. Students at every level, in every field, with every ambition can find what they are looking for among REA's publications.

REA's series presents tests that accurately depict the official exams in both degree of difficulty and types of questions. REA's practice tests are always based upon the most recently administered exams, and include every type of question that can be expected on the actual exams.

Today REA's wide-ranging catalog is a leading resource for teachers, students, and professionals.

We invite you to visit us at *www.rea.com* to find out how "REA is making the world smarter."

Acknowledgments

In addition to our author, we would like to thank Larry B. Kling, Vice President, Editorial, for his overall guidance, which brought this publication to completion; Pam Weston, Vice President, Publishing, for setting the quality standards for production integrity and managing the publication to completion; Diane Goldschmidt, Senior Editor, for project management; Alice Leonard, Senior Editor and Molly Solanki, Associate Editor, for pre-flight editorial review; Rachel DeMatteo, Graphic Artist, for designing the pages; Christine Saul, Senior Graphic Designer, for our cover design; and Jeff LoBalbo, Senior Graphic Designer, for post-production file mapping.

We also gratefully acknowledge Sandra Rush for copyediting the manuscript and Kathy Caratozzolo of Caragraphics for typesetting this edition.

Preface

You can do it!

You can learn enough from this book to pass the CLEP Financial Accounting exam.

This book contains all the information you would find in the first college semester of financial accounting. If you learn it well, you could move on to the second semester (usually managerial accounting) or on to intermediate financial accounting. Or . . . you can pass financial accounting, breathe a sigh of relief and call it the end of your accounting career.

Learning accounting is like learning to play the piano. Practice makes perfect. No matter what your background, grasping accounting from a book takes discipline. But this book is designed for you even if you have a special advantage such as:

- You studied accounting in high school, or

- You have used some accounting in your job, or

- You took a college financial accounting course and, unfortunately, flunked.

What you need now is a tool to help you store the necessary information in your brain so you can move on in your career. This book is that tool.

For more than twenty-five years, I have helped students like you pass tests like the CLEP Financial Accounting exam. I have encouraged and prodded hundreds of students who at first cried, "I can't!" but who in the end cheered, "I *did*!"

If you had the courage to pick up this book, I believe you are another successful CLEP candidate in the making.

My best wishes go with you.

Respectfully,

Donald P. Balla

CONTENTS

CLEP FINANCIAL ACCOUNTING
Independent Study Schedule

The following study schedule allows for thorough preparation for the CLEP Financial Accounting exam. Although it is designed for six weeks, it can be reduced to a three-week course by collapsing each two-week period into one. Be sure to set aside enough time—at least two hours each day—to study. But no matter which study schedule works best for you, the more time you spend studying, the more prepared and relaxed you will feel on the day of the exam.

Week	Activity
1	Read and study Chapter 1 of this book, which will introduce you to the CLEP Financial Accounting exam. Then take Practice Test 1 to determine your strengths and weaknesses. Assess your results by using our raw score conversion table. You can then determine the areas in which you need to strengthen your skills.
2 & 3	Carefully read and study Chapters 2 through 10 of the CLEP Financial Accounting review. Familiarize yourself with the Vocabulary List, Accounting Principles and Formulas, and Journal Entries sections found at the end of each chapter. Make memory cards for information you need to study more.
4 & 5	Carefully read and study Chapters 11 through 20 of the CLEP Financial Accounting review. Familiarize yourself with the Vocabulary List, Accounting Principles and Formulas, and Journal Entries sections found at the end of each chapter. Make memory cards for information you need to study more.
6	Take Practice Test 2 and carefully review the explanations for all incorrect answers. If there are any types of questions or particular subjects that seem difficult to you, review those subjects by again studying the appropriate sections of the review material in this book.

Note: If you care to, and time allows, retake Practice Tests 1 and 2. This will help strengthen the areas in which your performance may still be lagging and build your overall confidence.

CHAPTER 1

Passing the CLEP Financial Accounting Exam

Chapter 1

Passing the CLEP Financial Accounting Exam

ABOUT THIS BOOK

This book provides you with complete preparation for the CLEP Financial Accounting exam. Inside you will find a targeted review of the subject matter, as well as tips and strategies for test taking. We also give you two full-length practice tests, featuring content and formatting based on the official CLEP Financial Accounting exam. Our practice tests contain every type of question that you can expect to encounter on the actual exam. Following each practice test you will find an answer key with detailed explanations designed to help you more completely understand the test material.

All CLEP exams are computer-based. As you can see, the practice tests in our book are presented as paper-and-pencil exams. The content and format of the actual CLEP subject exams are faithfully mirrored. Later in this chapter you'll find a detailed outline of the format and content of the CLEP Financial Accounting exam.

ABOUT THE EXAM

Who takes CLEP exams and what are they used for?

CLEP (College-Level Examination Program) examinations are typically taken by people who have acquired knowledge outside the classroom and wish to bypass certain college courses and earn college credit. The CLEP is designed to reward students for learning—no matter where or how that knowledge was acquired. The CLEP is the most widely accepted credit-by-examination program in the country, with more than 2,900 colleges and universities granting credit for satisfactory scores on CLEP exams.

Although most CLEP examinees are adults returning to college, many graduating high school seniors, enrolled college students, military personnel, and international students also take the exams to earn college credit or to demonstrate their ability to perform at the college level. There are no prerequisites, such as age or educational status, for taking CLEP examinations. However, because policies on granting credits vary among colleges, you should contact the particular institution from which you wish to receive CLEP credit.

There are two categories of CLEP examinations:

1. **CLEP General Examinations** are five separate tests that cover material usually taken as requirements during the first two years of college. CLEP General Examinations are available for English Composition (with or without essay), Humanities, Mathematics, Natural Sciences, and Social Sciences and History.

2. **CLEP Subject Examinations** include material usually covered in an undergraduate course with a similar title. For a complete list of the subject examinations offered, visit the College Board website.

Who administers the exam?

The CLEP exams are developed by the College Board, administered by Educational Testing Service (ETS), and involve the assistance of educators throughout the United States. The test development process is designed and implemented to ensure that the content and difficulty level of the test are appropriate.

When and where is the exam given?

The CLEP Financial Accounting exam is administered each month throughout the year at more than 1,300 test centers in the United States and can be arranged for candidates abroad on request. To find the test center nearest you and to register for the exam, you should obtain a copy of the free booklets *CLEP Colleges* and *CLEP Information for Candidates and Registration Form*. They are available at most colleges where CLEP credit is granted, or by contacting:

CLEP Services
P.O. Box 6600
Princeton, NJ 08541-6600
Phone: (800) 257-9558 (8 a.m. to 6 p.m. ET)
Fax: (609) 771-7088
Website: *www.collegeboard.com/clep*

CLEP Options for Military Personnel and Veterans

CLEP exams are available free of charge to eligible military personnel and eligible civilian employees. All the CLEP exams are available at test centers on college campuses and military bases. In addition, the College Board has developed a paper-based version of 14 high-volume/high-pass-rate CLEP tests for DANTES Test Centers. Contact the Educational Services Officer or Navy College Education Specialist for more information. Visit the College Board website for details about CLEP opportunities for military personnel.

Eligible U.S. veterans can claim reimbursement for CLEP exams and administration fees pursuant to provisions of the Veterans Benefits Improvement Act of 2004. For details on eligibility and submitting a claim for reimbursement, visit the U.S. Department of Veterans Affairs website at *www. gibill.va.gov/pamphlets/testing.htm*.

SSD Accommodations for Students with Disabilities

Many students qualify for extra time to take the CLEP Financial Accounting exam, but you must make these arrangements in advance. For information, contact:

> College Board Services for Students with Disabilities
> P.O. Box 6226
> Princeton, NJ 08541-6226
> Phone: (609) 771-7137 (Monday through Friday, 8 a.m. to 6 p.m. ET)
> TTY: (609) 882-4118
> Fax: (609) 771-7944
> E-mail: ssd@info.collegeboard.org

HOW TO USE THIS BOOK

What do I study first?

Read over the course review and the suggestions for test-taking, take the first practice test to determine your area(s) of weakness, and then go back and focus your study on those specific problems. Studying the reviews thoroughly will reinforce the basic skills you will need to do well on the exam. Make sure to take the practice tests to become familiar with the format and procedures involved with taking the actual exam.

To best utilize your study time, follow our Independent Study Schedule, which you'll find in the front of this book. The schedule is based on a six-week program, but can be condensed if necessary by collapsing each two-week period into one.

When should I start studying?

It is never too early to start studying for the CLEP Financial Accounting exam. The earlier you begin, the more time you will have to sharpen your skills. Do not procrastinate! The sooner you learn the format of the exam, the more time you will have to familiarize yourself with it.

FORMAT AND CONTENT OF THE EXAM

The CLEP Financial Accounting exam covers the material one would find in a college-level Financial Accounting class. The exam assesses the student's knowledge and mastery of the skills and concepts found in an entry-level financial accounting course, including familiarity with accounting concepts and terminology, understanding and analyzing accounting data, and applying accounting techniques to problem-solving situations.

The exam consists of 75 multiple-choice questions, each with five possible answer choices, to be answered in 90 minutes.

The approximate breakdown of topics is as follows:

20–30%	General Topics
20–30%	The Income Statement
30–40%	The Balance Sheet
5–10%	Statement of Cash Flows
< 5%	Miscellaneous

ABOUT OUR COURSE REVIEW

The review in this book provides you with a complete background of all the important accounting principles and theories relevant to the exam. It will help reinforce the facts you have already learned while better shaping your understanding of the discipline as a whole. By using the review in conjunction with the practice tests, you should be well prepared to take the CLEP Financial Accounting exam.

SPECIAL TOOLS IN THIS BOOK

In addition to the thorough review provided, our book is filled with exercises, questions and answers to reinforce what you just learned about financial accounting. Special icons appear throughout the course review that highlight nuggets of information to help your studies. Look for the "CLEP Clues" and "Accounting Principle" icons throughout the review chapters.

CLEP Cram. To successfully pass the CLEP Financial Accounting exam, you will need to remember vocabulary, accounting principles, formulas and journal entries. All the necessary facts are conveniently listed at the end of each chapter under the "CLEP Cram" section. We suggest you make a memory card for each fact and review it until you feel confident and at ease with the information.

SCORING YOUR PRACTICE TESTS

How do I score my practice tests?

The CLEP Financial Accounting exam is scored on a scale of 20 to 80. To score your practice tests, count up the number of correct answers. This is your total raw score. Convert your raw score to a scaled score using the conversion table on the following page. (Note: The conversion table provides only an estimate of your scaled score. Scaled scores can and do vary over time, and in no case should a sample test be taken as a precise predictor of test performance. Nonetheless, our scoring table allows you to judge your level of performance within a reasonable scoring range.)

When will I receive my score report?

The test administrator will print out a full Candidate Score Report for you immediately upon your completion of the exam (except for CLEP English Composition with Essay). Your scores are reported only to you, unless you ask to have them sent elsewhere. If you want your scores reported to a college or other institution, you must say so when you take the examination. Since your scores are kept on file for 20 years, you can also request transcripts from Educational Testing Service at a later date.

STUDYING FOR THE CLEP

It is very important for you to choose the time and place for studying that works best for you. Some students may set aside a certain number of

PRACTICE-TEST RAW SCORE CONVERSION TABLE *

Raw Score	Scaled Score	Course Grade	Raw Score	Scaled Score	Course Grade
75	80	A	37	50	C
74	79	A	36	49	D
73	78	A	35	48	D
72	78	A	34	47	D
71	77	A	33	46	D
70	76	A	32	46	D
69	75	A	31	45	D
68	74	A	30	44	D
67	74	A	29	43	D
66	73	A	28	42	D
65	72	A	27	42	D
64	71	A	26	41	D
63	70	A	25	40	D
62	70	A	24	39	F
61	69	B	23	38	F
60	68	B	22	38	F
59	67	B	21	37	F
58	66	B	20	36	F
57	66	B	19	35	F
56	65	B	18	34	F
55	64	B	17	34	F
54	63	B	16	33	F
53	62	B	15	32	F
52	62	B	14	31	F
51	61	B	13	30	F
50	60	C	12	30	F
49	59	C	11	29	F
48	58	C	10	28	F
47	58	C	9	27	F
46	57	C	8	26	F
45	56	C	7	26	F
44	55	C	6	25	F
43	54	C	5	24	F
42	54	C	4	23	F
41	53	C	3	22	F
40	52	C	2	21	F
39	51	C	1	20	F
38	50	C	0	20	F

*This table is provided for scoring REA practice tests only. The American Council on Education recommends that colleges use a single across-the-board credit-granting score of 50 for all CLEP computer-based exams. Nonetheless, on account of the different skills being measured and the unique content requirements of each test, the actual number of correct answers needed to reach 50 will vary. A 50 is calibrated to equate with performance that would warrant the grade C in the corresponding introductory college course.

hours every morning, while others may choose to study at night before going to sleep. Other students may study during the day, while waiting on a line, or even while eating lunch. Only you can determine when and where your study time will be most effective. But be consistent and use your time wisely. Work out a study routine and stick to it!

When you take the practice tests, try to make your testing conditions as much like the actual test as possible. Turn your television and radio off, and sit down at a quiet table free from distraction. Make sure to time yourself. Start off by setting a timer for the time that is allotted for each section, and be sure to reset the timer for the appropriate amount of time when you start a new section.

As you complete each practice test, score your test and thoroughly review the explanations to the questions you answered incorrectly; however, do not review too much at one time. Concentrate on one problem area at a time by reviewing the question and explanation, and by studying our review until you are confident that you completely understand the material.

TEST-TAKING TIPS

Although you may not be familiar with computer-based standardized tests such as the CLEP Financial Accounting exam, there are many ways to acquaint yourself with this type of examination and to help alleviate your test-taking anxieties. Listed below are ways to help you become accustomed to the CLEP, some of which may be applied to other standardized tests as well.

Read all of the possible answers. Just because you think you have found the correct response, do not automatically assume that it is the best answer. Read through each choice to be sure that you are not making a mistake by jumping to conclusions.

Use the process of elimination. Go through each answer to a question and eliminate as many of the answer choices as possible. By eliminating just two answer choices, you give yourself a better chance of getting the item correct, since there will only be three choices left from which to make your guess. Remember, your score is based only on the number of questions you answer correctly.

Work quickly and steadily. You will have only 90 minutes to work on 75 questions, so work quickly and steadily to avoid focusing on any one question too long. Taking the practice tests in this book will help you learn to budget your time.

Acquaint yourself with the computer screen. Familiarize yourself with the CLEP computer screen beforehand by logging on to the College Board website. Waiting until test day to see what it looks like in the pretest tutorial risks injecting needless anxiety into your testing experience. Also, familiarizing yourself with the directions and format of the exam will save you valuable time on the day of the actual test.

Be sure that your answer registers before you go to the next item. Look at the screen to see that your mouse-click causes the pointer to darken the proper oval. This takes less effort than darkening an oval on paper, but don't lull yourself into taking less care!

THE DAY OF THE EXAM

On the day of the test, you should wake up early (hopefully after a decent night's rest) and have a good breakfast. Make sure to dress comfortably, so that you are not distracted by being too hot or too cold while taking the test. Also plan to arrive at the test center early. This will allow you to collect your thoughts and relax before the test, and will also spare you the anxiety that comes with being late. As an added incentive to make sure you arrive early, keep in mind that no one will be allowed into the test session after the test has begun.

Before you leave for the test center, make sure that you have your admission form and another form of identification, which must contain a recent photograph, your name, and signature (i.e., driver's license, student identification card, or current alien registration card). You will not be admitted to the test center if you do not have proper identification.

If you would like, you may wear a watch to the test center. However, you may not wear one that makes noise, because it may disturb the other test-takers. No dictionaries, textbooks, notebooks, briefcases, or packages will be permitted and drinking, smoking, and eating are prohibited.

Good luck on the CLEP Financial Accounting exam!

▼
CHAPTER 2
Getting Started

Chapter 2

Getting Started:
Discovering the Balance Sheet

Welcome to financial accounting. Financial accounting is the skill of producing financial statements from business transactions.

In this chapter you will learn:

- How to analyze business start-up transactions.
- How to present those transactions on a balance sheet.
- How to analyze the balance sheet.
- About the accounting cycle and the fiscal year.

2.1. BALLOON PARTY, LAUREN'S NEW BUSINESS

Lauren's business idea is to sell balloons at all the county fairs in the state. A supplier will provide balloons at prices from 2¢ to 25¢ each. A large tank of helium costs $500 initially and only $50 to fill. Cousin Lou agrees to sell his $2,000 Pontiac to Lauren for $100 down and 19 monthly payments at 12% interest. Lauren hands Lou a $100 bill.

Lauren transfers $800 from her savings account into a new checking account called "Balloon Party." She writes two checks. One for $550 goes to buy a filled helium tank. Another check for $70 buys balloons.

2.2. LAUREN'S FIRST ACCOUNTING

Accounting helps Lauren record her business transactions.

Accounting Principle

*Every transaction gets recorded twice: (1) where the money comes from, and (2) where it goes. This is called **double entry accounting**.*

13

Table 2-1. Analyzing Balance Sheet Transactions

Description	Amount of money	Where did it come from?	Where did it go?
Open the business checking account	$800	Owner's savings account	Business checking account
Buy the canister of helium	$550	Business checking account	Canister $500 Helium $50
Buy balloons	$70	Business checking account	Supplies of balloons
Buy the Pontiac	$2,000	Lauren $100 Loan $1,900	Car

The $500 that Lauren paid to buy the canister is not gone. It has simply transformed from cash into another useful item. The same happened with the car and the supplies of balloons and helium. The money was not expensed (gone forever) but **capitalized**—that is, changed into **capital**, another asset that helps you make money. In the next chapter, you will learn how to record a transaction in which the owner spends money and has nothing to show for it. For now, Lauren has not lost any money, as this analysis shows.

Where did the money go?
or
Here's what the business has.

Cash—business checking account (+$800 − $550 − $70)	$ 180
Supply of balloons	70
Helium supply	50
Canister	500
Car	2,000
Total	$2,800

Where did the money come from?
or
Here's who has a claim on what the business has.

What the business owes to Cousin Lou	$1,900
What belongs to Lauren (+$800 savings + $100 down payment)	900
Total	$2,800

This is Lauren's first accounting report—a **balance sheet**. What she has ($2,800) balances the *claims* on what she has (also $2,800).

> **QUESTION 1.** It must balance. Why? (The answers to these questions are always at the end of each chapter.)

When "Where did it go?" equals "Where did it come from?" Lauren has **balanced books**.

2.3. THE BALANCE SHEET INTRODUCED

Let's rewrite the balance sheet using some standard terminology.

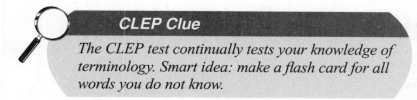

CLEP Clue

The CLEP test continually tests your knowledge of terminology. Smart idea: make a flash card for all words you do not know.

Figure 2-1. Balloon Party's Balance Sheet: 4/14/20x1

Balloon Party
Balance Sheet
As of April 14, 20x1

❶

❷ ASSETS

Cash—business checking account	$180
Supply of balloons	70
❸ Helium supply	50
Canister	500
Car	2,000
Total Assets	$2,800

❹ LIABILITIES

Loan Payable—Cousin Lou	$1,900

❺ OWNER'S EQUITY

❻ Owner's equity	900
Total Liabilities plus Owner's Equity	$2,800

❶ The **heading**. All financial statements have a three-line heading. The first line is the business name. The second is the name of the report. The third is the date or period of time. Balance sheets are always for a specific date. (In this book 20x1 represents the first year of Lauren's business, although in real life, of course, you would use the number of the actual year.)

Note that Lauren's name appears nowhere on the balance sheet. Lauren must not mix her personal financial information with the business information.

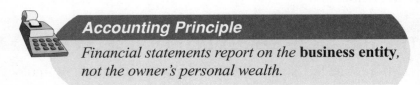

Accounting Principle

Financial statements report on the **business entity**, *not the owner's personal wealth.*

❷ **Assets** is now the official name for "Here's what your business has." Assets are economic resources that the business plans to use in the future to make money.

❸ Financial reports are primarily for the owner and should report assets the way the owner wants them. However, other people also use these financial statements, so you will be learning the standard names of common assets.

❹ **Liabilities** is now the official name for "What I owe other people." Lauren owes the money to **creditors**. **Loan payable** is the common term for reporting a loan. Lauren added "—Cousin Lou" to distinguish this loan from future loans.

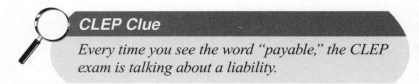

CLEP Clue

Every time you see the word "payable," the CLEP exam is talking about a liability.

Creditors do not own any part of the business assets. However, they do have a *claim* on the assets. In Lauren's case, Lou does not own the car. But if Balloon Party does not make its payments, Lou can ask a court to let him take the car back.

❺ **Owner's equity** is the official name for the owner's claim on the assets in the business.

❻ The total line for "Here's who has a claim on what your business has," is now called "total liabilities plus owner's equity." This number must equal total assets because all the assets that creditors do not claim belong to Lauren. Therefore, the fundamental **accounting equation** is:

Assets = Liabilities + Owner's equity
or: Owner's equity = Assets – Liabilities
or: Liabilities = Assets – Owner's equity

QUESTION 2: If Lauren has $2,800 of assets and owes $1,000, how much is her equity?

Exercise

The following numbers were taken from Lauren's books. Place them in the proper place on the balance sheet and give the numbers the proper names. Use today's date in the heading. Figure 2-1 shows the correct answer.

The part of the business that belongs to Lauren, the owner.	$900
What the business paid for the car	$2,000
What the business paid for the supply of helium it still has	$50
What the business owes Cousin Lou	$1,900
How much money is left in the business checking account	$180
How much the business paid for the helium canister	$500
How much the business paid for the supply of balloons	$70

2.4. ANALYZING THE BALANCE SHEET

Lauren analyzed her balance sheet and learned some interesting facts, as shown in Table 2.2.

Table 2.2. Analyzing the Balance Sheet: 4/14/20x1

Description	Formula	Balloon Party's Example	Result
Measure ability to pay debts: debt ratio	Total liabilities / Total assets	1900 / 2800	68%
Equity ratio is owner's portion	Equity / Total assets	900 / 2800	32%
Compute current liabilities (debts due within the next year)	Bills due within 1 year + Current portion of loan	$0 + $100/mo to Lou × 12 months	$1,200
Compute current assets	Cash + Supplies	$180 + 70 + 50	$300
Measure ability to pay bills when they come due: current ratio	Total current assets / Total current liabilities	300 / 1200	25%

Lauren's **debt ratio** measures the portion of her business that creditors claim. Balloon Party's 68% debt ratio is high. It is more than twice Lauren's 32% **equity ratio**, which measures the owner's claim on the business assets. The higher the debt ratio, the higher the risk for the business.

QUESTION 3. When you add the debt ratio and the equity ratio, what number do you always get?

CLEP Clue

If given one of these ratios on the CLEP test, subtract that number from 100% to quickly find the other.

Example: *If the debt ratio is 55%, the equity ratio is 100% – 55% = 45%.*

Current liabilities are those debts that must be paid in the coming 12 months, or longer if a business has a natural operating cycle (see Section 2.5) that is longer than one year. The most common current liabilities are invoices the business receives for goods and services it has purchased but not yet paid. Although Balloon Party has no bills like that, it does owe Cousin Lou $1,900. Of that amount, $1,200 is due within one year (12 payments of $100/month).

Current assets are those that the business can use to pay current liabilities. Cash, of course, is easy to use to pay bills. The company's inventory of helium and balloons will probably be sold in the coming year and turned into cash. The easier it is to turn an asset into cash, the more **liquid** the asset is. Current assets are the most liquid assets of the business. Since the business will probably not change the canister and the car into cash in the coming year, they are not current assets.

The **current ratio** measures a company's ability to pay coming bills. A healthy ratio is anything over 100%. That would mean the company already has more current assets than current liabilities. In Balloon Party's case, its ratio of 25% is a warning sign. Unless Balloon Party makes some money this summer, in three months it will run out of cash to pay Lou!

2.5. OPERATING CYCLE AND FISCAL YEAR

An **operating cycle** is a natural period of time before certain business activity tends to repeat. Balloon Party sells balloons at fairs during the summer, so its income starts in April, drops off in September, and does not get going again until the next April. Accordingly, one year makes a good business cycle for Lauren's business. For retail stores, a business cycle may be one or two months. A whiskey company that ages its product 18 years before selling it might have an 18-year cycle.

Accounting Principle

"Current" liabilities are those debts that must be paid within one year or one business cycle, whichever is longer.

Businesses have less freedom in choosing when their cycle starts and ends, called the **fiscal year**. Lauren, as an individual owner (called a **sole proprietor**), must use the calendar year as her fiscal year. Partnerships and limited liability companies have complex tax rules limiting when their fiscal year may end. Corporations may select the end of any month as the end of their fiscal year.

CLEP Cram

A. *VOCABULARY*

Assets—Economic resources that the business plans to use in the future to make money.

Balance sheet—The financial report that shows business assets, liabilities, and owner's equity as of a particular day.

Balanced books—When "Where did it go?" equals "Where did it come from?" or when a company's assets equal its liabilities plus owner's equity.

Capital—Assets that help a business or a person make money.

Capitalized—When money is changed into another asset that helps the business make money.

Creditors—Outsiders to whom the company owes money.

Current assets—Assets that can be used to pay current liabilities.

Current liabilities—Debts that must be paid within one year or one operating cycle, whichever is longer.

Financial accounting—The skill of producing financial statements from business transactions.

Fiscal year—The 12-month period a business uses to report the results of its operations.

Heading—All financial statements have a standard 3-line heading as follows:

Name of the Company
Name of the Report
Date (balance sheet) or Period of Time (all other statements)

Liabilities—Debts owed to people outside the company.

Liquid—The easier it is to change an asset into cash, the more liquid that asset is.

Operating cycle—The natural period of time before certain business activities tend to repeat—normally one year.

Owner's equity—That portion of the business the owner gets to keep after paying off all creditors.

Sole proprietor—The individual owner (without partners) of an unincorporated business.

B. *ACCOUNTING PRINCIPLES AND FORMULAS*

Basic accounting equation.

$$\text{Assets} = \text{Liabilities} + \text{Owner's equity}$$
Or: $\text{Owner's equity} = \text{Assets} - \text{Liabilities}$
Or: $\text{Liabilities} = \text{Assets} - \text{Owner's equity}$

Business entity—The financial statements report about a single business. Every business gets its own set of books. Accountants do not mix in the owner's personal financial information.

Current—"Current" liabilities are those debts that must be paid within one year or one operating cycle, whichever is longer.

Current ratio— $\dfrac{\text{Current assets}}{\text{Current liabilities}} = \text{Current ratio}$

Debt ratio— $\dfrac{\text{Total liabilities}}{\text{Total assets}} = \text{Debt ratio}$
Or: $100\% - \text{Equity ratio} = \text{Debt ratio}$

Double entry accounting—Recording business transactions twice: once to show where the money came from, and another time to show where the money went.

Equity ratio— $\dfrac{\text{Total equity}}{\text{Total assets}} = \text{Equity ratio}$
Or: $100\% - \text{Debt ratio} = \text{Equity ratio}$

ANSWERS TO QUESTIONS FOUND IN THIS CHAPTER

Q1: Double entry accounting system. Lauren recorded the same entry twice: once showing where the money came from, and once showing where the money went. So, of course, one equals the other.

Q2: Owner's Equity = Assets – Liabilities. $1,800 = $2,800 – $1,000

Q3: 100%. The owner and the creditors together always claim 100% of the assets.

CHAPTER 3
Making Money

Chapter 3

Making Money:
Discovering the Income Statement and the Statement of Owner's Equity

Lauren has sold her balloons at all the fairs in the state. She happily discovers that she made a modest profit. Lauren learns how well her business operated, and how those operations affect the financial condition of her business.

In this chapter you will learn:

- How to analyze business operational transactions.

- How to adjust the results of operations for depreciation expense and changes in inventory.

- How to report those transactions on an income statement.

- How to calculate cost of goods sold, gross profit, and net income.

- How to analyze the income statement.

- How to make a statement of owner's equity.

- How to make a chart of accounts.

- What T-accounts are.

- Three ways to present totals on financial statements.

3.1. OPERATING THE BUSINESS

Lauren loads the balloons and the canister into the Pontiac and heads out to the county fairs. She works all summer. At the end of the summer season, she looks at the business checking account and finds $2,385 in it. To celebrate, Lauren and her friend Bill go out and enjoy a great meal.

The day after her celebration, Lauren analyzes the transactions in Balloon Party's checkbook, and this is what she finds:

Table 3-1. Balloon Party's Checkbook Analysis: Summer 20x1

Description	Amount	Where did it come from?	Where did it go?
a. Income from selling balloons	+$3,700	Customers	Business checking account
b. Total of all the checks written to motels for fair weekends	−$500	Business checking account	Motel owners
c. 5 car payments to Cousin Lou	−$535	Business checking account	$500 to Lou to lower debt. $35 for interest[1]
d. Gasoline and car repair	−$240	Business checking account	Various gas stations
e. Purchase $70 of balloons and $50 of helium	−$120	Business checking account	Balloon and helium sellers
f. Celebration dinner	−$100	Business checking account	Lauren and Bill

See how these transactions differ from the ones shown in the last chapter:

1. They all happened as part of the process of earning money.

2. In all these transactions, one asset (in this case cash) went up or down and the other column explained why. When the cash went up, the "Where did it come from" column explained that the business earned income. When cash went down, the "Where did it go" column explained that the business incurred expenses. **Income** explains why assets go up during operations. **Expenses** explain why assets go down during operations.

3. Unlike the transactions in the last chapter where the money was capitalized into other useful assets, money this time was **expensed**, meaning it is gone forever.

3.2. MAKING ADJUSTMENTS

Four other expenses did not affect the business checking account.

1. At the start of summer, the canister held $50 of helium. At the end of the summer (after filling the tank once again), the tank is only half full. That means in addition to the helium purchased during the summer, Balloon Party also used up $25 (½ × $50) of the helium that was in the canister at the beginning of the summer.

---

[1] Later you will learn to calculate interest.

2. Balloon Party started the summer with $70 of balloons. During the year it purchased $70 more. At the end of the summer $80 of balloons were left. That means that $10 of the balloons purchased during the summer got added to inventory.

3. The Pontiac took a beating. Lauren decided the car might last only 4 summers. The first summer just finished, so ¼ of the car (¼ × $2,000 = $500) got used up.

4. The helium tank is tough. It should last 25 years. That means this summer ¹⁄₂₅ of the tank (¹⁄₂₅ of $500 = $20) got used up.

Lauren analyzed these four events this way:

Table 3-2. Balloon Party's Non-cash Adjustments: Summer 20x1

Description	Amount of money	Where did it come from?	Where did it go?
g. Using up half the helium in the tank	$25	Supply of helium	Into the balloons sold
h. The supply of balloons went up $10	$10	Balloons bought during summer	Into inventory of balloons remaining
i. Using up ¼ of the car	¼ × $2000 = $500	The car	Used up on the road
j. Using up ¹⁄₂₅ of the canister	¹⁄₂₅ of $500 = $20	The canister	Used up through rust, etc.

Now that we have analyzed the operations, let's see how Balloon Party did.

How Well Balloon Party Did

Income from selling the balloons		$3,700
Cost of the motels	$ 500	
Cost of gasoline and repairs to the car	240	
Cost of loan interest	35	
Cost of balloons (+70 bought –10 that went into inventory)	60	
Cost of helium (+50 bought +25 used from inventory)	75	
Cost of using up the car and the canister (500 + 20)	520	
Total cost necessary to earn income		1,430
Money left over—what the owner gets to keep!		$2,270

Not only did Lauren make a nice profit, but she made her second financial statement. Her **income statement** reports on how well her business operated over a period of time. In contrast, the balance sheet shows the financial position of the business on a single date. Think of it this way: If you were driving on a long trip and got lost, you would look at the map. The balance sheet would tell you where you are. The income statement would tell you how far you have come.

3.3. THE INCOME STATEMENT REFINED

Let's take Lauren's report and rewrite it using standard financial accounting terms.

Figure 3-1. Balloon Party's Income Statement: Summer 20x1

❶	**BALLOON PARTY**	
	Income Statement	
	For the 5 months ended August 31, 20x1	

❷ Sales		$3,700	100% **❽**
Less cost of goods sold			
❸ Helium	$ 75		2%
Balloons	60		2%
Total cost of goods sold		135	4%
❹ Gross profit		$3,565	96%
Expenses			
Car expense	$ 240		6%
❺ Depreciation expense	520		14%
Interest expense	35		1%
❻ Travel expense	500		14%
Total expenses		1,295	35%
❼ NET INCOME		$2,270	61%

❶ The heading for an income statement has three lines. The first line is the business name. The second line is "Income Statement." The third is a period of time with an ending date.

❷ **Sales** is the common name given the income earned by selling goods.

❸ **Cost of goods sold** (CGS) is a handy accounting concept that every business calculates on the income statement. For businesses that buy and resell goods, cost of goods sold usually is a single number. For manufacturers, cost of goods sold usually includes three amounts: materials, labor, and overhead. Other businesses, such as doctors and lawyers, sell services, so they do not calculate cost of goods sold.

❹ **Gross profit** (GP) is the special term given to the result of this equation:

Sales − Cost of goods sold = Gross profit

Example: Find gross profit if sales are \$10,000 and cost of goods sold is \$7,000.

$$\text{Sales} - \text{CGS} = \text{GP}$$
$$\$10,000 - \$7,000 = \$3,000$$

QUESTION 1. Find sales if cost of goods sold is \$6,000 and gross profit is \$7,000.

QUESTION 2. Find cost of goods sold if sales are \$55,000 and gross profit is \$22,000.

5 **Depreciation expense** is now the official name for recording the amount of long-lived assets used up during operations. Chapter 15 discusses what depreciation involves.

6 **Travel expense** is the official name for the cost of living while away from home on business. It includes meals and lodging and local transportation. The cost of airplane fares, trains, and long-distance buses is called **transportation expense**.

7 **Net income** (NI) is the name given to the result of this calculation:

$$\text{Income} - \text{Expenses} = \text{Net income}$$

8 **Percentage analysis**. Owners analyze their income statements to gain extra information to make intelligent decisions about the business. A percentage analysis of the income statement assigns 100% to the sales amount and then compares all the other numbers to sales. Balloon Party's 4% cost of goods sold percentage (CGS%) is very low. Low is good! A 96% gross profit percentage (GP%) is great. Many companies hope for only 50%.

QUESTION 3. When you add the CGS% + GP%, what number do you always get?

Balloon Party's 62% net income percentage (NI%) is also very good. Many companies with sales in the millions are quite happy with a NI% of 2% to 6%. On the other hand, a lawyer can have a NI% of 90%.

Percentage analyses are even more valuable when compared with previous periods or similar companies.

CLEP Clue

You will be tested on the entire income statement equation. Memorize it and be able to fill in any missing number:

$$Sales - CGS = GP$$
$$GP - Exp = NI$$

Example: If sales are $100, net income is $10, and expenses are $20, find the cost of goods sold and gross profit.

$$Sales - CGS = GP$$
$$GP - Exp = NI$$

	Given	Step 1	Step 2
Sales	100	100	100
– CGS	– ?	– ?	– 70
GP	?	30	30
–Exp	– 20	– 20	– 20
NI	10	10	10

QUESTION 4: If gross profit is $40,000, cost of goods sold is $35,000 and expenses are $25,000, find the missing key income statement numbers.

3.4. THE STATEMENT OF OWNER'S EQUITY

After the good summer season, Lauren wants to know how her equity has changed. This is shown on her third financial statement, the statement of owner's equity.

Figure 3-2. Balloon Party's Statement of Owner's Equity: 8/31/20x1

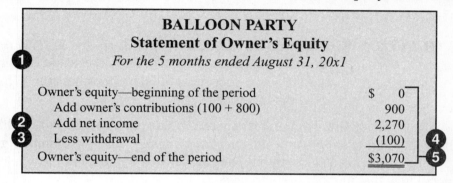

BALLOON PARTY
Statement of Owner's Equity
For the 5 months ended August 31, 20x1

Owner's equity—beginning of the period	$ 0
Add owner's contributions (100 + 800)	900
Add net income	2,270
Less withdrawal	(100)
Owner's equity—end of the period	$3,070

1 The statement of owner's equity contains net income from the income statement (shown in Figure 3-1), and that number covers a period of time; therefore, the statement of owner's equity covers the same period of time as the income statement.

2 The flow of information. The income statement summarizes all the revenue and expense accounts into a single number called "net income," as shown in Figure 3-1. That number appears in the statement of owner's equity and gets combined into the final number called "owner's equity—end of period," which ends up in the balance sheet, as you will soon see.

3 **Withdrawal** (or **draw**) is money the owner takes out of the business. It would have been better, or "cleaner," if Lauren had transferred the money from her business checking account to her personal checking account and paid for the celebration meal out of her personal account. Using business checks to pay for personal bills violates the Business Entity Principle, which requires no mixing of the owner's personal information with the business entity books. However, as long as Lauren records her personal spending as a withdrawal and not an expense, the accounting will be accurate.

QUESTION 5: Sales are $10,000, cost of goods sold is $5,000, depreciation expense is $1,000, and other expenses are $2,400. The owner spent $600 on personal rent. What is the net income?

4 The withdrawal amount is reported inside parentheses: (100). This is the standard method of showing a *negative number*. Placing a minus sign before the number is also common. The phrase "*less* withdrawal" also helps readers know that number is subtracted.

5 The equation of the statement of owner's equity is always the same. You must memorize it.

Equity—beginning + Net Income – Withdrawal = Equity—ending

3.5. KEEPING TRACK OF NUMBERS IN ACCOUNTS

Balloon Party's checking account had a lot of activity. Lauren needs a simple way to keep track of all the ups and downs. To do this, she uses an account.

An **account** is a place to keep track of financial information that the owner wants to know. All transactions get recorded in appropriate accounts. Balloon Party has already used the accounts listed in the **chart of accounts** in Figure 3-3.

Figure 3-3. Balloon Party's Chart of Accounts: 8/31/20x1

> **BALLOON PARTY**
> **Chart of Accounts**
>
> ASSET ACCOUNTS
>   Cash—business checking account
> **❶**   Balloons inventory
>   Helium inventory
>   Canister
> **❷**   Accumulated depreciation—canister
>   Car
>   Accumulated depreciation—car
> LIABILITY ACCOUNTS
>   Loan Payable—Lou
> EQUITY ACCOUNTS
>   Lauren's Equity
>   Lauren's Withdrawal
> INCOME ACCOUNTS
>   Sales
> **❸** COST OF GOODS SOLD ACCOUNTS
>   Helium expense
>   Balloons expense
> EXPENSE ACCOUNTS
> **❹**   Car expense
>   Depreciation expense
>   Interest expense
>   Travel expense

❶ **Inventory** is the official name for the supply of items a business keeps on hand.

❷ The **accumulated depreciation** accounts are shown for the first time on the balance sheet shown later in Figure 3-5. Business people have decided it is useful to always see the historic purchase price of long-lived assets. Therefore, when these assets get used up, we show the reduction in a separate account called accumulated depreciation account. This account keeps growing as it accumulates each new year's depreciation. This is discussed further in Chapter 15.

❸ Notice that certain items on the financial statements, such as gross profit and cost of goods sold, do not have their own account. These items are calculated right on the financial statement from information in other accounts.

4 A smart chart of accounts will have special words within each account name to tell readers what type of account it is. For example, Balloon Inventory is an asset account, but Balloon Expense is an expense account.

CLEP Clue

The CLEP test will use certain key words to describe the types of account. Some of these account types you already know; some you will study later. Make flash cards of the following:

Liability account: Payable or Deferred.

Equity account: Owner's name, Withdrawal, Dividend, Stock.

Income account: Sales, Income or Revenue.

Expense account: Expense. (Every expense account on the CLEP exam should have "exp." at the end, such as "rent exp.")

Asset account: Receivable, Prepaid, Investment, Inventory. Many asset accounts merely list the name of the asset, such as "land" and "equipment" without any special identifying word. Whenever CLEP questions list an account without one of these key words, you should assume that it is an asset account.

3.6. USING T-ACCOUNTS

Of course, businesses keep track of all the account activity on a computer. On the CLEP exam, you should use a T-account. A **T-account** is a quick tool to keep track of the additions and subtractions within an account. In the case of Balloon Party, the cash account had the activity shown in Figure 3-4. You can see the T. One side records the increases, and the other records the decreases.

Figure 3-4. Cash T-account: 8/31/20x1

Cash Account				
Increases in cash			Decreases in cash	
Lauren's original deposit	800	(550)	Buy canister & helium	
		(70)	Buy balloons	
Totals:	800	(620)		
Balance, April 14, 20x1	180			
Sales income for summer	3,700	(500)	Motels	
		(535)	Payments to Lou	
		(240)	Gasoline and car repair	
		(120)	Purchases of supplies	
		(100)	Withdraw—celebration meal	
Totals:	3,880	(1,495)		
Balance, Aug 31, 20x1	2,385			

3.7. HOW OPERATIONS AFFECT THE BALANCE SHEET

Take a look at how operations have affected Balloon Party's balance sheet, as shown in Figure 3-5.

Figure 3-5. Balloon Party's Balance Sheet: 8/31/20x1

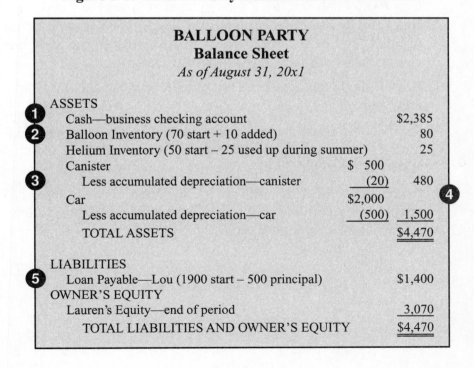

BALLOON PARTY
Balance Sheet
As of August 31, 20x1

① ASSETS

② Cash—business checking account $2,385
Balloon Inventory (70 start + 10 added) 80
Helium Inventory (50 start – 25 used up during summer) 25
Canister $ 500

③ Less accumulated depreciation—canister (20) 480
Car $2,000 **④**
Less accumulated depreciation—car (500) 1,500
TOTAL ASSETS $4,470

LIABILITIES

⑤ Loan Payable—Lou (1900 start – 500 principal) $1,400
OWNER'S EQUITY
Lauren's Equity—end of period 3,070
TOTAL LIABILITIES AND OWNER'S EQUITY $4,470

1 For the cash account, see the T-account calculation in Figure 3-4.

2 Balloon Party uses the new term "inventory" for its balloons and helium that remain unsold.

3 The accumulated depreciation account is not like the inventory accounts. In inventory accounts, the increases and decreases combine in the same account. For long-lived assets, businesses keep the historical cost in one account and the using-up of those assets (called depreciation) in another account. Notice that the accumulated depreciation numbers are in parentheses, meaning they are negative numbers. They are **contra-asset accounts**. Contra accounts get subtracted from other accounts. Accountants display a contra account directly under its related account and the two are **netted together**. When numbers net together, they combine so the negative numbers get subtracted from the positive numbers.

4 Here are some more basic rules about making financial statements.

1. Start computations by placing numbers in the column farthest to the right. In Balloon Party's balance sheet, the first calculation is the totaling of assets in the far right column.

2. To make a sub-calculation, move one column to the left. In Balloon Party's balance sheet, Lauren wanted to see the canister account and its associated accumulated depreciation account netted together (500 − 20 = 480). To do that, she placed the $500 one column to the left with the (20) directly under it.

3. Draw a single line under the last number in a calculation. Lauren drew a line under the (20).

4. Put a double underline under final numbers: net income (see Figure 3-1), owner's equity—end of period (see Figure 3-2) and total assets, and total liabilities and owner's equity (see Figure 3-5).

5. Accountants place the results of a calculation in one of three different places as shown in Figure 3-6. Use the method that allows for the clearest communication.

Figure 3-6. Three Ways to Present a Total

a. Result goes under the final number. Each number gets an identifying name.

Canister	$ 500
Less accumulated depreciation	(20)
Book value of canister	$ 480

b. Result goes under the final number one column to the right.

Canister	$ 500	
Less accumulated depreciation	(20)	
Book value of canister		480

(Note: Use method b. when the final number needs to go into another calculation off to the right and the result needs an identifying name.)

c. Result goes on the same line as the final number one column to the right.

Canister	$ 500	
Less accumulated depreciation	(20)	480

(Note: Use method c. when there is no need to give the result an identifying name.)

5 The loan payable went down by the amount of principal paid. According to Lauren's deal with Cousin Lou, she was to pay $100 per month plus 5% interest on any remaining balance. Over the first five payments, Lauren paid $535, of which $35 was interest. Notice that interest is an expense. It does not pay back the loan. Only the $500 of principal reduces the loan.

CLEP Cram

A. *VOCABULARY*

Account—A place on the financial books to keep track of financial information that the owner wants to know.

Accumulated depreciation—The contra-asset account that accumulates all the depreciation of long-lived assets over the years.

Chart of accounts—The official list of all business accounts.

Contra account—An account that gets subtracted from its related account. Contra accounts always get reported as negative numbers.

Contra-asset account—An account that gets subtracted from an asset account.

Cost of goods sold—The cost to the business of the goods that it sells.

Depreciation expense—The amount of long-lived assets used up during operations.

Draw—See *Withdrawal*.

Expensed—Money is "expensed" if it is gone forever—if there remains no useful asset as a result of the spending. The opposite of *capitalized*.

Expenses—Accounts that explain why assets went down from operations.

Income—Accounts that explain why assets went up from operations.

Income statement—The financial report that shows the result of business operations over a period of time.

Inventory—A supply of items a business has on hand.

Net—A word that means a subtraction has occurred.

Net income—Income – Expenses = Net Income.

Netted—When numbers are "netted," they combine so that the negative numbers get subtracted from the positive numbers.

Percentage analysis—A financial statement analysis technique in which one number is assigned as 100% and all other numbers are expressed as a percentage of the first number. In balance sheets, the key number is total assets. In income statements, the key number is sales.

Sales—An income account that explains the increase in business assets as a result of selling goods.

Statement of owner's equity—A financial statement that calculates an end-of-period balance of the owner's equity account.

T-account—A tool to keep track of the ups and downs in accounts. The ups go on one side of the T and the downs on the other side.

Transportation expense—The cost of business airplane fares, trains, and long-distance buses.

Travel expense—The cost of living while away from home on business.

Withdrawal—Money that the owner takes from the business, or money in the business account that the owner spends on personal bills.

B. *ACCOUNTING PRINCIPLES AND FORMULAS*

Book value of a long-lived asset.

Purchase price – Accumulated depreciation = Book value

Ending owner's equity formula.

Equity—beginning + Net Income – Withdrawal = Equity—ending

Gross profit.

Sales – Cost of goods sold = Gross profit.

Income statement formula.

Sales – Cost of goods sold = Gross profit
Gross profit – Expenses = Net income

ANSWERS TO QUESTIONS FOUND IN THIS CHAPTER

Q1: $13,000. GP + CGS = Sales. 7,000 + 6,000 = 13,000.

Q2: $33,000. Sales − GP = CGS. 55,000 − 22,000 = 33,000.

Q3: 100%

Q4: Sales − CGS = GP
and GP − Exp = NI.
75,000 − 40,000 = 35,000
and 35,000 − 25,000 = *10,000*,
so Sales = $75,000
and NI = $10,000.

Q5: Sales − CGS = GP
and GP − Exp = NI.
10,000 − 5,000 = 5,000
and 5,000 − 1,000 − 2400 = 1,600.
so net income is $1,600.
Do *not* mix in the $600 personal rent with the business net income.

CHAPTER 4
Watching Over Cash

Chapter 4

Watching Over Cash:
Discovering the Cash Flow Statement

In the last two chapters, Lauren started a business and operated it profitably all summer. She has been wondering how much money she should leave in the business and how much she can take out. She wants to make sure she has enough money to pay Cousin Lou during the slow winter months of her operating cycle.

In this chapter you will learn:

- Reasons for watching over business cash flow.

- How to make a statement of cash flows from a worksheet.

4.1. LAUREN DECIDES SHE NEEDS TO WATCH OVER CASH

Lauren looks at Balloon Party's income statement and balance sheet when she suddenly realizes that they tell her nothing about the cash flow in her business. For example, the net income number includes some expenses that did not require any cash during operations. Depreciation expense did not involve spending money. She distinctly remembers buying $140 of balloons, yet the income statement shows a balloon expense of only $60. She sees $35 of interest expense on the income statement, but she knows she paid Lou $535. What gives?

In addition, Lauren has taken out only $100 from the business checking account. How much more can she take out? How much should she leave in? Lauren has heard of other companies that were on the edge of disaster not because they were losing money, but because they did not have enough cash. She might want to get another loan and hire an employee next summer. How can she show the bank that she will make enough money to repay the loan?

Figure 4-1. Balloon Party's Calculation of Cash Flow: 8/31/20x1

BALLOON PARTY
Cash Flow Worksheet
For the summer ended August 31, 20x1

	A Begin Bal	B End Bal	C Change (A – B)	
ASSETS	❶			❸
Cash—checking acct.	0	2,385	(2,385)	k
Balloon inventory	0	80	(80)	c
Helium inventory	0	25	(25)	d
Canister	0	500	(500)	e
Accumulated depreciation—canister	0	(20)	20	b
Car	0	2,000	(2,000)	f
Accumulated depreciation—car	0	(500)	500	b
TOTAL ASSETS	0	4,470	❸	
LIABILITIES			(B – A)	
Loan payable—Lou: 1900 in, (500) out	0	1,400	1,400	g
EQUITY				
Lauren's equity—beginning	0	0	0	j
Lauren's contributions	0	900	900	h
Lauren's withdrawal	0	(100)	(100)	i
Net income	0	2,270	2,270	a
TOTAL LIAB & OWNER'S EQUITY		4,470		

❷

BALLOON PARTY
Cash Flow Statement
For the summer ended August 31, 20x1

❹

Cash flow from operations		
❺ Net income	$ 2,270	a ❻
Add back depreciation expense	520	b
Increase in balloon inventory	(80)	c
Increase in helium inventory	(25)	d
Net cash flow from operations	$ 2,685	
❼ Cash flow from investing activities		
Purchase canister	$ (500)	e
Purchase car	(2,000)	f
Net cash flow from investing activities	$(2,500)	
❽ Cash flow from financing activities		
Borrowed from cousin Lou	$ 1,900	g
Paid back loan	(500)	g ❾
Owner's investment in the business	900	h
Owner's withdrawal	(100)	i
Net cash flow from financing activities	$ 2,200	
TOTAL NET CASH FLOW	$ 2,385	k
Cash—beginning of period	0	j ❿
Cash—end of period	$ 2,385	

4.2. CASH FROM OPERATIONS

Figure 4-1 has two parts. The top part is a worksheet necessary to calculate the cash flow statement. The bottom part is the **cash flow statement**, which reports on where the business cash came from and where it went. Arrows show how the amounts in the worksheet go onto the cash flow statement. In the worksheet, Lauren first analyzes the *changes* in Balloon Party's accounts.

> ### CLEP Clue
>
> *Know where to look for the information to make a financial statement:*
>
> *Balance sheet: assets, liability, and equity accounts*
>
> *Income statement: income and expense accounts*
>
> *Statement of cash flow: the **change** over the period in all the accounts*

Let's go through Balloon Party's calculation.

1 Write in column (A) the balances in all the accounts on April 14, 20x1, when the business began. Because it is a new business, the balances are all zero. Next year, there will be numbers in column (A). Column (B) shows the balances in all the accounts at the end of the period—in this case, August 31, 20x1.

2 The equity section contains all the accounts that would be in the statement of owner's equity. No income or expense accounts are on this worksheet. Instead, Lauren combined all those accounts into a single number—net income.

3 Column C is the change in the accounts from the beginning of the period to the end. If you get a negative number, place it inside parentheses.

Example: 0 − 80 = (80)

> ### CLEP Clue
>
> *Handy trick: When calculating the change in column C, use Column (A) − Column (B) to calculate the change in **asset** accounts. Use Column (B) − Column (A) for the change in **liability** and **equity** accounts. The resulting positive numbers are all increases in cash, and negative numbers are all decreases in cash.*

4 Like all report headings, the **cash flow statement** has three lines. Because it reports on a period of time, the third line of the heading is exactly the same as that for the income statement and the statement of owner's equity. It is a period of time with an ending date.

QUESTION 1: Which financial statement is for a single date?

5 The statement of cash flow has three sections. The first reports on cash from **operations**. "Operations" refers to what a business normally does to make money. Balloon Party's normal operations is selling balloons at fairs. Start with net income. Because net income includes some non-cash expenses that did not originate in the checking account (Table 3-2), Lauren must back those out in order find cash flow from operations. Right now Lauren has three adjustments: depreciation expense and the change in the two inventories. Eventually she will have more.

6 Every number in the change column must go somewhere on the cash flow statement. Use each number only once. The first number is always Net Income. Put a letter "a" by the net income number in the cash flow statement and an "a" by the net income number above in the worksheet. Do the same with the numbers for depreciation (use b) and the changes in the inventory accounts (use c and d). When done, net the numbers together to get a cash flow of $2,685 from operations.

This section reveals that the company made $2,270 of net income, but $520 of the expenses came from depreciation expense, which does not cost the company any cash. However, the company spent an additional $80 on balloons and $25 on helium, which is not shown in net income. $2,270 + 520 - 80 - 25 = 2,685$. A positive number here is always good.

4.3. CASH FROM INVESTING ACTIVITIES

7 The second section of the cash flow statement is cash flow from investing activities. **Investments** are uses of a business' money to buy assets that make more money. A negative number here is normal. It means the business is investing in income-producing property. Sometimes businesses sell these assets, and that brings money into the business. Balloon Party invested in two long-lived assets: the canister and the car. In the "change" column, these numbers are in parentheses, meaning they are negative numbers. This means that cash went out of the company to buy these two assets. Place an "e" by the (500) canister amount above in the worksheet and below in the cash flow statement. Mark the car amount with an "f" in both places.

4.4. CASH FROM FINANCING ACTIVITIES

8 The third section of the cash flow statement shows cash flow from financing activities. **Financing** is the process of finding money for the business from sources other than normal operations. Financing comes from lenders and investors. This section also reports on money returned to investors, like Lauren's withdrawal.

9 For the loan payable—Lou account, the $1,400 change is explained by analyzing both the increases and decreases in the account. In this case, loans payable went up when Balloon Party borrowed $1,900, and it went down when Lauren made payments of $500 on the principal. The interest expense portion of the payments to Lou shows up in the income statement. Leave it there. It is part of cash from operations.

CLEP Clue

The CLEP exam likes to test your knowledge of the interest expense rule. Remember that the interest expense is included in the net income number at the start of the cash flow from operations section and is not backed out. (There will never be a line adjusting for interest expense.) Principal paid is a negative number in the cash flow from financing activities section.

QUESTION 2. This year, Company A borrowed $50,000. It made twelve $1,000 payments, of which $10,000 went to pay principal and $2,000 went for interest. How do these transactions affect cash flow from financing activities?

QUESTION 3. How do the transactions in Question 2 affect cash flow from operations?

QUESTION 4. Is there a line called "adjustment for interest expense" in the cash flow statement?

You will analyze the ups and down of all the accounts in the cash flow from investing activities section and the cash flow from financing activities section. In Balloon Party's case, only the "Loans payable—Lou" account has both ups and downs.

QUESTION 5. When will Lauren's car account or the canister account go down?

CLEP Clue

There is no need to memorize whether a number should be positive or negative. Just determine whether cash is coming in or going out. (All accounting students intuitively know this.) If it is coming in, show it as a positive number. If it is going out, show it as a negative number by putting it in parentheses.

⑩ The line for total cash flow from financing activities, $2,200, has a single line under it. You will notice that all the totals have a single line under them. This single line means that the total is not part of the calculation immediately below it. Adding the three totals produces Balloon Party's net cash flow for the summer. This number *must* equal the change in cash for the period. Write a "k" by total net cash flow and a "k" by the change in the cash (checking) account to make sure they are the same. By adding total net cash flow to the beginning cash account balance, we get the value for "cash—end of period." This number must equal the balance in the cash account at the end of the period.

4.5. THE DIRECT METHOD OF PRESENTING THE CASH FLOW STATEMENT

There are two methods of preparing the cash flow statement. The method presented above is the **indirect method**. There is also a **direct method**.

CLEP Clue

Good news! The CLEP test will test your skill only of the indirect method. All you need to know about the direct method is presented next.

1. The difference in the two methods involves only the first section, cash flow from operations. The presentation of the other two sections is the same for both methods.

2. The direct method does not start with net income.

3. The direct method lists several cash-in categories for income, and several cash-out categories for expenses. It then nets these amounts into a single "cash flow from operations" number.

4. Both methods produce the same total "cash flow from operations."

5. The direct method is more difficult because most accounting computer programs cannot automatically produce it. Most companies use the indirect method.

Exercise

Given the changes in the accounts for the period, you must be able to place those changes in the proper section of the cash flow statement. Using the account changes for Balloon Party given below, fill in the blanks in the cash flow statement. The period is for the five months ending August 31, 20x1. The numbers came from using the trick of calculating Column (A) – Column (B) for the asset accounts, and Column (B) – Column (A) for the equity and liability accounts. Check Figure 4-1 for the correct answer.

Account	Change	Account	Change
Balloon inventory	(80)	Loan payable (up)	1,900
Helium inventory	(25)	Loan payable (down)	(500)
Canister	(500)	Equity—beginning	0
Accum depr—canister	20	Owner's contribution	900
Car	(2,000)	Owner's withdrawal	(100)
Accum depr—car	500	Net income	2,270

_____

_____

_____

Cash flow from _____

_____ _____ $_____

  Add back _____ _____   _____

  Increase in _____ _____   _____

  Increase in _____ _____   _____

Net cash flow from _____ $_____

Cash flow from _____ activities

  Purchase _____ $_____

  Purchase _____   _____

Net cash flow from _____ activities $_____

Cash flow from _____ activities

_____ $_____

  Paid back _____   _____

_____ invested in the business   _____

  Owner's _____   (_____)

Net cash flow from _____ activities $_____

    TOTAL _____ _____ _____ $_____

Cash—_____ of the period   _____

Cash—_____ of the period $_____

CLEP Cram

A. *VOCABULARY*

Cash flow statement—The business financial statement that shows where the cash came from and where it went during the period. It has four major sections.

- Cash flow from operations
- Cash flow from investing activities
- Cash flow from financing activities
- A calculation of (1) net cash flow, and (2) cash—end of period.

Direct method—The method of calculating cash flow from operations that does not start with net income, but does show cash-in and cash-out categories.

Financing—The process of finding money for the business from sources other than normal operations.

Indirect method—The usual method of computing cash flow from operations. It starts with net income and uses the *changes* in the asset and liability accounts to adjust net income into cash flow from operations.

Investments—Uses of money to buy assets that make more money. Long-term investments are in assets such as buildings and equipment. Short-term investments are in assets such as certificates of deposit or stock.

Operations—What a business normally does to make money.

B. *ACCOUNTING PRINCIPLES AND FORMULAS*

Cash flow statement formula.

Cash from operations

+ Cash from investing activities

+ Cash from financing activities

= Total change in cash

+ Cash—beginning of period

= Cash—end of period

ANSWERS TO QUESTIONS FOUND IN THIS CHAPTER

Q1: The balance sheet is the only one. All the other financial statements are for a period of time.

Q2: Cash flow from financing activities goes up $40,000 ($50,000 borrowed – $10,000 in payments).

Q3: Cash flow from operations goes down by the interest expense, $2,000.

Q4: No. There will never be a line adjusting for interest expense in a cash flow statement.

Q5: These long-lived asset accounts go down when they are disposed of. If Lauren sells the car for $1,000, then cash flow from investing activities will go up $1,000.

CHAPTER 5

Accounting Reports
and the Outside World

Chapter 5

Accounting Reports and the Outside World:
Accounting Like Everyone Else Does

Lauren will not be the only person to look at her financial statements. She will have to follow accounting standards so that others can have the assurance that her financial statements present her business fairly.

In this chapter you will learn:

- Who else may read your business financial statements.

- What authorities define generally accepted accounting principles.

- Five basic accounting principles.

- How auditing can add credibility to financial statements.

5.1. OTHER USERS OF LAUREN'S FINANCIAL STATEMENTS

Accounting is called the language of business. If other people want to learn about Lauren's business, they will look at her financial statements. All these people may have an interest in Balloon Party:

- *Individuals*. Lauren's landlord may want to see whether Lauren makes enough money to pay rent.

- *Bankers*. Lauren's banker may want to know whether Lauren makes enough to pay back the business loan or to buy that house she has her eye on.

- *Suppliers*. As Lauren negotiates with Balloon Party's suppliers, they may want to look at her books to decide whether they should let her buy on credit.

- *Government.* Lauren must include her income statement on her tax return.

- *Investors/owners.* When Lauren tries to raise money for business expansion, the new investors will check her financial statements. After they invest, they will want regular reports to see how their investment is going.

A whole other area of accounting is **managerial accounting**, which specializes in providing information to run a large business. The CLEP test you are studying for is **financial accounting**, the skill of producing financial statements from business transactions.

5.2. MAKING SURE THE STATEMENTS ARE ACCURATE

Because outsiders look at business financial statements, there must be some assurance that the financial statements fairly reflect the business. One way to make financial information more dependable is to require accountants to all use the same principles. Accounting authorities have created this set of guiding principles. To assure readers that these principles were followed, businesses often hire auditors to check their accounting records.

Authorities

Accounting authorities have defined the accounting rules we use. If businesses each created their own accounting systems, users of financial statements could never be sure if the financial statements were accurate. False accounting reports could cost millions of dollars in bad decisions. The **Financial Accounting Standards Board** (FASB) has defined **generally accepted accounting principles** (GAAP). Don't let the words "generally accepted" fool you. If a company does not use GAAP, outsiders consider the company's financial statements worthless.

Other authorities exist that may influence accounting. When it comes to defining taxable net income, the Internal Revenue Service (IRS) is the authority. For companies that want to sell stock across state lines, the Securities and Exchange Commission (SEC) has its own set of rules. Governments and nonprofit organizations also have their own accounting principles. For this book, we consider only the rules set by FASB.

Principles

Chapter 2 introduced three accounting principles:

- Every transaction gets recorded twice.

- Financial statements report on the business entity, not the owner's personal wealth.

- "Current" liabilities are those debts that must be paid within one year or one business cycle, whichever is longer.

Principles are basic values that shape accounting rules. Throughout this book, you will see these principles in action.

CLEP Clue

Two good reasons to memorize these principles: (1) some CLEP questions directly cover these principles, and (2) when you do not know an answer, accounting principles will many times guide you to a correct educated guess.

Here are some more accounting principles:

The Conservative Principle. Accountants are less likely to do harm if they under-report net income or assets compared to over-report. If there is uncertainty, this principle requires accountants to select the result that is least favorable.

The Historical Cost Principle. Record assets at their historical cost rather than their current value. Current value is a subjective guess that is difficult to verify.

QUESTION 1. If a car is worth $16,000, but Company A pays $7,000 for it, and Company B offers $8,000 for it, at what value will Company A report the car on the balance sheet?

QUESTION 2. Assuming Company B buys it for $8,000, at what value will it appear on Company B's balance sheet?

The Going-Concern Principle. Assume that a business will remain in existence a long time. As a result, accountants do not show long-lived assets at the current fair value on the assumption that the owner is not planning to sell those assets.

QUESTION 3. NewCo bought a building for $500,000. In its first year, the company lost $50,000. After one year, the current value of the building is $560,000. What is the net income for NewCo in the first year?

The Objectivity Principle. Accountants record transactions using the best objective evidence. Use a documented amount instead of an estimated amount. Do not guess at all if the estimate is too unreliable.

QUESTION 4. Your company paid $100,000 for a patent. The man who sold you the patent said it was worth $700,000. Your lawyer wrote you an opinion that the patent was worth $200,000. At what amount will you show the patent on your balance sheet?

QUESTION 5. Your company was sued for $1,000,000 by an irate customer. Your lawyer thinks you may have to settle for $50,000 to $150,000. What amount do you show in the liability account, lawsuits payable?

The Stable Monetary Unit Principle. Accountants assume the dollar does not change with inflation. This allows consistency over the years. Of course, the dollar does change with time, and accountants have complicated ways to handle the effects of inflation. These computations, however, do not appear on basic financial statements—for which all CLEP takers should be eternally grateful. Because of this principle, old financial statements are never restated in terms of the current buying power of the dollar.

QUESTION 6. Last year NewCo earned $100,000. This year NewCo earned $106,000. The inflation rate for the year is 10%. On NewCo's income statement, will it report that income went up 6% or down 4%?

Auditors

Suppose Lauren wants a loan from a bank. She prepares Balloon Party's financial statements accurately according to GAAP and follows all the accounting principles. The banker likes what he reads, but he wants some assurance that Lauren did not just invent the numbers. The banker may ask Lauren to have her financial statements audited.

Lauren must go to a **certified public accountant** (CPA). The banker will probably not accept an audit from anyone who is not a CPA. CPAs are licensed by the state as professional independent verifiers. The CPA will **audit** the books, meaning that she will do various tests of accuracy on the basic accounting records. The CPA will also check to see if Balloon Party created its financial statements according to GAAP. If everything checks out, the auditor will give a written opinion about the financial statements. That opinion stapled to the front of financial statements carries a lot of weight, although auditors do not guarantee the accuracy of financial statements.

> **QUESTION 7.** If Lauren's banker requires an audit, and the auditor finds that Lauren has reported her car at the Blue Book value of $10,000 instead of the accounting value of $1,500, what will the auditor do?

CLEP Cram

A. *VOCABULARY*

Audit—The check of business accounting records in order to give an opinion on whether the financial statements present the business fairly.

Auditors—Certified public accountants who audit accounting records.

Certified public accountants (CPAs)—Accountants licensed by the state as professional independent verifiers of business financial statements.

Financial accounting—The skill of producing financial statements from business transactions.

Financial Accounting Standards Board (FASB)—The organization of accountants that has the responsibility of creating accounting rules.

Generally accepted accounting principles (GAAP)—The rules of accounting that everyone must follow.

Managerial accounting—The skill of providing financial information to run a large business.

B. *ACCOUNTING PRINCIPLES*

Conservative Principle—The accounting principle that requires accountants to resolve financial statement uncertainty in the least favorable way.

Going-Concern Principle—The accounting principle that requires that financial statements be based on the assumption that the business will last indefinitely.

Historical Cost Principle—The accounting principle that requires assets to be reported on balance sheets at their historical cost.

Objectivity Principle—The accounting principle that requires business transactions to be recorded using the best objective evidence.

Stable Monetary Unit Principle—The accounting principle that assumes that the value of money stays the same year after year.

ANSWERS TO QUESTIONS FOUND IN THIS CHAPTER

Q1: $7,000, the historical cost.

Q2: $8,000, the historical cost.

Q3: A $50,000 loss. Accountants do not consider the $60,000 increase in value of the building. Accountants assume NewCo will keep the building until it is torn down. In that case, the business will never realize the $60,000 increase in value.

Q4: $100,000, the objective amount of your check. Even if you plan to sell the patent very soon, the other amounts are too subjective to use in your financial statements.

Q5: Nothing. The Objectivity Principle requires that you use clear objective evidence before you place any amounts on the financial statements. Wait until the amount is more certain. (You may, however, have to mention the existence of the lawsuit in some attached notes to the financial statements.)

Q6: Up 6%. The Stable Monetary Unit Principle requires accountants to ignore inflation on basic financial statements.

Q7: The auditor will mention to Lauren that her decision to report her car at $10,000 violates some accounting principles. The auditor will allow Lauren to change the financial statements. If Lauren refuses, the auditor will write an unfavorable opinion and require Lauren to add that opinion to the front of her financial statements.

▼

CHAPTER 6
Debits and Credits

Chapter 6

Debits and Credits:
Entering the Heart of Accounting

The time is December 31, 20x1. Lauren has done nothing in her business since August 31, 20x1, when she produced her last set of financial statements. Now she is preparing for a new year. Her business has grown and the accounting is becoming time-consuming. She would like a method that would make recording business transactions easier, faster, and more accurate.

In this chapter you will learn:

- How debits and credits make balances in accounts go up or down.

- How to enter transactions into T-accounts.

- How to prepare a trial balance.

- How to make closing entries and a post-closing trial balance.

6.1. INTRODUCING DEBITS AND CREDITS

In Chapters 2 and 3, Lauren analyzed transactions by looking at "Where did the money come from?" and "Where did the money go?" We called this system double entry accounting. To speed up and assure more accuracy to this double entry system, accountants developed a system of debits and credits. For every transaction, some dollar amounts will be debits and some credits.

Debits = Credits. Always.

If for every transaction the debits equal the credits, the books will always be in balance. These T-accounts will help you learn about debits and credits. Figure 6-1 shows the balance sheet T-accounts. It reflects the basic accounting equation:

Assets = Liabilities + Owner's equity.

Figure 6-1. T-accounts with Debits and Credits

Asset Accounts		=	Liability Accounts		+	Equity Accounts	
debit	credit		debit	credit		debit	credit
increase	decrease		decrease	increase		decrease	increase

These T-accounts reveal two basic rules:

1. The left side of every T-account is *always* the debit side, and the right side is *always* the credit side.

2. Debits make assets go up; credits make assets go down. For liabilities and equity accounts, debits and credits have just the opposite effect. Since every business transaction must keep the accounting equation in balance, that means that every debit on the asset side of the equation must be balanced by an equal credit on the liability/equity side of the equation, and vice versa.

CLEP Clue

Learn these T-accounts as if your CLEP exam depends on it! Study until the phrase "debit cash" makes your heart leap in your chest, but "credit cash" makes you weep, "debit liabilities" makes you feel warm, but "credit liabilities" makes you grit your teeth.

QUESTION 1. Why should debiting cash and liabilities make you happy?

6.2. POSTING THE START-UP TRANSACTIONS IN THE T-ACCOUNTS

When amounts are placed into accounts, they are **posted**. Figure 6-2 shows how the start-up transactions go into the T-accounts. Let's analyze the debits and credits of these transactions.

Figure 6-2. Balloon Party's Start-up Transactions in T-accounts

Asset Accounts		=	Liability Accounts		+	Equity Accounts	
debit increase	credit decrease		debit decrease	credit increase		debit decrease	credit increase
a. 800 cash		=					a. 800 Lauren's equity
b. 500 canister 50 helium	b. 550 cash	=	(nothing)				
c. 70 balloons	c. 70 balloons	=	(nothing)				
d. 2000 car		=		d. 1900 loan	+		d. 100 Lauren's equity

CLEP Clue

Repeat out loud the pattern used here to analyze the debits and credits. The more this pattern of analysis gets into your brain, the more thoroughly you will analyze CLEP questions.

a. In transaction (a), the asset "cash" is increased by a debit of $800; this is balanced when Lauren's Equity is increased by a credit of $800. Both sides of the accounting equation went up by the same amount.

b. In transaction (b), the asset "canister" and the asset "helium inventory" increased by a total debit of $550; this is balanced when the asset "cash" is decreased by a credit of $550. The accounting equation stays in balance because the asset side goes up and down by equal amounts.

c. In transaction (c), the asset "balloons inventory" is increased by a debit of $70; this is balanced when the asset "cash" is decreased by a credit of $70. Again, the asset side of the equation goes up and down by equal amounts.

d. In transaction (d), the asset "car" is increased by a debit of $2,000; this is balanced when the liability "loans payable" is increased by a credit of $1,900 and Lauren's equity is increased by a credit of $100. The accounting equation is kept in balance by a debit on the asset side and two credits on the liability/equity side.

QUESTION 2. Suppose that immediately after buying the car, Lauren sells it to a friend for $2,000. Analyze the debits and credits.

6.3. T-ACCOUNTS FOR INCOME AND EXPENSES

In Chapter 3, Lauren recorded income and expenses and computed her net income in the income statement. Then, on the statement of owner's equity, Lauren added the net income to her equity account. Here's the equation from the statement of owner's equity:

Equity—beginning + Net income – Withdrawal = Equity—ending

Net income goes into Lauren's equity account because it all belongs to her. Therefore, income and expense accounts are actually just part of equity. Income accounts explain the increases in equity as a result of earning. Expense accounts explain the decreases in equity as a result of using up assets. The accounting equation with T-accounts now looks like that shown in Figure 6-3.

Figure 6-3. Basic Accounting Equation with All T-accounts

Asset Accts	=	Liability Accts	+	ALL EQUITY ACCOUNTS	
debit | credit		debit | credit		debit, decrease	credit, increase
incr | decr		decr | incr		– Withdrawal	Equity—beginning
				debit |	debit | credit
				incr |	decr | incr
				– Expense Accts	Income Accts
				debit |	| credit
				incr |	| incr

These T-accounts reveal some more debit and credit rules.

1. The withdrawal and expense accounts increase with debits, but because debits make equity go down, these two types of accounts decrease equity. They are **contra-equity accounts**. The minus signs in front of these two accounts are to help you imagine withdrawal and expense accounts as groups of negative numbers. The larger the number you subtract, the smaller the remainder.

QUESTION 3. In the equation A – B = C, if B gets larger, what happens to C?

2. Withdrawal, expense accounts, and income accounts have only an increase side. This is to remind you that these accounts *almost always* go up. The withdrawal and expense accounts specialize in collecting the debits for the equity part of the equation. Those debits explain why equity has gone down. Income accounts specialize in collecting credits for the equity part of the equation. Those credits explain why equity has gone up.

The withdrawal, expense, and income accounts go down for only two reasons:

a. To correct mistakes or make adjustments.

b. When these accounts are **closed** (start over every year), they go down to zero (see Section 6.5).

CLEP Clue

Unless you see the words "mistake," "adjust," or "close" in a CLEP question, debit all expense and withdrawal accounts, and credit all income accounts.

6.4. POSTING OPERATIONS TO T-ACCOUNTS

Figure 6-4 shows Balloon Party's summer transactions in T-accounts. Some accounts have a "start" balance because Lauren has already posted the start-up transactions. The letters to the left of each number correspond to the transaction described at the bottom of Figure 6-4. For example, in transaction (c) (the one marked by the arrows) there is a $535 credit to cash, a $500 debit to loans payable, and a $35 debit to Interest Expense. This transaction records the five car payments to Cousin Lou. Trace each transaction to see how the posted debits always equal the credits.

After posting the transactions, sum the debit column and the credit column of each account. If there is a balance on both the debit and credit sides, such as in the cash account, the two amounts are netted together. **Netted together** means the two numbers are subtracted and the side with the larger number gets the remainder. For example, the debits in the cash account total to $3,880. Total credits equal $1,495. The debits are greater, so the $2,385 difference (3,880 – 1,495) goes on the debit side. A double underline goes under this new balance.

Figure 6-4. Balloon Party T-accounts: 8/31/20x1

BALLOON PARTY
T-accounts
For the summer ended August 31, 20x1

ASSETS	=	LIABILITIES	+	OWNER'S EQUITY
+ debits − credits		− debits + credits		− debits + credits

ASSETS (+ debits | − credits)

Cash
	180	start		
a	3,700	b	500
		c	535
		d	240
		e	120
		f	100
	3,880		1,495
	2,385		

Balloon Inventory
	70	start	
h	10		
	80		

Canister
| | 500 | start |

Car
| | 2,000 | start |

LIABILITIES (− debits | + credits)

Loans Payable
		start	1,900
c	500		
	500		1,900
			1,400

Helium Inventory
	50	start	
		g	25
	50		25
	25		

Accum. Depr—Canister
| | | j | 20 |

Accum. Depr—Car
| | | i | 500 |

OWNER'S EQUITY (− debits | + credits)

Lauren's Withdrawal (+ debits)
| f | 100 |

Lauren Equity— Beginning (+ credits)
| | start | 900 |

EXPENSE ACCTS (+ debits)

Travel Exp
| b | 500 |

Interest Exp
| c | 35 |

Car Exp
| d | 240 |

Helium Exp
e	50
g	25
	75

Balloon Exp
| e | 70 | h | 10 |
| | 60 | | |

Depreciation Exp
i	500
j	20
	520

INCOME ACCTS (+ credits)

Sales Income
| | a | 3,700 |

a. Cash sales deposited in checkbook
b. Checks written to pay for motels and other travel expenses
c. Paid Cousin Lou five car payments: $500 of principal and $35 of interest
d. Checks written to pay for gas and car repairs
e. Checks written to buy balloons ($70) and helium ($50)
f. Spent on celebration dinner after the summer
g. Adjusted the helium inventory to reflect $25 of helium was used up
h. Adjusted the balloon inventory to reflect that it increased $10
i. Depreciated the car $500
j. Depreciated the canister $20

To prove that we posted an equal amount of debits and credits, we make a trial balance. In a **trial balance**, list every account. If the account has a debit balance, the amount goes in the debit column; if it has a credit balance, the amount goes in the credit column. In Figure 6-5, the debits equal the credits both at the start and at the end. This means the books are **in balance**.

QUESTION 4. If the books are in balance, does that mean all the accounting was correctly done?

Figure 6-5. Balloon Party Trial Balances: 4/14/x1 and 8/31/x1

BALLOON PARTY
Trial Balances
At April 14, 20x1 and August 31, 20x1

	4/14/x1 Debits	4/14/x1 Credits	8/31/x1 Debits	8/31/x1 Credits
Cash	$ 180		$2,385	
Balloon Inventory	70		80	
Helium Inventory	50		25	
Canister	500		500	
Accum Depr—Canister				$20
Car	2,000		2,000	
Accum Depr—Car				500
Loans Payable		$1,900		1,400
Lauren's Equity—Beginning		900		900
Lauren's Withdrawal			100	
Sales Income				3,700
Balloon Expense			60	
Car Expense			240	
Depreciation Expense			520	
Helium Expense			75	
Interest Expense			35	
Travel Expense			500	
TOTALS	$2,800	$2,800	$6,520	$6,520

CLEP Clue

The CLEP exam may describe a posting error and ask whether the trial balance will catch the error. Rule: If the posted debits equal the posted credits, the trial balance will not *catch the error. The types of errors a trial balance will catch are when a debit is not posted (balance will be off by that amount), or is posted as a credit (balance will be off by double that amount).*

QUESTION 5. When Lauren bought balloons, she debited balloon inventory for $70 and debited cash for $70. By how much will the trial balance be off, if at all?

6.5. CLOSING TEMPORARY ACCOUNTS

After preparing the trial balance, accountants prepare the financial statements. In Balloon Party's case, those statements will look exactly as already shown in Chapters 3 and 4. Because those statements were for the five summer months, they were interim statements. **Interim statements** are for any period less than a year. A good idea is to prepare interim statements every month or every quarter (3 months).

In December, at the end of Balloon Party's fiscal year, Lauren wants the income, expense, and withdrawal accounts to go down to zero. She does not want to mix the second year's operations with the first year's results. She wants to see how each year is doing in order to compare the progress from year to year. She does this by closing the accounts.

Closing accounts is the process of bringing the temporary accounts to zero. The **temporary accounts** are withdrawal, income, and expense accounts—those accounts that specialize in explaining the ups and downs of equity. To bring an account to a zero balance, you must post to that account an amount *opposite* to its current balance. For example, if the account has a $240 debit balance, close it out by posting to it a $240 credit. Withdrawal and expense accounts will always have a debit balance at the end of the year. Debit is their **normal balance**. Therefore, to close these accounts, credit them. Income accounts normally have a credit balance. To close income accounts, debit them.

Of course, we cannot simply erase these balances from the books. If we do, the books will go out of balance. So we must place these debits and credits some place. Therefore, all temporary accounts get closed out "to" another account.

Here are the three closing entries:

1. Income and expense accounts get closed out to a new account called income summary.

2. The income summary account gets closed out to Lauren's equity— beginning.

3. The withdrawal account gets closed out to Lauren's equity— beginning.

Check Figure 6-6 to see these closing entries in action.

Figure 6-6. Balloon Party Closing T-accounts: 12/31/20x1

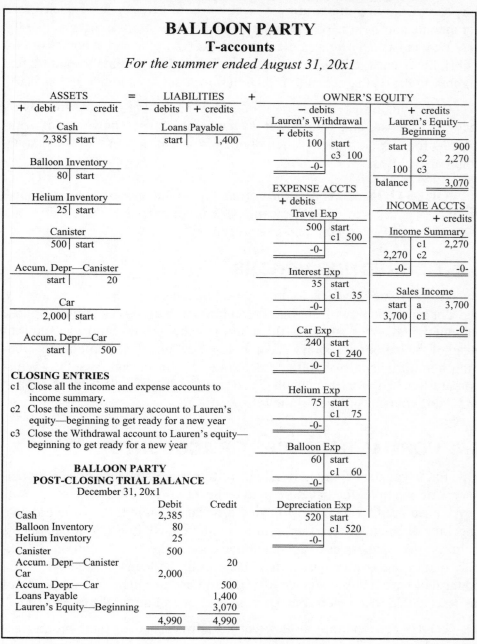

BALLOON PARTY
T-accounts
For the summer ended August 31, 20x1

ASSETS = LIABILITIES + OWNER'S EQUITY

ASSETS

+ debit	– credit
Cash	
2,385	start

Balloon Inventory	
80	start

Helium Inventory	
25	start

Canister	
500	start

Accum. Depr—Canister	
start	20

Car	
2,000	start

Accum. Depr—Car	
start	500

LIABILITIES

– debits	+ credits
Loans Payable	
start	1,400

OWNER'S EQUITY

– debits

Lauren's Withdrawal

+ debits	
100	start
	c3 100
-0-	

EXPENSE ACCTS

+ debits

Travel Exp

500	start
	c1 500
-0-	

Interest Exp

35	start
	c1 35
-0-	

Car Exp

240	start
	c1 240
-0-	

Helium Exp

75	start
	c1 75
-0-	

Balloon Exp

60	start
	c1 60
-0-	

Depreciation Exp

520	start
	c1 520
-0-	

+ credits

Lauren's Equity— Beginning

start	900
	c2 2,270
100	c3
balance	3,070

INCOME ACCTS

+ credits

Income Summary

	c1 2,270
2,270	c2
-0-	-0-

Sales Income

start	a 3,700
3,700	c1
	-0-

CLOSING ENTRIES

c1 Close all the income and expense accounts to income summary.
c2 Close the income summary account to Lauren's equity—beginning to get ready for a new year
c3 Close the Withdrawal account to Lauren's equity—beginning to get ready for a new year

BALLOON PARTY
POST-CLOSING TRIAL BALANCE
December 31, 20x1

	Debit	Credit
Cash	2,385	
Balloon Inventory	80	
Helium Inventory	25	
Canister	500	
Accum. Depr—Canister		20
Car	2,000	
Accum. Depr—Car		500
Loans Payable		1,400
Lauren's Equity—Beginning		3,070
	4,990	4,990

The "start" balances of the accounts are the current balance just before the closing entries. The credit of $2,270 to income summary in closing entry c1 is exactly the same as Balloon Party's net income as shown on the income statement. Netting together all the credits from income accounts and debits from expense accounts always produces net income. In fact, the only purpose of the **income summary** account is to keep track of each year's net income somewhere on the business books. Income summary is like the mayfly; it exists only for a single day each year. At year-end, it comes out for its brief existence, taking in a single number and immediately sending that number to the equity account. It then lies dormant for another 364 days.

Asset, liabilities, and Lauren's equity—beginning do not close. Only income, expense, and withdrawal accounts close. The equivalent of withdrawals for corporations is called dividends, and later you will see that account also closes.

> **QUESTION 6.** What is the normal type of balance of asset accounts? Liability accounts? Contra-asset accounts, such as accumulated depreciation?

6.6. CORRECTING ERRORS

In the same way that Lauren closed accounts "to" income summary, she can move amounts from one account to another. For example, suppose Lauren mistakenly posted a $100 debit to the helium inventory account instead of the balloon inventory account. She can "move" the amount by crediting helium inventory $100 and debiting balloon inventory $100. (When you are finished with this chapter, you may credit yourself from the couch and debit yourself in front of the refrigerator.)

6.7. NORMAL BALANCES OF ACCOUNTS

Each type of account normally has either a debit balance or a credit balance. For example, the balances in asset accounts are always debits. Assets never have credit balances. (Imagine a negative building!) An overdrawn checking account will end up with a credit balance, but then it becomes a liability; the business owes money to the bank. Likewise, if Lauren mistakenly makes one extra payment to Cousin Lou, the loans payable—Lou account will have a debit balance of $100. In that case, that amount becomes an asset called loan receivable, because Lou owes Lauren the extra $100.

Contra accounts are sisters that are always tied to their brother accounts. For example, accumulated depreciation—car is always tied to the car account. Contra accounts always have normal balances the opposite of their brother accounts. Since the asset car always has a debit balance, accumulated depreciation—car always has a credit balance. Contra accounts get reported under their brother accounts.

Car	$2,000
Less accumulated depreciation—car	− 500
Book value of car	$1,500

Here are four facts for normal balances:

- Accounts with debit normal balances are assets, withdrawal, and expenses.

- Accounts with credit normal balances are liabilities and income.

- Equity accounts normally have a credit balance, but when the company loses money, an equity account can be negative and have a debit balance.

- Contra accounts have a normal balance that is the opposite of their brother account.

CLEP Clue

If your answer on the CLEP test has an account with an abnormal balance (for example, debit when it should be credit), change your answer.

CLEP CRAM

A. *VOCABULARY*

Closing—End-of-year posting to bring the temporary accounts to zero and transfer their balances into the owner's equity account.

Contra accounts—Sister accounts that have a normal balance the opposite of their brother account. Contra accounts are reported under their brother account and have the effect of lowering the brother account.

Credit—The right side of T-accounts. Credits increase liabilities and equity and income accounts, but decrease assets.

Debit—The left side of T-accounts. Debits increase assets, withdrawal and expense accounts, but decrease liabilities and equity.

Income summary—An account used once a year for closing entries. Its purpose is to record net income for the year.

Interim financial statements—Financial reports for any period less than one year.

Normal balance—All accounts normally keep balances that are either debits or credits.

Post-closing trial balance—A trial balance prepared after the books have been closed at the end of the year.

Posting—The process of taking amounts from recorded business transactions and placing those amounts as debits or credits in the various accounts.

Temporary accounts—Accounts that get closed (brought to zero) at the end of each year. The temporary accounts are income, expenses, withdrawal, and dividends.

Trial balance—A listing of all accounts with their balances. Debit balances go in the debit column; credit balances go in the credit column. The debit column must equal the credit column for the books to be in balance.

B. *ACCOUNTING PRINCIPLES AND FORMULAS*

Debit and credit formula.

Debits = Credits. Always.

ANSWERS TO QUESTIONS FOUND IN THIS CHAPTER

Q1: When you debit cash, cash goes up. Every business owner likes that. When you debit liabilities, debts go down. The fewer debts, the more business assets belong to you.

Q2: The asset "cash" increases by a debit of $2,000, which is balanced when the asset "car" decreases by a credit of $2,000. The equation stays in balance because assets go up and down by the same amount. The question said nothing about paying back Cousin Lou.

Q3: C gets smaller. That is the nature of contra accounts. The larger a contra-equity account gets, the smaller equity gets. The larger a contra-asset account gets, the smaller some asset gets. The larger a contra-sales account gets, the smaller net sales gets.

Q4: No. If the books are in balance, it means that the accountant posted an equal number of debits and credits. However, it is possible that the accountant placed a credit or a debit in the wrong account. A trial balance will not catch this type of mistake.

Q5: It was a mistake to debit cash. The books will be off by $140 because there are $70 too many debits and $70 too few credits.

Q6: Assets normally have debit balances. Liabilities normally have credit balances. Because contra-asset accounts are like negative assets, they normally have credit balances.

CHAPTER 7

Journals and Ledgers

Chapter 7

Journals and Ledgers:
Speeding Up Data Entry

The time is April 1, 20x2. Lauren is getting ready for another summer season. This year Lauren expects a lot more income and expenses. She would like some method that would make recording business transactions easier and faster.

In this chapter you will learn:

- How to record entries in the general journal.
- How to post entries from the general journal to the general ledger.
- How specialized journals work.
- How to write all the types of transactions you have learned about so far as journal entries.
- How to write vertical journal entries.

7.1. THE GENERAL JOURNAL

There is a simpler way to record transactions than writing them in T-accounts. Record them in a **general journal**, the book (or computer subroutine) that can be used to record any type of accounting entry. A general journal entry looks like this:

		(a)	Debit	Credit
8/31/x1	Cash		3,700	
	Sales Income			3,700

(To record cash sales for the summer of 20x1)

Every general journal entry has at least five items.

1. An identifying number or letter, in this case (a),

2. The date of the entry (in this case 8/31/x1),

3. A debit entry with the number in the debit column,

4. An indented credit entry with the number in the credit column, and

5. An explanation commonly placed inside parentheses or underlined.

Figure 7-1 shows the general journal entries for the ten entries shown on the T-accounts in Figure 6-4.

There is no harm in having more debit entries than credit entries or vice versa, as long as the total debits equal the total credits. There is also no harm in combining multiple transactions into a single journal entry, such as combining transactions (i) and (j).

This general journal has a post column. Place a check when you have taken a number from the general journal and posted it to the individual T-account. With accounting software, the computer automatically posts to the accounts.

CLEP Clue

General journal entries are the CLEP exam's main ingredients. From this chapter forward, every chapter will have critical journal entries for you to memorize. For each journal entry, you should make a memory card. The front should read "What is the journal entry to record ... " and describe the entry. On the back will be debits and credits like those found in CLEP Cram Section B of this chapter. From now on, the end of each chapter will present the journal entries you will need to memorize. The end of this chapter presents the journal entries recording the activities illustrated in all prior chapters.

Figure 7-1. Balloon Party General Journal Entries: 8/31/x1

BALLOON PARTY
General Journal

Date	Account	Debit	Credit	Post
	(a)			
8/31/x1	Cash	3,700		✓
	Sales Income		3,700	✓
	(To record cash sales for the summer of 20x1)			
	(b)			
8/31/x1	Travel Exp	500		✓
	Cash		500	✓
	(To record checks to motels and other travel costs)			
	(c)			
8/31/x1	Loans Payable—Lou	500		✓
	Interest Exp	35		✓
	Cash		535	✓
	(To record 5 loan payments to Lou)			
	(d)			
8/31/x1	Car Exp	240		✓
	Cash		240	✓
	(To record gasoline and repairs for summer of 20x1)			
	(e)			
8/31/x1	Helium Exp	50		✓
	Balloon Exp	70		✓
	Cash		120	✓
	(To record checks written to buy helium and balloons)			
	(f)			
8/31/x1	Lauren's Withdrawal	100		✓
	Cash		100	✓
	(To record check written to restaurant for celebration dinner)			
	(g)			
8/31/x1	Helium Exp	25		✓
	Helium Inventory		25	✓
	(To adjust helium inventory for amount used up at end of summer)			
	(h)			
8/31/x1	Balloon Inventory	10		✓
	Balloon Expense		10	✓
	(To adjust balloon inventory for amount added during summer)			
	(i & j)			
8/31/x1	Depreciation Exp	520		✓
	Accumulated Depreciation—Canister		20	✓
	Accumulated Depreciation—Car		500	✓
	(To record depreciation expense for the summer)			

QUESTION 1. After doing a physical inventory of Balloon Party's balloons on December 31, 20x2, Lauren discovers that she has $500 of balloons on hand. The balance in her balloon inventory account is $564. What journal entry will correct this?

	(a)	<u>Debit</u>	<u>Credit</u>
_____	_____	_____	_____
	_____	_____	_____

(To _____)

7.2. THE GENERAL LEDGER

When all accounting was done on paper in books, the **general ledger** was a binder with removable pages. It contained all the individual accounts. Each account had its own page. After entries were written in the general journal, the debit and credit amounts were posted to the individual accounts.

In accounting software, the collection of individual accounts is still commonly called the general ledger. Instead of a "ledger page," computers let you see "account activity" for each account. The ledger pages look somewhat like T-accounts. Old ledger pages and some software reports on account activity look like Figure 7-2.

Figure 7-2. A Sample Ledger Page

General Ledger					
❶ No. 555	HELIUM EXPENSE				
❷ Date	Description	Debit	Credit	Balance	Source
7/11/x1	Purchased helium	50		50	Ch
8/31/x1	Adjusted helium to end of yr	20		70	GJ
❹ 12/31/x1	Closing entry		70	0	GJ
				❸	❺

❶ *Account number and name.* This ledger page contains an account number (No. 555). Account numbers made manual posting faster, and they are still used in large accounting systems. Some smaller programs use only account names. The problem with just using account names is that these systems let any user make up the account name. It works best if the chart of accounts is created by the accountant with input from the owner. Owners should ask for separate accounts for every type of information that helps the owner make useful business decisions.

2 *Date.* The transaction date should be the same as that shown in the journal. This ledger shows the purchase of additional helium on 7/11/x1. Closing entries are always shown on the last day of the year, even if the entries were actually written later.

3 *Running balance.* The ledger keeps a running balance for each account.

4 *Closing entry.* The final entry at the end of each year for income, expense, and withdrawal accounts is the closing entry. The proper closing entry is whatever is necessary to bring the balance in the account to zero.

5 *Source.* In order to keep an audit trail that shows where all the numbers came from, record the source—the original journal in which the transaction was first recorded. Common sources are:

- Ch = check register
- GJ = general journal
- CR = cash register
- SJ = sales journal

Some software programs have a Report of Account Activity that uses positive numbers as debits and numbers in parentheses as credits. Other programs use positive numbers to mean whatever is that account's normal balance. For example, in Figure 7-3, because you know the normal balances of all accounts, you know that the first entry in the balloon expense account is a debit and the second is a credit.

Figure 7-3. Sample Report of Account Activity

Report of Account Activity: Balloon Expense		
Date	Description	
7/11/x1	Purchased balloons	70
8/31/x1	Adjusted helium for inventory	(10)
12/31/x1	Closing entry	(60)
12/31/x1	Balance	0

CLEP Clue

If you know the types of normal balances for all the accounts, you will not be confused no matter how the CLEP exam displays the activity inside an account.

7.3. SPECIALIZED JOURNALS

You will probably not be required to record entries in specialized journals on the CLEP exam. **Specialized journals** are designed to save time when recording certain very common transactions. Common specialized journals are:

- The check register. Recording all cash-out transactions.

- The sales journal. For businesses that commonly have 10–100 sales per day. For high-volume businesses, the cash register functions as the sales journal by recording all sales on rolls of tape.

- The purchases journal. For manufacturing businesses or retail stores that buy many items every day.

Common features of special journals are:

- Each transaction takes one line, unlike the general journal that takes at least 4 lines.

- The dollar amount is written once but posted twice. For example, by recording "sales $100," you know to debit cash $100 and credit sales $100. Manual systems have places for two check marks to remind the accountant to post twice.

7.4. HOW TO WRITE VERTICAL JOURNAL ENTRIES

Chapter 6 showed how to record business transactions in a general journal and then post the debits and credits into T-accounts—a simplified form of the general ledger. The CLEP exam may ask you questions about T-accounts, so retain your understanding of them. However, general journal entries and T-accounts are not the fastest way to do the accounting during the CLEP test. Vertical journal entries (VJEs) are faster because you journalize and post at the same time. VJEs are more computer/calculator friendly and more commonly used in business. They will help you learn your accounts faster and remember more easily where they go in the financial statements. For these reasons, this book uses VJEs from this point forward.

CLEP Clue

*Although VJEs are a test-taking trick, the CLEP exam will probably **not** test your skill with them. Most introductory financial accounting books do not discuss VJEs. However, learning VJEs will help you go faster on the CLEP test and improve your score.*

Figure 7-4 is identical to Figure 6-4 from last chapter, only with vertical journal entries instead of T-accounts. Look at the differences.

Figure 7-4. Balloon Party VJEs: 8/31/x1

BALLOON PARTY
Vertical Journal Entries
For the summer ended August 31, 20x1

	Start	a	b	c	d	e	f	g & h	i	j	TOTAL
ASSETS											
Cash	180	3,700	(500)	(535)	(240)	(120)	(100)				2,385
Balloon Inventory	70							h 10			80
Helium Inventory	50							g (25)			25
Canister	500										500
Accum. Depr.—Canister										(20)	(20)
Car	2,000										2,000
Accum. Depr.—Car									(500)		(500)
LIABILITIES											
Loan Payable—Lou	(1,900)			500							(1,400)
OWNER'S EQUITY											
Lauren's Equity	(900)										(900)
Lauren's Withdrawal							100				100
INCOME											
Sales		(3,700)									(3,700)
EXPENSES											
Balloon Exp						70		h (10)			60
Car Exp					240						240
Depreciation Exp									500	20	520
Helium Exp						50		g 25			75
Interest Exp				35							35
Travel Exp			500								500
TOTALS	—	—	—	—	—	—	—	—	—	—	—

a. Cash sales deposited in checkbook.
b. Checks written to pay for motels and other travel expenses.
c. Paid Cousin Lou 5 car payments: $500 of principal and $35 of interest.
d. Checks written to pay for gas and car repairs.
e. Checks written to buy balloons ($70) and helium ($50).
f. Spent on celebration dinner after the summer.
g. Adjusted the helium inventory to reflect that $25 of helium was used up.
h. Adjusted the balloon inventory to reflect that it increased $10.
i. Depreciated the car $500.
j. Depreciated the canister $20.

1 All the accounts are easy to find in the left column. They are listed by type, and always in the same order: assets, liabilities, equity, income, and expenses. The expense accounts are in alphabetical order.

> **CLEP Clue**
>
> *Visualize these accounts always in this order. A large number of points on the CLEP test come from knowing the official name of an account and knowing what kind of account it is.*

2 The second column is always the balance of the accounts at the start. Here is the first difference about VJEs. The credits are in parentheses! On reports, amounts within parentheses are negative numbers, but in VJEs amounts in parentheses are credits. Credits make some types of accounts go up and some types of accounts go down. Don't worry. With a little practice, students get to see the debits and credits in VJEs very easily.

3 There are two credits in the Start column: (1,900) in loans payable and (900) in Lauren's equity. They total up to a credit of (2,800).

QUESTION 2. What must the total debits in the Start column equal?

4 The accounts are in the same order as they appear on the balance sheet and income statement. The major headings (assets, liabilities, equity, income, and expense) are not accounts and so never get any numbers. Accordingly, in VJE's, the major headings are shaded in gray.

5 It is possible to combine several transactions in one column, as shown for transactions g and h. When that happens, you can avoid confusion by placing the letter of the transaction by the number. For example, in transaction h, you can see that the debit of $10 to the balloon inventory account is balanced by the ($10) credit to balloon expense.

> **CLEP Clue**
>
> *On the CLEP exam, you will be making VJEs in the margin to do quick analyses. Feel free to squeeze as many transactions as you want into one column, but make sure to clearly letter them. A little bit of time spent lettering your transactions saves time in the long run.*

6 The "total" column at the far right is the same as calculating the balance in T-accounts, except it is designed better for calculators. Start in "Start" column, then add all amounts without parentheses and subtract all amounts within parentheses. If the result is negative, it is a credit balance. For example, calculate the balance for balloon expense by typing into your calculator: $70 - 10 = 60$ debit balance. When the number in the "Start" column is a credit, some calculators require you to start with a zero. For example, to calculate the balance in the loan payable—Lou account, type: $0 - 1,900 + 500 = -1,400$ credit balance. Because the number shown on your calculator is negative, place it inside parentheses (1,400) and show it as a credit in the "total" column.

CLEP Clue

Because accounts keep the same normal balance, if the number in the start column is a debit, the number in the total column will be a debit. The same with credits. If you start with a debit and end with a credit, there is a 99% probability you made a mistake.

7 The total column at the bottom makes sure debits equal credits in every column. This is something T-accounts cannot do. Add the debit amounts and subtract the credit amounts in the column. The total of every column must equal zero.

QUESTION 3. Why must the total of every column equal zero?

CLEP CRAM

A. VOCABULARY

General journal—The book or computer subroutine that can be used to record any type of accounting entry.

General ledger—The book or computer subroutine that contains all the individual accounts.

Specialized journal—A book or computer subroutine that is designed for quick input of a frequent type of business transaction.

Vertical journal entries—A method of journalizing and posting accounts at the same time by recording transactions vertically in columns.

B. JOURNAL ENTRIES

Show the journal entry (JE) to record:

Owner contributes $100 to the business	Cash Owner's equity	100	100
Buy a $7,000 machine with cash	Machines Cash	7,000	7,000

Buy a $2,000 car on time with a $100 cash down payment	Car
	    Cash
	    Loans payable
		2,000	100
			1,900

Borrow $1,000	Cash Loans payable	1,000	1,000
Earn $4,000 of cash income from sales	Cash Sales	4,000	4,000
Pay loan payment of $535, of which $35 is interest	Loans payable Interest expense Cash	500 35	535
Owner buys $150 of personal groceries	Withdrawal Cash	150	150
Adjust balloon inventory to make it $500 bigger	Balloon inventory Balloon expense	500	500
Adjust balloon inventory to make it $500 smaller	Balloon expense Balloon inventory	500	500

Record $1,500 of car depreciation	Depreciation expense Accumulated depreciation—car	1,500	1,500
Correct $50 wrongly debited to car expense instead of travel expense	Travel expense Car expense	50	50

Close out $10,000 of income and $6,000 of expense accounts	Income accounts
	  Expense accounts
	  Income summary
		10,000	6,000
			4,000

ANSWERS TO QUESTIONS FOUND IN THIS CHAPTER

Q1:   (a)   Debit Credit
  12/31/x2   Balloons Expense   64
                 Balloon Inventory (564 – 64 = 500)   64

(To adjust the Balloon Inventory account to equal the physical count $500)

Q2: A debit balance of $2,800. The debits always equal the credits.

Q3: The debits you add must equal the credits you subtract.

CHAPTER 8

Controls and Ethics

Chapter 8

Controls and Ethics:
$1 of Prevention Is Worth $10,000 of Cure

Lauren built two more balloon stands and planned to ask her friends Karen and Bill to sell balloons across the state. She also hired Diane, an outside accountant, to give her advice about how to organize her business. Diane recommended a series of controls to reduce the possibility of theft.

"I trust Karen and Bill," insisted Lauren.

"Of course, you do," Diane answered, "but we always design our internal controls as if we don't trust anyone. That's our job. Good internal controls make for good long-term relationships."

In this chapter you will learn:

- Why have internal controls.

- The basic business internal controls that every business ought to have.

- The difference between legal and ethical.

- What types of dangers internal controls cannot catch.

- To look for internal controls in the remaining chapters of this book.

8.1. WHY BALLOON PARTY SHOULD HAVE INTERNAL CONTROLS

"But I trusted him." Every business person who has ever been robbed has said those same words. Normally fine people, given economic stresses and put in an environment where it is easy to steal, will be tempted. Protect your employees with good internal controls. **Internal controls** are company procedures that make it hard to get away with wrong behavior. For example:

- After starting the practice of taking the day's cash sales to the bank after work instead of leaving it at the store and depositing it in the morning, the flower shop owner's net income went up $1,000/ month.

- After requiring a printed cash register receipt instead of a hand-written receipt before reimbursing the salesman for gasoline, the cost of gasoline dropped $100/week.

- After insisting that the bookkeeper no longer open the mail, the utility company discovered $100,000 missing.

- After insisting on a complete list of all vendor names, addresses, and identification numbers, the company discovered that the bookkeeper had set up a bogus "vendor" and paid it $250,000.

There are other reasons to have good internal controls besides safeguarding business assets.

- *Accurate financial statements*. Cheaters cover their tracks by falsifying financial records, causing owners to make bad business decisions.

- *Adherence to policies*. Good controls make people more likely to do what owners want them to do.

- *Legal protection*. Certain laws make owners responsible for the crimes of employees if weak internal controls allowed the crimes to happen.

QUESTION 1. How do you respond to an employee who, when you put an internal control into practice, says with a hurt voice, "You don't trust me?"

8.2. LAUREN DESIGNS BALLOON PARTY'S INTERNAL CONTROLS

Lauren put in place the following common controls:

- *Hire honest people*. Lauren realized Karen was an inexperienced salesperson who has always been in debt. Instead of hiring Karen, Lauren hired Jake, an experienced salesperson who was bonded. **Bonded** means an insurance company has promised to pay Lauren if Jake steals anything. Insurance companies do not bond anyone with a history of stealing. Lauren checked Jake's references and discovered that he has no economic stressors in his life. People whose economic lives are out of control are not good people to handle your books or assets.

- *Require authorization.* Lauren authorized her new salespeople to spend up to $500, but larger purchases would require her authorization. Lauren is the only check signer.

- *Everyone gets oversight.* Managers supervise employees. Owners supervise managers. Laws govern owners. Lauren checks her salespeople's work at random.

- *Separate accounting from operations.* A person who keeps the books and authorizes payment can steal without getting caught. Lauren handles operations and uses an outside accountant to keep the books.

- *Separate accounting from custody of assets.* A person who can take assets and remove any record of them from the books can steal without getting caught. Lauren opens all the mail. The outside accountant reconciles cash each month and maintains a list of all assets.

- *Have regular audits.* Just knowing that an auditor will check their work makes thieves think twice. Lauren counts petty cash at random intervals.

- *Use prenumbered documents.* Prenumbered sales receipts prevent an employee from writing a receipt and pocketing the money. Prenumbered purchase orders prevent an employee from ordering nonexistent supplies from a fake company. Lauren bought an inexpensive cash register to number all sales. To make sure Jake and Bill use the cash register for all purchases, Lauren affixed a sign on the front saying, "Free balloon with specially marked receipt."

- *Physical security.* Lauren bolted the cash register to the counter of the balloon stand. The cash drawer does not open without a key. The extra balloons are in lockable cabinets in the stand.

- *Policy.* Because the cash box often has more than $1,000 after a day of sales, Lauren requires the salespeople to count the money in private and compare it with the written cash register tape. They then must place the tape in the glove compartment of the truck and take the money in a lockable money bag to the nearest bank, which has already agreed for a fee to wire the money the next day to Lauren's bank.

- *Budgets and comparisons.* Lauren has a good idea of how much money each salesperson should bring in. She investigates any regular shortages. She gives her salespeople a travel budget and expects them not to exceed it.

QUESTION 2. Why do lunch buffets give you your ticket as you leave the line, but have you pay on your way out?

8.3. ETHICS

Ethics are internalized standards that define what you do when no one is looking. For most issues, ethical and legal are the same. It is ethical to follow the rules of the game. Stealing seems ethically wrong, but baseball rules allow it. Some rules are unethical, and your own ethics system may not let you follow them. There are some ethical issues you must learn for the CLEP test. Other ethical issues you must learn for life. For the CLEP test, remember these:

- *Sarbanes-Oxley Act (SOX)*. When someone in a corporation commits a crime, SOX says corporate managers may be criminally responsible if they do not have an enforced ethical policy in place. Companies must have a system of internal controls that auditors must test and evaluate.

- *Code of ethics*. The American Institute of Certified Public Accountants (AICPA), accounting's professional organization, has issued a code of ethics for accountants. Your company needs a code of ethics that spells out what to do in certain circumstances.

- *Law.* Nothing unlawful is ethical. Not everything lawful is necessarily ethical, however.

- *Full disclosure.* Do not hide from users of financial statements anything that makes your business look worse. When accounting rules require you *not* to put something on the balance sheet (the results of an uncertain pending lawsuit, for example), attach a note to your financial statements explaining the uncertainty. Accounting information is not complete without notes that disclose what the financial statements do not.

- *Conflicts of interest.* Reveal to all readers of financial statements any conflict of interest the owners have. For example, the $5 million building on the balance sheet that the corporation bought from the major stockholder was appraised at $1 million.

- *Reveal important contracts.* A corporation is not worth $10 million if the CEO has a golden parachute contract giving her $5 million should she be fired.

For life, a good ethical rule of thumb is the Golden Rule: "Do unto others as you would have them do unto you."

QUESTION 3. Corporation A sells all its widgets with a 100% markup to Corporation B. Cecilia Smith owns 80% of both corporations. Do you reveal this relationship on Corporation A financial statements?

CLEP Clue

Accounting ethical issues mainly have to do with hiding information. **Accounting principles** *define what numbers go on the financial statements.* **Accounting ethics** *say that companies must disclose even more in the notes to the financial statements. On the CLEP exam, you must be able to distinguish between the two.*

8.4. ALL INTERNAL CONTROLS ARE IMPERFECT

Accounting itself is an internal control only if managers look at the financial statements and make intelligent decisions that increase profit more than the cost of the accounting. Lauren wants monthly accounting reports. Her outside CPA is expensive. Lauren is willing to pay $200 to discover a $2,000 theft, but she is not interested in paying $200 for her books to be accurate to the penny. She wants to pay only for **material** information.

Accounting Principle

The **Materiality Principle** *says that businesses should pay for more accurate information only if it is material to making business decisions. "Material" means large enough to affect decision making. What is material differs for each business. For a small business such as Balloon Party, $1,000 of sales is material, but $100,000 of sales may be immaterial to Microsoft.*

The purpose of a business is to make money, and the purpose of internal controls is to increase profit. Every control costs may. Build a fence around your shipping yard only if you save more money from theft reduction than the cost of the fence. If not, consider buying a loud dog.

The internal controls that Lauren set up are also not perfect.

- *Collusion.* Separation of duties will not prevent theft if the different people plot together to steal.

- *Time.* Controls are time-consuming to monitor.

- *Prevention versus apprehension.* Some controls catch theft only after it happens.

- *Unsophisticated managers.* Accounting controls will catch problems only if the people reading the information know how to analyze it and spot the problems.

All of these internal control problems can be fixed with additional controls, but eventually there comes a point at which the additional controls are not worth the cost. It is an owner's job to know when to quit.

> **QUESTION 4.** A movie house has one employee inside an enclosed room selling tickets. A different person in the theater tears the tickets in two. How does this prevent theft? How can theft still happen?

8.5. THIS CHAPTER HAS NOT TOLD EVERYTHING

This chapter has described several ways to steal. In case you are wondering, I have omitted the techniques auditors use to catch this theft.

> **QUESTION 5.** How is the previous paragraph an internal control?

CLEP CRAM

A. *VOCABULARY*

AICPA—American Institute of Certified Public Accountants. Accounting's professional organization that issues the code of ethics for accountants.

Bonded—An employee is bonded when an insurance company has issued a policy saying it will pay the employer should the employee ever steal.

Ethics—Standards that define how to act in business situations.

Internal controls—Business procedures that make it difficult to get away with wrong behavior.

Material—Information significant enough to affect decision making.

B. *ACCOUNTING PRINCIPLES*

Materiality Principle—The accounting principle that says that businesses should pay for more accurate information only if the information is useful for making business decisions.

ANSWERS TO QUESTIONS FOUND IN THIS CHAPTER

Q1: You answer with, "Of course, I trust you, but I design the controls of the company as if I trust no one. Good controls make for good relationships." In general, most honest people do not mind controls, and most dishonest people appear offended when internal controls go into place. Watch out! If anyone gets so offended that he quits, immediately audit his past work.

Q2: Separation of duties prevents theft. The person who both rings up the cash register and collects the money can pocket any payment just by not truly entering the information in the cash register. The way to prevent this type of theft is to make the payer ask for the cash register receipt. That's why Lauren offers a free balloon for specially marked receipts.

Q3: Although the rules of accounting do not call for it, good ethics requires this disclosure. Corporation A's income statement looks good only because Cecilia Smith "sold" the widgets to herself. To any reader of Corporation A's financial statements, the connection between the two corporations is material to making good decisions.

Q4: If the same person sold the tickets and also tore them up, that person could steal. He tears up one ticket but throws away only one half. He palms the next ticket and tears up the second half of the first ticket. The third time, he resells the palmed ticket in his hand, pocketing the money. *Collusion* defeats all internal controls. The ticket tearer could palm a few good tickets, saunter over to the ticket seller and pass on the untorn tickets. The ticket seller could then resell these and split the money later with the ticket tearer.

Q5: By adding the final paragraph, I hope to keep people from trying any of the theft techniques described in this chapter.

CHAPTER 9

Cash and Short-Term Investments

Chapter 9

Cash and Short-Term Investments:
Keeping Track of Your Easiest-to-Lose Assets

The fair season has started, and Balloon Party plans to sell balloons at every fair in three states. Lauren has constructed three traveling balloon booths and has hired two salespeople and Katie, a part-time office helper. This year, Lauren expects her accounting to be much more complicated than last year. She hired an outside accountant, Diane, who advised her about establishing good policies and internal controls. Lauren expects sales to exceed $80,000! That is a lot of cash to look after. Lauren plans to invest excess cash during the summer so she can earn some interest on it.

In this chapter you will learn:

- How to record a bank reconciliation.

- How to handle petty cash.

- How to invest idle cash in short-term investments.

9.1. RECONCILING THE BANK STATEMENT

This summer, Lauren is writing many checks. The person who writes a check is called the **maker**. At the end of each month, Lauren gets a statement from her bank. It shows all the checks that **cleared the bank**. A check clears Lauren's bank when the **payee**, the person Lauren wrote the check to, presents the check to her bank and her bank pays the payee from money in Balloon Party's account. The bank statement also shows all deposits made into the account as of a certain date.

The bank statement is an excellent internal control for Lauren's cash. Hopefully, the amount in Balloon Party's cash account exactly equals what the bank shows it has in the checking account.

Unfortunately, this rarely happens due to timing differences. Payees are often slow in presenting checks to Lauren's bank. Checks that Lauren wrote but the bank has not yet paid are termed **outstanding**. The same happens with deposits. Fairs usually end on Sundays. According to arrangements with local banks, Lauren's salespeople deposit amounts into the bank on Saturday and Sunday evenings. The following Monday, the banks transfer these amounts to Lauren's bank by wire. If the end of the month falls on a weekend, there are **deposits not shown** (DNS) in Lauren's bank account.

Three other differences can occur between the bank statement and Lauren's books.

- Balloon Party's cash account may be too low by the amount of interest income earned in the account.

- Balloon Party's cash account may be too high by the amount of bank fees charged.

- Balloon Party's books may be off either high or low by mistakes Lauren made.

Figure 9-1 shows the method to reconcile the bank statement with Lauren's cash account.

Figure 9-1. Bank Reconciliation Formula

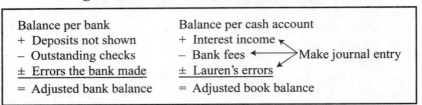

If the two balances are equal, then the adjusted book balance is the amount Balloon Party's cash account should be. Lauren makes no adjustment for deposits not shown or outstanding checks. She already has these amounts in her books. However, Lauren's books may lack the interest income, bank fees, and error corrections, and she must make an adjusting journal entry to record these items.

Example: In early July, 20x2, Lauren receives her bank statement for the end of June. It shows a balance of $3,500. The deposits for the last two days of June, $1,600 and $2,400, are not shown. Lauren discovers that the following checks had not cleared the bank before the bank statement was printed:

Check # 1201 for $300

Check # 1202 for $500

Check # 1204 for $170

The bank statement reported that she earned $75 of interest income and that the bank had taken $80 from her account to pay for wire charges.

Lauren also found two mistakes: (1) Lauren had written a check for $90 that the bank had mistakenly recorded as $9. A call to the payee revealed that the payee had gotten his full $90, so Lauren called the bank and told them to take the additional money from her account. (2) Jake had deposited $1,650 in the bank, but Lauren had mistakenly recorded it as $1,560. Before any reconciling, Balloon Party's cash account showed a debit balance of $6,364.

Try the reconciliation yourself first. Make sure you clearly mark which numbers are positive, and so increase cash, and which are negative, and so reduce cash. Check your answer with Figure 9-2.

```
┌─────────────────────────────────────────────────────────────────────┐
│                        Bank _____                       │
│                            June 30, 20x2                              │
│                                                                       │
│  Balance per bank statement    _____   Balance per cash account  _____ │
│  + _____ _____ _____                    + _____       _____ │
│    _____                             _____                      │
│    _____                             _____                      │
│  - _____ _____                     - _____       (___)  │
│    _____                             _____                      │
│    _____                                                           │
│    _____                                                           │
│                                                                       │
│  Error: Bank recorded check                Error: Lauren recorded deposit  │
│    #1198 as $9 instead of $90   _____     as $1,560 instead of $1,650 ____ │
│  Adjusted cash balance          _____   Adjusted cash balance    ____   │
└─────────────────────────────────────────────────────────────────────┘
```

What is the general journal entry to correct Balloon Party's books? Try here first, then check Figure 9-3.

```
┌─────────────────────────────────────────────────────────────────────┐
│                  General Journal Adjusting Entry                       │
│                                                                       │
│                                        Debit          Credit          │
│                                                                       │
│   _____  _____                ____                          │
│             _____                ____                          │
│             _____                               ____          │
│             _____                                              │
│         (                                    )         ____          │
└─────────────────────────────────────────────────────────────────────┘
```

Figure 9-2. Balloon Party's Bank Reconciliation: 6/30/x2

BALLOON PARTY
Bank Reconciliation
June 30, 20x2

Balance per bank statement	$3,500	Balance per cash account	$6,364
+ Deposits not shown		+ Interest income earned	75
Saturday	1,600		
Sunday	2,400		
– Outstanding checks		– Bank wire fee	(80)
#1201	(300)		
#1202	(500)	Error. Lauren recorded	
#1204	(170)	deposit as $1,560 instead	
Error. Bank recorded check		of $1,650	90
#1198 as $9 instead of $90	(81)		$6,449
	$6,449		

Figure 9-3. General Journal Entry for Bank Reconciliation: 6/30/x2

BALLOON PARTY
General Journal Adjusting Entry

		Debit	Credit
6/30/20x2	Cash	85	
	Bank Exp	80	
	Sales revenue		90
	Interest revenue		75
	(To adjust cash for bank reconciliation)		

Column (a) in Figure 9-4 also shows the same bank reconciliation entry as a vertical journal entry.

Figure 9-4. VJEs to Reconcile Cash and Handle Petty Cash: 6/30/x2

BALLOON PARTY
VJE Adjusting Entry
June 30, 20x2

	Start (partial)	a Adjust for bank reconciliation	b New balance (start + a)	c Start petty cash	d Replenish petty cash	End (b+c+d)
ASSET						
Cash	6,364	85	6,449	(100)	(72)	6,277
Petty Cash			—	100		100
LIABILITY						
EQUITY						
Lauren's Equity	(4,804)		(4,804)			(4,804)
REVENUE						
Sales (Jake's deposit)	(1,560)	(90)	(1,650)			(1,650)
Interest revenue		(75)	(75)			(75)
EXPENSE						
Bank expense		80	80			80
Office supplies expense					46	46
Postage expense					6	6
Miscellaneous expense					20	20
TOTAL	0	0	0	0	0	0

Notice these important points in the VJE:

- Only the corrections to Lauren's books get recorded—the interest income and the bank fees that had not yet been recorded on Balloon Party's books.

- After this adjusting entry, the bank balance is a $6,449 debit, which is what the bank reconciliation said the account should be.

- The sales from Jake's deposit, (shown separately for illustration purposes only) is corrected to a ($1,650) credit.

- The ($4,804) credit in the equity account is merely to balance the partial list of numbers in the start column.

CLEP Clue

Look for these three slick ways to spot accounting mistakes on the CLEP exam.

1. *Find out how much your books are off and look for a transaction with that number in it. You probably forgot to post either the debit or the credit.*

2. *Look for an answer that is half the number you are off. When you post a debit as a credit or vice versa, your books will be off by double the amount you posted.*

3. *When the amount off is divisible by 9, look for a decimal mistake (such as recording $90 as $9) or a transposition of two numbers (such as recording $1,650 as $1,560).*

9.2. SETTING UP A PETTY CASH SYSTEM

Lauren's CPA told her how to set up the **petty cash system**, a system for paying small bills with cash.

Step 1. Lauren took $100 of cash out of Balloon Party's bank account, placed it into an unmarked envelope, and gave the envelope to Katie, the office worker, to store in an inconspicuous place somewhere in the office. The petty cash amount should be small enough to discourage stealing, but large enough to cover most small cash purchases during a month.

Step 2. Lauren created a spending policy. Only Katie can spend petty cash, and only for items less than $20.

Step 3. Every time money comes out of the envelope, a piece of paper with the same amount and payee written on it goes into the envelope. Katie had to go to the post office to buy $6 of stamps. She took a $10 bill from the envelope and placed a note in the envelope saying, "Took $10 to buy stamps." After buying the stamps, she returned to the office, removed the first note from the envelope, and put the $4 change and a sales receipt for $6 of stamps into the envelope.

Step 4. At an unannounced time, Lauren counts the money and receipts in the envelope. In July, Lauren found the following in the envelope:

- Cash = $28
- $72 of receipts:
  - Stamps: $6
  - Get well card for Jake: $2
  - Office supplies: $11 + $15 + 20 = $46
  - Pizzas for a staff conference: $18

$28 of money + $72 of receipts = $100, the original petty cash amount. Money + receipts must always equal the original amount.

Step 5. Once a month Lauren replenishes the fund. Lauren goes to the bank and gets $72 of cash for the exact amount of the receipts. Placing that cash into the envelope brings the petty cash amount up to the original amount of $100. Lauren removes the $72 of receipts, staples them together and places them with the paid bills.

Step 6. On the books, Lauren records the $72 reduction in the cash account and the expenses.

There are only two types of petty cash journal entries: (1) when the cash account is set up, and (2) when the account is replenished. Figure 9-4 shows these entries in columns (c) and (d). Many times, the spending of petty cash will be for small items that Lauren really does not care to keep individual track of. For example, she doesn't want a get well card account or a pizza account. She therefore puts both amounts into a **miscellaneous** expense account. The miscellaneous expense account, by tradition, is always the last expense account.

CLEP Clue

The CLEP exam tries to trick students into guessing that the petty cash account goes up and down as the money is spent and replenished. It does not. The account usually has only a single entry in it. Picture a single lonely debit dated 10 years ago when the account was created. Maybe in 10 more years the owner will want to increase the balance in the petty cash account and debit it a second time.

QUESTION 1. In 20x1, a business set up a petty cash system by debiting Petty Cash and crediting Cash. When will be the next time that the business debits the Petty Cash account?

9.3. INVESTING IN SHORT-TERM SECURITIES

Lauren has some extra cash. She decides to invest it in stock so her money can work for her. On July 1, 20x2, she buys $3,000 of Corporation A stock and $2,500 of Corporation B stock. Below is the General Journal Entry. Figure 9-5 shows the VJEs.

7/1/20x2	Short-term investments	5,500	
	Cash		5,500
	[To invest short-term in Corp A ($3,000) and Corp B ($2,500)]		

Figure 9-5. VJEs to Handle Short-Term Investments: July, 20x2

BALLOON PARTY
VJE Adjusting Entry
July, 20x2

	Start (partial)	a Buy stock for ST invest	b Rec'd cash dividend	c Unrealized gain on A stock	d Sold B stock for $1,800	End
ASSET						
Cash	6,277	(5,500)	30		1,800	2,607
Petty cash	100					100
ST invest in A stock		3,000		300		3,300
ST invest in B stock		2,500			(2,500)	—
LIABILITY						
EQUITY						
Lauren's equity	(4,804)					(4,804)
REVENUE						
Sales	(1,650)					(1,650)
EXPENSE						
Bank expense	80					80
Office supplies expense	46					46
Postage expense	6					6
Miscellaneous expense	20					20
OTHER REVENUES, GAINS & LOSSES						
Interest revenue	(75)					(75)
Dividend revenue			(30)			(30)
Unrealized (gains)/losses				(300)		(300)
Realized (gains)/losses					700	700
TOTAL	0	0	0	0	0	0

During the month, Corporation A paid a $30 dividend. By July 31, Corporation A stock had gone up to $3,300 and Corporation B stock had gone down to $1,800. Lauren decided to sell the Corporation B stock.

Short-term investments are assets that the business plans to change into cash within one year. The accounting profession defines three types of investments:

- **Trading investments.** The business buys and sells stock to make money on idle cash. These are always short-term investments.

- **Available-for-sale investments.** The business is willing to sell these investments when the price is right, but it may keep these investments for more than one year (see Section 20.1, note 14).

- **Held-to-maturity investments.** These are investments that the business does not intend to sell.

The accounting method for each type of investment is different. This chapter considers only trading investments.

CLEP Clue

As soon as you see the word "investment" in a problem, check immediately for how long the business intends to keep the investment. Remind yourself of the proper rule before continuing to read the problem.

Figure 9-5 shows the vertical journal entries to record these transactions.

Start column. These VJEs start where Figure 9-4 ended.

Column (a). Balloon Party takes $5,500 from the cash account to invest in the stock. Lauren chose to show a separate account for each type of stock. More commonly, businesses use a single account called "short-term investments" or "investments in marketable securities." **Marketable securities** are stocks, bonds, and other types of investments that are easy to buy and sell in public markets such as the New York Stock Exchange.

Column (b). Balloon Party received a $30 check from Corporation A. Non-operating revenue and expenses have their own section that is located after operating revenue and expenses (see other revenues, gains and losses in Figure 9-5). **Non-operating** means that the income or expenses come from transactions that are not a normal part of the business. Balloon Party's business is selling balloons and not investing in stock, so income from dividends is a non-operating revenue.

Column (c). Lauren checked the New York Stock Exchange and found that Corporation A stock experienced an unrealized gain. The "gain" part comes from Corporation A stock going up in value from $3,000 to $3,300. The gain is $300. An **unrealized gain** happens when a business asset goes up in value, but the business still owns the asset. Once Corporation A stock is sold, the gain will be "realized." With this adjusting entry, the balance of the Corporation A stock account will equal the market value of the stock.

Adjust the value of securities only where the recent value is easily determinable. Some stock investments are in companies that are not publicly traded. Make no adjustment for those stocks.

> ### CLEP Clue
>
> *On the CLEP exam, the words "stock exchange" will clue you that the security is "marketable" and so you must adjust the value of the stock to its market value.*

Column (d). Balloon Party realized the loss on Corporation B stock because it sold the stock. Lauren removed the original value of the stock from the books by crediting the ST investment in B stock account ($2,500). She then debited the Cash account $1,800 for the cash received. The transaction needs $700 more debits. Lauren places the $700 debit in the realized loss account.

> ### CLEP Clue
>
> *On the CLEP exam, always record cash first. Students can almost always figure out whether cash goes up or down. Then remove the old investment at the original price. The gain or loss is whatever is necessary to make the debits equal the credits. If you need more debits, there is a loss; more credits, a gain.*

QUESTION 2. If you buy stock at $2,000 and sell it at $3,000, is the gain a debit or a credit? Realized or unrealized?

CLEP CRAM

A. *VOCABULARY*

Clear the bank—A check has cleared the bank if the *payee* has presented the check to the bank and the bank has paid it by taking money out of the *maker's* account.

Deposit not shown—A deposit not shown is a bank deposit made too late to show up on the bank statement.

Maker—The person who writes a check.

Marketable securities—Securities (pieces of paper that represent ownership in investments such as stocks, bonds, etc.) that are traded on public exchanges, such as the New York Stock Exchange.

Miscellaneous expense—An expense account for small expenses that are not important enough to have their own account.

Non-operating—Non-operating expenses or revenues come from transactions that are not part of normal business operations.

Outstanding—A check is outstanding when it has not yet *cleared the bank.*

Payee—The person to whom a check is written.

Petty cash system—A system for making small payments with cash.

Realized gain/loss—A gain or loss that happens when an asset is sold.

Short-term investments—Investments that the business plans to resell within one year. Also called *investments in marketable securities.*

Trading investments—Short-term investments for which the purpose is to resell them for a profit.

Unrealized gain/loss—A gain or loss as a result of a business asset going up or down in value, but the asset has not been sold.

B. *ACCOUNTING PRINCIPLES AND FORMULAS*

Bank reconciliation formula.

Balance per bank   Balance per cash account
+ Deposits not shown   + Interest income
− Outstanding checks   − Bank fees   ←⎯⎯⎯→ Make journal entry
± bank errors   ± business errors
= Adjusted bank balance   = Adjusted book balance

C. *JOURNAL ENTRIES*

Show the journal entry (JE) to record:

Bank reconciliation	Cash (adjusted either up or down) xxx xxx Bank fee xx Interest income xx
Set up a $100 petty cash fund	Petty cash 100 Cash 100
Reimburse petty cash	Various expense accounts (from receipts) xxx Cash xxx
Buy $1,000 of short-term investments	Short-term investment 1,000 Cash 1,000
Receive a $100 dividend on stock	Cash 100 Dividend revenue 100
Reflect that short-term investments have gone up $300	Short-term investments 300 Unrealized gain in ST investments 300
Sell for $900 stock that was bought for $1,000	Cash 900 Realized loss on sale of stock 100 Short-term investment 1,000

ANSWERS TO QUESTIONS FOUND IN THIS CHAPTER

Q1: Maybe never. The next time the petty cash account will go up will be when the business decides to increase the amount in petty cash on hand.

Q2: Gains are always credits. Losses are always debits. Since you sold the stock, the gain is realized.

▼
CHAPTER 10
Accounts Receivable

Chapter 10

Accounts Receivable:
Increasing Profit by
Selling to Customers on Credit

Balloon Party has grown to where Lauren buys balloons in bulk and resells them to other businesses. She has sold a few of her mobile balloon vending stands. Now she has good customers who pay regularly every month. Some have asked her to extend credit—to sell them the balloons and wait a month before getting paid. Lauren believes she can increase her profit by accommodating her good customers.

In this chapter, you will learn:

• The difference between accrual basis and cash basis accounting.

• How to record sales on account.

• How to record collections from customers on account.

• Two methods of estimating an allowance for uncollectible accounts.

• The direct write-off method of recognizing bad debt expense.

10.1. ACCRUAL ACCOUNTING
FOR ACCOUNTS RECEIVABLE

Adams, Baker, and Cortez have asked to buy balloons in bulk from Balloon Party on account. Buying **on account** means buying now and paying later. Should Lauren record the sales revenue when she ships the balloons (known as accrual basis accounting), or should she wait until she receives the money (known as cash basis accounting)?

GAAP requires accrual accounting. **Accrual accounting** recognizes revenues when they are earned and expenses when they are incurred—not when cash changes hands. **Cash basis accounting** recognizes income when a business receives cash and recognizes expenses when a business pays cash. The problem with cash basis financial statements is that they do not show how much outsiders owe the company, or how much the company owes outsiders.

During the month of July, Balloon Party made the following sales on account: $2,000 to Adams, $3,000 to Baker, $5,000 to Cortez, and $4,000 to others. The general journal entry Lauren made is shown in Figure 10-1.

Figure 10-1. Balloon Party General Journal Entry to Sell on Account

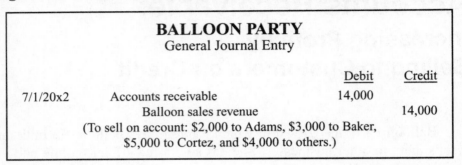

		Debit	Credit
7/1/20x2	Accounts receivable	14,000	
	Balloon sales revenue		14,000
	(To sell on account: $2,000 to Adams, $3,000 to Baker, $5,000 to Cortez, and $4,000 to others.)		

Accounts receivable (universally abbreviated as A/R) is the **control account** that contains the amounts that all customers owe the business. The individual record for each customer is kept in a **subsidiary record**, as Figure 10-2 shows. In computerized systems, every time a journal entry involves the Accounts Receivable control account, the computer handles the details for individual customers as well.

Figure 10-2. T-accounts for Accounts Receivable

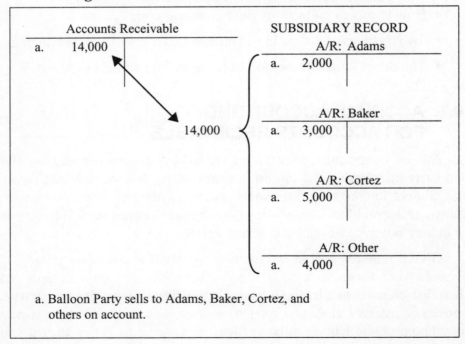

a. Balloon Party sells to Adams, Baker, Cortez, and
   others on account.

Figure 10-3 shows the VJEs for accounts receivable.

Figure 10-3. Accrual Basis VJEs for Accounts Receivable: June, 20x2

BALLOON PARTY
Accrual Basis Vertical Journal Entries
For the month of June, 20x2

		a	b	c	d	e	f	
(partial list of accounts)	Start	Sell balloons on account	Rec'd $4,200 from Baker	Estimate $1,000 of bad debts	Collect $4,000 from Cortez	Write off bad debt	Estimate 2% of A/R as uncol	End
ASSETS								
Current Assets								
Cash	2,607		4,200		4,000			10,807
Petty Cash	100							100
ST Investments	3,300							3,300
Accounts Receivable		14,000	(4,200)		(4,000)	(1,000)		4,800
Allowance for uncollectible accounts				(1,000)		1,000	(96)	(96)
Fixed Assets								
Car	2,000							2,000
Accumulated Depr	(500)							(500)
Equipment	10,000							10,000
Accumulated Depr	(437)							(437)
LIABILITIES								
EQUITY								
Lauren—Equity	(3,070)							(3,070)
Lauren—Withdrawal	10,000							10,000
REVENUE								
Balloon Sales	(35,000)	(14,000)						(49,000)
EXPENSES								
Uncollectible accts exp				1,000			96	1,096
Other expenses	11,000							11,000
TOTALS	—	—	—	—	—	—	—	—

a. Sold $14,000 of balloons on account to Adams ($2,000), Baker ($3,000), Cortez ($5,000), and others ($4,000).
b. Collected $3,000 from Baker and $1,200 from others.
c. Cortez informed us that all he can pay is $4,000 next month.
d. Cortez paid $4,000.
e. Wrote off the $1,000 that we estimated Cortez would never pay.
f. Estimate that 2% of accounts receivable will never be collected.
    Accounts receivable balance: $14000 - 4200 - 4000 - 1000 = 4{,}800 \times 2\% = 96$

Start column. This column shows the numbers from the end column from the Chapter 9 VJEs, with some new information for income, expenses, and withdrawals. The asset section of the balance sheet accounts has been broken down into two subsections: current assets and fixed assets. **Current**

assets are available for spending within a year. **Fixed assets**, or **plant assets**, are expected to last longer than one year.

Column (a)—Sell on account. This column shows a $14,000 debit to accounts receivable and a ($14,000) credit to balloon sales revenue.

CLEP Clue

In a CLEP problem, if the business uses accounts receivable or any other "receivable," the business uses accrual accounting.

Column (b)—Collect from customers. When a business collects cash on account, debit Cash and credit accounts receivable. You will be tempted to credit sales revenue. RESIST. You already counted this revenue in column (a) when you recorded accounts receivable.

Column (c)—Warning of uncollectability. As soon as a business debits accounts receivable, there is a probability that some customers will never pay their accounts. Accrual accounting recognizes expenses in the period they are incurred. Cortez told Balloon Party that it could not pay more than $4,000. Accordingly, Lauren immediately recognized $1,000 of uncollectible accounts expense and credited "Allowance for uncollectible accounts" for ($1,000). The allowance for doubtful accounts is a contra-asset account. It measures the decrease in value of accounts receivable. The account name is indented. Contra-asset accounts have credit balances.

Column (d)—A customer pays. Cortez pays $4,000 of the $5,000 he owes.

Column (e)—Write-off of an account. Even though Lauren estimated that Cortez would not pay $1,000, she did not remove Cortez from accounts receivable. If she had, the computer would no longer bill Cortez. Eventually, Lauren got word that Cortez was bankrupt, so she decided to **write off** his account to remove him from her books. This VJE lowers both accounts receivable and the allowance for uncollectible accounts.

Column (f)—Estimate uncollectible accounts. Even though Lauren has no indication of problems at this time, she learns that in the balloon industry, 2% of accounts receivable is commonly not collected. So Lauren recognizes the uncollectible accounts expense in the same month she recorded the related revenue.

Accounting Principle

The **Matching Principle** *says that a company's income and the expenses associated with earning that income should be matched with each other and reported in the same period.*

Lauren checks the end column and sees that accounts receivable is $4,800. She computes the estimated uncollectible accounts expense this way: $4,800 × 2% = $96. There are two ways to estimate uncollectible accounts expense. Companies are free to choose either of the following methods:

- A percentage of accounts receivable (as Balloon Party has done), or

- A percentage of sales.

The **percentage of accounts receivable method** estimates what the *allowance* should be. The formula for calculating the adjustment is:

A/R × Est % = What allowance should be
− What allowance is = Adjustment

Example: Suppose your allowance for uncollectible accounts already has a credit balance of ($5,000) in it. Your sales on account is $170,000. Your accounts receivable is $140,000. You estimate that 5% of accounts receivable, or $7,000, is uncollectible (140,000 × 5% = 7,000).

A/R × Est % = What allowance should be − What allowance is = Adjustment
140,000 × 5% = 7,000 − 5,000 = 2,000 bigger

The general journal entry is:

6/30/20x1   Uncollectible accounts expense   2,000
                        Allowance for uncollectible accounts   2,000
               (To adjust the allowance to be 5% of accounts receivable)

The **percentage of sales method** estimates what the *uncollectible accounts expense* should be. The formula to calculate the adjustment is:

Sales on account × Est % = Uncollectible accounts expense

Use only sales on account in this method. Cash sales are always 100% collected. Assuming the same facts as above, your collection history indicates that 2% of sales on account is probably uncollectible. The calculation is:

Sales on account × Est % = Uncollectible accounts expense
 $170,000 × 2% = $3,400

The general journal entry is:

6/30/20x1	Uncollectible accounts expense	3,400	
	Allowance for uncollectible accounts		3,400
	(To record uncollectible accounts expense of		
	2% of sales on account)		

QUESTION 1. Why do accountants estimate uncollectible accounts expense long before the business gives up trying to collect the account?

10.2. CASH BASIS ACCOUNTING FOR SALES ON ACCOUNT

Figure 10-4 shows what the books would look like if Balloon Party kept cash basis books instead of accrual basis books.

Column (a)—Ignore sales on account. Since cash basis accounting records income when the money comes in, accounts receivable never gets recorded. This is a shortcoming of cash basis accounting.

Columns (b) and (d)—Record revenue. Cash basis accounting records revenue when the cash comes in.

Columns (c) and (f)—Ignore estimates of bad debts. Without accounts receivable, a business does not need the allowance account to warn about potential bad accounts. Cash basis accounting does not record bad debts. Unpaid accounts never get recorded as revenue.

Column (e)—Write-off. Without accounts receivable, there is no need to remove bad accounts from the books.

QUESTION 2. When it comes to recording sales on accounts, three accounts in accrual basis accounting never show up in cash basis accounting. What are they?

10.3. THE DIRECT WRITE-OFF METHOD FOR BAD DEBTS

There is another method for reporting the money that a business cannot collect from customers. The **direct write-off method** shows the bad-debt expense when the business finally gives up trying to collect. Because the bad-debt expense shows up many periods after the revenue was recognized, this method violates the matching principle, and so is not GAAP. Figure 10-5 shows the VJEs for this method.

Figure 10-4. Cash Basis VJEs for Sales on Account

BALLOON PARTY
Cash Basis Vertical Journal Entries
For the month of June, 20x2

(partial list of accounts)	Start	a Sell balloons on account	b Rec'd $4,200 from Baker	c Estimate $1,000 of bad debts	d Collect $4,000 from Cortez	e Write off bad debt	f Estimate 2% of A/R as uncol	End
ASSETS								
Current Assets								
Cash	2,607		4,200		4,000			10,807
Petty Cash	100							100
ST Investments	3,300							3,300
Accounts Receivable								—
Allowance for uncollectible accounts								—
Fixed Assets								
Car	2,000							2,000
Accumulated Depr	(500)							(500)
Equipment	10,000							10,000
Accumulated Depr	(437)							(437)
LIABILITIES								
EQUITY								
Lauren—Equity	(3,070)							(3,070)
Lauren—Withdrawal	10,000							10,000
REVENUE								
Balloon Sales	(35,000)		(4,200)		(4,000)			(43,200)
EXPENSES								
Doubtful accts exp								—
Other expenses	11,000							11,000
TOTALS	—	—	—	—	—	—	—	—

a. Sold $14,000 of balloons on account to Adams ($2,000), Baker ($3,000), Cortez ($5,000), and others ($4,000).
b. Collected $3,000 from Baker and $1,200 from others.
c. Cortez informed us that all he can pay is $4,000 next month.
d. Cortez paid $4,000.
e. Wrote off the $1,000 that we estimated Cortez would never pay.
f. Estimate that 2% of accounts receivable will never be collected.
   Accounts receivable balance: $14000 - 4200 - 4000 - 1000 = 4,800 \times 2\% = 96$

Figure 10-5. Direct Write-off Method of Handling Bad Debts

BALLOON PARTY
Accrual Basis VJEs—Direct Write-off Method
For the month of June, 20x2

(partial list of accounts)	Start	a Sell balloons on account	b Rec'd $4,200 from Baker	c Estimate $1,000 of bad debts	d Collect $4,000 from Cortez	e Write off bad debt	f Estimate 2% of A/R as uncol	End
ASSETS								
Current Assets								
Cash	2,607		4,200		4,000			10,807
Petty Cash	100							100
ST Investments	3,300							3,300
Accounts Receivable		14,000	(4,200)		(4,000)	(1,000)		4,800
Allowance for uncollectible accounts								—
Fixed Assets								
Car	2,000							2,000
Accumulated Depr	(500)							(500)
Equipment	10,000							10,000
Accumulated Depr	(437)							(437)
LIABILITIES								
EQUITY								
Lauren—Equity	(3,070)							(3,070)
Lauren—Withdrawal	10,000							10,000
REVENUE								
Balloon Sales	(35,000)	(14,000)						(49,000)
EXPENSES								
Bad debt expense						1,000		1,000
Other expenses	11,000							11,000
TOTALS	—	—	—	—	—	—	—	—

a. Sold $14,000 of balloons on account to Adams ($2,000), Baker ($3,000), Cortez ($5,000), and others ($4,000).
b. Collected $3,000 from Baker and $1,200 from others.
c. Cortez informed us that all he can pay is $4,000 next month.
d. Cortez paid $4,000.
e. Wrote off the $1,000 that we estimated Cortez would never pay.
f. Estimate that 2% of accounts receivable will never be collected.
   Accounts receivable balance: $14000 - 4200 - 4000 - 1000 = 4,800 \times 2\% = 96$

Columns (a), (b), and (d)—Accrual accounting. Recording sales on account and receipt of payments on account are the same as the accrual method. The only difference in this method is the way the business records the bad debt.

Columns (c) and (f)—No estimating expenses. Unlike accrual accounting, the direct write-off method does not estimate the amounts in accounts receivable that are likely never to come in.

Column (e)—The direct write-off. When the account is finally hopeless, the business removes the account from the books and shows the bad debt. Compare this entry with column (e) in Figure 10-3.

The allowance for uncollectible accounts is totally missing in this method. Nothing is more misleading to a reader of a balance sheet than accounts receivable swollen with old accounts that will never be collected.

QUESTION 3. The IRS wants to collect as much income tax as it can. Tax law requires that businesses use the direct write-off method. Why?

CLEP CRAM

A. *VOCABULARY*

Accrual basis accounting—The system in which income is recognized when earned and expenses are recognized when incurred.

Cash basis accounting—The system in which income and expenses are recognized when cash changes hands. Cash basis accounting does not meet GAAP.

Control account—The account that shows the total of all the individual records in the *subsidiary record*.

Current assets—Assets that are available to spend within a year.

Direct write-off method—The method that recognizes bad-debt expenses in the period the business writes off the accounts receivable. Not GAAP.

Fixed assets—Assets that are expected to last longer than one year. Also called *plant assets*.

On account—A sale for which payment is to be made later.

Plant assets—The same as *fixed assets*.

Subsidiary record—A separate record containing the details of a control account. Example: The accounts receivable subsidiary record lists all who owe the company money, the total of which is reflected in accounts receivable.

Write-off—When a company gives up collecting an account receivable, it writes off the account by removing it from company records.

B. ACCOUNTING PRINCIPLES AND FORMULAS

Matching Principle—The company's income and expenses associated with that income should be matched with each other and reported in the same period.

Percentage of accounts receivable method—The method of estimating the allowance for uncollectible accounts.

$$A/R \times Est \% = \text{What allowance should be}$$
$$- \text{ What allowance is } = \text{Adjustment}$$

Percentage of sales method—The method of estimating uncollectible accounts expense.

$$Sales \times Est \% = \text{Uncollectible accounts expense}$$

C. JOURNAL ENTRIES

Show the journal entry (JE) to:

Record $100 of sales on account	Accounts receivable Sales revenue	100	100
Record $100 collected on account	Cash Accounts receivable	100	100
Adjust allowance to be $1,000 when it is $800	Uncollectible accounts expense Allowance for uncollectible accounts	200	200
Record uncollectible accts exp estimated at 2% of $100,000 sales	Uncollectible accounts expense Allowance for uncollectible accounts	2,000	2,000

Write off $1,000 bad debt (allowance method)	Allowance for uncollectible accounts	1,000	
	Accounts receivable		1,000
Write off $1,000 bad debt (direct write-off method)	Bad debt expense	1,000	
	Accounts receivable		1,000

ANSWERS TO QUESTIONS FOUND IN THIS CHAPTER

Q1: The Matching Principle requires that a business report expenses in the same period as the revenue those expenses generate. An estimate of the uncollectible accounts expense appears in the same period that the business recognizes the sales revenue, even though the business doesn't give up trying to collect the account until many periods later.

Q2: Accounts receivable, allowance for uncollectible accounts, and uncollectible accounts expense.

Q3: The direct write-off method delays recognizing the bad debt expense until long in the future. That means the business income will be higher now. Higher income means higher taxes. You are correct in thinking that in some future year the bad debt will be recognized and the income will be lower. However, for the IRS, tax money received this year is more valuable than tax money received next year.

CHAPTER 11

Other Receivables

Chapter 11

Other Receivables:
Making Sure You Collect the Money People Owe You

Duncan and Elkins together buy a mobile balloon sales booth from Balloon Party for $20,000. They ask Balloon Party to let them pay six months later.

"I don't know," Lauren hesitates. "I had to borrow to build that booth."

"We'll each give you a $10,000 note," Duncan says. "You can get your cash at the bank."

Lauren is not sure what a note is, but she agrees to take the slips of paper.

In the meantime, Lauren checks petty cash and finds it $55 short! Tearfully, the office assistant Katie confesses that she took it. Katie agrees that Lauren could take the amount from her next paycheck. Lauren removes petty cash from Katie's control.

In this chapter, you will learn:

- How to account for notes receivable.

- What other types of receivables exist.

- How to further analyze current assets.

11.1. DISCOUNTING A NOTE RECEIVABLE AT THE BANK

Figure 11-1 shows the two notes from Duncan and Elkins, the **makers** of the notes. You will notice that the two notes look slightly different. Duncan's note has a **face interest** rate of 10%. Both notes have different **face amounts**.

Figure 11-1. Duncan's and Elkins's notes to Balloon Party: 8/1/20x2

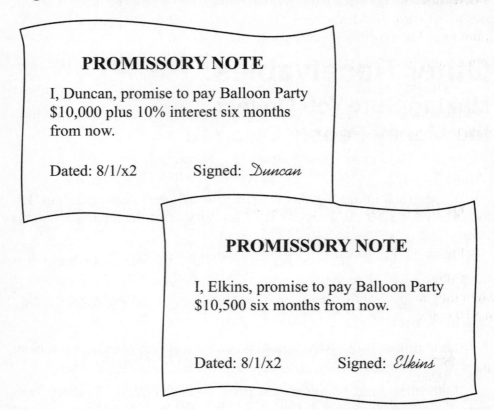

Duncan's note is an **interest-bearing** note, meaning that written on the face of the note is a rate of interest. The formula to calculate interest is:

Loan amount (or **principal**) × Rate% × Years (or fraction thereof) = Interest

$10,000 × 10% × 6/12 of a year = $500

Therefore Duncan promised to pay Balloon Party $10,500 six months from now.

Elkins also promised to pay Balloon Party $10,500 six months from now. The two notes are financially equal. Elkins's note is a **non-interest-bearing** note because there is no interest rate written on the face of the note. The face amount of Elkins's non-interest-bearing note is the **future value** or **maturity value**—$10,500—on the maturity date. Future values always contain the interest. The face amount of Duncan's interest-bearing note—$10,000—is the **present value**, the principal without any interest.

If Duncan and Elkins are stable businesses, Balloon Party will sell, or **discount**, the note at a bank. Two months after getting the notes, Lauren goes to her bank and discounts Duncan's note. The bank charges a 12% discount rate. The formula for calculating the discount is:

Future value of the note × Discount% × Years (or fraction thereof) = Discount

$10,500   ×   12%   ×   4/12 of a year   = $420

The amount the bank gives for a note is called the **proceeds**. The formula to calculate the proceeds is:

Future value – Discount = Proceeds
$10,500 – $420 = $10,080

QUESTION 1. Which represents a greater expense: 10% interest or 10% discount?

Figure 11-2 shows the VJEs for handling notes receivable.

Column (a)—Receiving a note. Notes receivable are a current asset when they mature within one year. Record both notes at their present value of $10,000 each.

Accounting Principle

The Present Value Principle requires notes to be shown at their present value. When given a future value, GAAP requires that the interest be backed out.

CLEP Clue

Don't worry about calculating the interest. The CLEP exam will give you the present value.

Example: Suppose Bill bought a car from you with a $22,000 note. If he had cash, he could have bought the car for $20,000. On the books, show the car at $20,000. The $2,000 difference is interest.

Column (b)—Discounting a note at the bank. As calculated above, the bank gave Lauren $10,080 for Duncan's note. The $80 is the interest that Balloon Party earned while holding the note for two months.

> ### CLEP Clue
>
> *Sharp students often think they see a shortcut to calculating the $80. The CLEP exam will hint that you can subtract the interest rate from the discount rate or vice versa. Take no shortcuts! They are traps.*

Figure 11-2. VJEs for Handling Notes Receivable

BALLOON PARTY
Vertical Journal Entries
From August 20x2 to January 20x3

		a	b & c	d	e & f	
(partial list of accounts)	Start	8/1 Sold a booth for 20,000 of notes	b. Disc note c. Accrue interest	2/1/x3 Eakins pays note	e. Duncan defaults f. Katie steals	End
ASSETS **Current Assets**						
Cash	14,107		b 10,080	10,500	e (10,600) f (55)	24,032
Petty Cash	100					100
Accounts Receivable	4,800				e 10,600	15,400
Allowance for uncollectible accounts	(96)					(96)
Notes receivable		20,000	b (10,000)	(10,000)		—
Interest receivable			c 417	(417)		—
Loan rec—Katie					f 55	55
Inventories	95					95
Fixed Assets						
All fixed asset accts	11,064					11,064
LIABILITIES						
All current liabilities	(21,000)					(21,000)
EQUITY						
Lauren—Equity	(3,070)					(3,070)
Lauren—Withdrawal	21,000					21,000
REVENUE						
Balloon Sales	(49,000)					(49,000)
Booth Sales		(20,000)				(20,000)
Interest revenue			b (80) c (417)	(83)		(580)
EXPENSES						
All expense accts	22,000					22,000
TOTALS	—	—	—	—	—	—

a. Balloon Party sold a booth for $20,000 to Duncan and Elkins; each gave a $10,000 note.

b. Two months later, Lauren discounted Duncan's note at the bank and got $10,080 cash.

c. At the end of the year, Lauren calculated how much interest Elkins owes.

d. Elkins pays the full amount of the note.

e. The bank tried to collect from Duncan when the note matured, but Duncan could not pay.

f. Lauren discovered the $55 missing from petty cash. Lauren replenished the missing money and agreed to take the amount from Katie's next paycheck.

QUESTION 2. What is the maturity value of a $1,000 one-year 13% note?

11.2. ACCRUING INTEREST RECEIVABLE

Column (c)—Accrued interest. Accrual accounting recognizes income when it is earned. Interest revenue is earned as time passes. At the end of the year, Lauren wants to recognize five months of interest revenue on Elkins's note. Using the formula for calculating interest, Lauren computes:

Principal × Rate% × Years (or fraction thereof) = Interest

$10,000 ×   10%   ×   5/12 of a year   = $417[1]

CLEP Clue

Don't count days on the CLEP exam unless the question asks you to do so. Months will do.

Column (d)—Payment on a note. When Balloon Party receives Elkins's $10,500, it must deliver the note to Elkins, marking it paid. Because it no longer has the note, Balloon Party must remove the $10,000 from notes receivable by crediting it. It also must remove the interest receivable because the cash is now received. The $83 difference between the $500 of interest that Elkins paid and the interest receivable on December 31, 20x2 is the interest income for January, 20x3.

QUESTION 3. What is the journal entry to accrue 3 months of interest on a $1,000 12% note?

11.3. A CUSTOMER DISHONORS A NOTE

Column (e)—Default on a note. Even though Balloon Party "sold" its note receivable to the bank, all bank agreements require the discounter to guarantee collection on the note. Unfortunately, Duncan defaulted on the note and the bank charged Balloon party $10,500 for the maturity value of the note plus a $100 default fee! Balloon Party intends to get this money from Duncan eventually. A dishonored note has no value, though, so the $10,600 that Duncan now owes goes into accounts receivable, not back to notes receivable.

---

[1] Actually, $416.67, but for simplicity rounded to the nearest dollar.

11.4. LOANS RECEIVABLE

Column (f)—Loans Receivable. Most of the time when an employee steals, the money is gone for good, and often so is the employee! Katie was so insistent she would pay back Balloon Party, Lauren decided to show the debit as a loan receivable instead of an expense.

> **QUESTION 4.** If Lauren fires Katie without ever recovering the money, how would she show the journal entry to replenish petty cash?

11.5. ANALYSIS OF CURRENT ASSETS

Figure 11-3 presents new ways to analyze financial statements. Use the numbers in the end column in Figure 11-2 to make these new analyses.

Figure 11-3. Analysis of Balloon Party's Balance Sheet: 2/1/20x3

Description	Formula	Balloon Party's Example	Result
Compute **Quick Assets**, those quickly changed into cash	Cash + Petty Cash + ST Investments + Net A/R	24,032 + 100 + 0 + 15,400 + (96)	$39,436
Compute **Current Assets**	Quick + all other current assets	39,436 + 55 + 95	$39,586
Compute the **Quick Ratio** (**Acid Test Ratio**)	Total quick assets / Total current liabilities	39,436/21,000	188%
Current Ratio: Measure ability to pay bills when they come due	Total current assets / Total current liabilities	39,586/21,000	189%
Average Net A/R: Measure average customer debt	(Beginning net A/R + Ending net A/R) / 2	[(0 – 0) + (15,400 – 96)] / 2	$7,652
One day's sales: Measure average sales per day	Net sales on account / 365 days	69,000 / 365	$189
Days' sales in A/R: Measure how long it takes to collect A/R	Average net receivables / One day's sales	7,652 / 189	40.5

Quick assets are those assets quickly changed into cash: Cash (including petty cash), short-term investments, and net receivables (A/R – allowance). Large amounts of quick assets help a business pay its bills. Too much may indicate the business is not investing enough in business assets.

The **quick ratio** is quick assets divided by current liabilities. A good number is 20%. Too low indicates a future difficulty in paying current bills. Balloon Party's 188% is very high. Lauren has her cash tied up in quick assets that are not earning much money for her.

For a discussion of current assets and current ratio, see Chapter 2.

Days' sales in A/R measures how quickly the business collects on accounts receivable. It is easiest to visualize this in three steps:

Step 1. Calculate average net accounts receivables

[(Beginning A/R – allowance) + (Ending A/R – allowance)] / 2 = Avg. net A/R

[($0   – $0   ) + (15,400   –   86   )] / 2 = $7,652

Step 2. Calculate one day's sales.

Net sales on account / 365 days = One day's sales on account

(49,000 + 20,000) /   365   = $189

Step 3. Calculate Days' Sales in Accounts Receivable

Average net receivables / One day's sales = Days' sales in A/R

7,652   /   189   =   40.5 days

Since Balloon Party just started selling on account, beginning net accounts receivable was zero. The 41 days in accounts receivable tells financial statement readers that it takes an average of 41 days to collect a sale on account. A good number is 30 days, although each industry has a different standard.

QUESTION 5. Calculate days' sales in A/R from the following information:

Beginning A/R = $40,000 with an allowance of ($6,000)

Ending A/R = $50,000 with an allowance of ($8,000)

Sales on account for the year were $365,000.

CLEP CRAM

A. *VOCABULARY*

Discount a note—To sell a note to a bank that subtracts a *discount*, giving the seller the *proceeds*.

Face amount—The dollar amount written on the face of a note.

Face interest—The interest rate written on the face of a note.

Future value of a note—The amount borrowed plus the interest up to the maturity date.

Interest-bearing note—A note with an interest rate written on the face, whose face amount is the present value.

Maker—The person who borrows money and writes a note promising to pay in the future.

Maturity value—The future value of a note.

Non-interest-bearing note—A note without an interest rate written on the face, whose face amount is the future value.

Present value of a note—The amount borrowed, or the *principal*. *Interest-bearing notes* show the present value as the face amount.

Principal—The loan amount that remains unpaid.

Proceeds of a note—The amount a bank gives in exchange for a note.

Quick assets—Assets quickly changeable into cash: cash, short-term investments, and net accounts receivable.

B. *ACCOUNTING PRINCIPLES AND FORMULAS*

Acid test ratio formula. The same as *quick ratio formula*.

Average net accounts receivable (A/R) formula.

$$\frac{(\text{Beginning net A/R} + \text{Ending net A/R})}{2} = \text{Average net A/R}$$

Days' sales in A/R formula.

$$\frac{\text{Average net A/R}}{\text{One day's sales}} = \text{Days' sales in A/R}$$

Discount on a note.

Future value of the note $\times$ Discount% $\times$ Years (or fraction thereof) = Discount

Interest formula.

Loan amount (or *principal*) $\times$ Rate% $\times$ Years (or fraction thereof) = Interest

One day's sales formula.

$$\frac{\text{Net sales on account}}{365 \text{ days}} = \text{One day's sales}$$

Present Value Principle. Financial assets are shown on the balance sheet at their present value. When given a non-interest-bearing note (which has interest in the face amount), GAAP requires that the interest be backed out.

Proceeds from a discounted note formula.

Future value – Discount = Proceeds.

Quick ratio formula.

$$\frac{\text{Total quick assets}}{\text{Total current liabilities}} = \text{Quick ratio}$$

C. JOURNAL ENTRIES

Show the journal entry (JE) to:

Accept a $1,000 note in payment for goods	Note receivable Sales revenue	1,000	 1,000

Discount a $1,000 note at the bank for $1,070	Cash
	    Note receivable
	    Interest revenue
		1,070	
			1,000
			70

Accrue $400 of interest on a note	Interest receivable Interest revenue	400	 400

Receive $1,100 payment on a $1,000 note. $60 of interest receivable was already accrued.	Cash
	    Note receivable
	    Interest receivable
	    Interest revenue
		1,100	
			1000
			60
			40

Record customer default on $1,000 note held to maturity. $100 of interest had been accrued.	Accounts receivable
	    Interest receivable
	    Note receivable
		1,100	
			100
			1,000

Employer loans $100 to employee	Loan receivable Cash	100	 100

ANSWERS TO QUESTIONS FOUND IN THIS CHAPTER

Q1: A 10% discount. The interest rate multiplies against the principal. The discount rate multiplies against the maturity value, which is principal + interest, and therefore always a larger number.

Q2: Interest on the $1,000 note is $130 (1,000 $\times$ 13% $\times$ 1 year = 130). The maturity value is principal + interest, or $1,130.

Q3: Interest receivable   30

Interest income (1,000 $\times$ 12% $\times$ 3/12)   30

(To accrue 3 months of interest on note)

Q4: Theft expense   55

Cash   55

(To replenish petty cash after Katie stole $55)

Lauren uses theft expense because the $55 is gone for good.

Q5: Step 1. [Beginning net A/R + Ending net A/R] / 2 = Average net A/R

[(40,000 − 6,000) + (50,000 − 8,000)] / 2 = $38,000

Step 2. Sales on account / 365 = 1 day's sales =
$365,000 / 365 = $1,000

Step 3. Average net A/R / 1 day's sales = Days' sales in A/R

$38,000 / $1,000 = 38 days

CHAPTER 12
Merchandise Inventories

Chapter 12

Merchandise Inventories:
Storing the Goods You Plan to Sell

As her business expands, Lauren must move out of her garage into a rented business space. In it, she sets up an office and warehouse. In the warehouse, she stores hundreds of boxes of balloons and supplies. Her inventory system pushes the newest box onto the shelf on one side and pulls the oldest box from the other side of the shelf to sell.

In this chapter, you will learn:

- Four systems for keeping track of inventory costs.

- Two alternate methods for journalizing inventory transactions.

- To estimate ending inventory using the gross profit method.

- Formulas for analyzing how well you handle your inventory.

12.1. TWO METHODS FOR HANDLING INVENTORY

When a business buys inventory for resale, it has an asset. When it sells the inventory, that inventory becomes an expense called **cost of goods sold**. For example, suppose a business bought Product A for $2,500 two months ago and sells it this month for $4,000.

Cash	4,000	
Sales		4,000
Cost of goods sold	2,500	
Inventory		2,500
(To record the sale of Product A)		

QUESTION 1. What accounting principle is upheld by not recording the $2,500 as an expense until the product is sold?

At the end of 20x1, Lauren counted Balloon Party's inventory. The business had 800 balloons at an average of 10¢ each, for a total inventory of $80. The canister of helium held 25 units at $1.00 per unit, for a total inventory of $25.

There are two methods for keeping inventory records. The **perpetual inventory** method records all the ups and downs directly in the inventory account. The **periodic inventory** method does not. It records all merchandise purchases in a purchases account and adjusts inventory only once a year.

12.2. THE PERPETUAL INVENTORY METHOD

Balloon Party keeps a perpetual inventory. During the summer, Balloon Party's inventory of balloons and supplies went up whenever the business bought merchandise and it went down whenever the business sold merchandise. Businesses need a system of determining which merchandise was sold and which stayed in the inventory. There are four allowable systems for doing this.

- *FIFO–First-in, first-out.* Picture the milk cooler in the grocery store. New cartons of milk come in from the back pushing older cartons of milk to the front for customers to buy first.

- *LIFO–Last-in, first-out.* Picture a bin of coal. New layers of coal get dumped on top. When sold, the coal gets shoveled off the top. The oldest coal at the bottom of the pile may never get sold.

- *Specific unit.* Picture a used car lot. When the dealership sells a car, it looks up the cost of that specific car and removes that amount from the inventory.

- *Weighted average.* Picture an underground tank of gasoline. When the station adds new gasoline to the tank, it mixes with the gasoline already there. The gasoline that gets pumped into a car is a mixture of all previous purchases.

Surprisingly, the accounting profession allows any business to select any inventory system as long as it presents inventory with reasonable accuracy.

CLEP Clue

If the CLEP test gives you facts for which one inventory system seems the most logical, expect a trap! For example, if the question is about a lettuce vendor, do not assume the business must use FIFO. The business may use any of the four systems.

12.2.1. Balloon Inventory Models the FIFO System

Figure 12-1 shows Balloon Party's inventory record for balloon merchandise. Lauren opted for the FIFO system

Figure 12-1. Balloon Party's Inventory Record: 20x2

Date	Quantity Bought/Sold	Price	Amount	1st Layer	Unit Cost	2nd Layer	Unit Cost	3rd Layer	Unit Cost	4th Layer	Unit Cost	Total
12/31/x1	800	$0.10	$80.00	800	$0.10							$ 80.00
New Year: 20x2												
3/1/x2	3,000	0.11	330.00	800	0.10	3,000	0.11					410.00
4/6/x2	(800)	0.10	(80.00)	0	0.10	1,800	0.11					198.00
	(1,200)	0.11	(132.00)	First layer permanently gone								
5/1/x2	4,000	0.13	520.00			1,800	0.11	4,000	0.13			718.00
6/1/x2	1,000	0.14	140.00			1,800	0.11	4,000	0.13	1,000	0.14	858.00
6/10/x2	(1,800)	0.11	(198.00)			—	0.11	—	0.13	900	0.14	126.00
	(4,000)	0.13	(520.00)									
	(100)	0.14	(14.00)									
TOTALS	900		126.00					2nd and 3rd layers permanently gone				

❶ The first row shows the inventory at the beginning of the year. Balloon Party has 800 balloons at a cost of 10¢ per balloon for a total inventory of $80. That becomes the first layer of inventory.

❷ In March, when Balloon Party purchases 3,000 balloons, the price has gone up to 11¢ per balloon. The inventory record keeps track of the 10¢ balloons and the 11¢ balloons separately. Visualize the 11¢ balloons stacked as a layer on top of the 10¢ balloons.

❸ On 4/6/x2 the business sells 2,000 balloons. Since this inventory uses FIFO, the first balloons in (the 800 balloons purchased at 10¢) are the first out. Next comes 1,200 of the 11¢ balloons. The total cost of goods sold is $212 [80 (800 × 10¢) + 132 (1,200 × 11¢)]. The 10¢ balloons are gone. Only 1,800 of the 11¢ balloons are left in inventory.

❹ In May and June, Balloon Party buys two more shipments of balloons at 13¢ and 14¢. These become two more layers on top of the 11¢ balloons.

❺ On June 10, Balloon Party sells 5,900 balloons. The oldest balloons (the 1,800 at 11¢) are the first to go out. Next are all 4,000 of the 13¢ balloons. Those two layers are now completely gone. One hundred of the 14¢ balloons also sell, leaving 900 of the 14¢ balloons in inventory. Ending inventory is 900 balloons × 14¢ = $126.

⑥ As a proof, net the numbers in the Quantity Bought/Sold column and the Amount column. The result is 900 units with a total cost of $126.

> **QUESTION 2.** When a business uses a FIFO inventory system, will the cost of the most recently purchased merchandise be in inventory or in cost of goods sold?

12.2.2. Helium Inventory Models the LIFO System

Figure 12-2 shows Balloon Party's inventory record for helium, which uses the LIFO system.

Figure 12-2. Balloon Party's Helium Inventory Record: 20x2

	Date	Quantity Bought/ Sold	Price	Amount	1st Layer	Unit Cost	2nd Layer	Unit Cost	3rd Layer	Unit Cost	Total
①	12/31/x1	25	$1.00	$25.00	25	$1.00	–	$ –		$ –	$ 25.00
	New Year: 20x2										
②	3/15/x2	100	1.10	110.00	25	1.00	100	1.10			135.00
③	5/1/x2	(50)	1.10	(55.00)	25	1.00	50	1.10			80.00
④	6/1/x2	400	1.15	460.00	25	1.00	50	1.10	400	1.15	540.00
⑤	6/15/x2	(100)	1.15	(115.00)	25	1.00	50	1.10	300	1.15	425.00
	7/1/x2	(300)	1.15	(345.00)	25	1.00	50	1.10	–	1.15	80.00
⑥		(20)	1.10	(22.00)	25	1.00	30	1.10	Layer removed		58.00
	TOTALS	55		58.00							

① The first row shows the inventory on 12/31/20x1 as the first layer.

② The purchases on March 15 form the second layer.

③ Under LIFO, the last units purchased are the first ones sold. The 50 units of helium sold on 5/1/x2 come from the second layer.

④ The 400 units of helium at $1.15/unit purchased on 6/1/x2 become the third layer.

⑤ The 100 units sold on 6/15/x2 come out of the third layer, leaving 300 in that layer. On July 1 when the business sells 320 units, that completely eliminates the remaining 300 units of $1.15 helium. In addition, 20 units of the $1.10 helium also sell.

⑥ As proof, total the Quantity Bought/Sold column and the Amount column to come up with 55 remaining units at a total cost of $58.

> **QUESTION 3.** After 10 years of operations, which inventory system would have more layers, FIFO or LIFO?

12.2.3. Balloon Party Doesn't Use Specific Unit System

Rather than the specific unit system, in which the cost of each unit sold is considered separately, Lauren chooses to use the weighted average system.

12.2.4. The Booth Inventory Models the Weighted Average System

This year Balloon Party added a product. The company constructs mobile booths for selling balloons and markets them to balloon vendors in other states. Figure 12-3 shows Balloon Party's inventory record for booths.

Figure 12-3. Balloon Party's Booth Inventory Record: 20x2

Date	Quantity Bought/ Sold	Unit Price	Inventory Balance	Total Units	Avg Cost	
① New Year: 20x2						
② 7/1/x2	2	4,000	8,000	2	4,000	
7/15/x2	(1)	(4,000)	4,000	1	4,000	
7/25/x2	1	3,500	7,500	2	3,750	(7,500 / 2)
③ 8/12/x2	3	3,000	16,500	5	3,300	(16,500 / 5)
④ 8/15/x2	(1)	(3,300)	13,200	4	3,300	
TOTALS	4	**⑤**				

① There is no beginning inventory. The first two booths cost $4,000 each for a total inventory of $8,000.

② The business sells one of the booths and makes another one. As Lauren improves her construction techniques, the booths get less expensive to make. As of July 25, there are two booths in inventory. The first cost $4,000, and the second cost $3,500. That averages to $3,750 [(4,000 + 3,500) / 2 = 3,750]. From here on, whenever a product is sold, use the average cost from the previous row.

③ The business constructs three more booths at a cost of $3,000 each for a total of $9,000 (3 × 3,000). Adding $9,000 to the inventory brings the total dollar amount to $16,500 for five booths. That averages to $3,300 each (16,500 / 5 = 3,300).

④ When a booth sells on 8/15/x2, the inventory lowers by $3,300, the weighted average per booth. Note that the $3,300 on this row comes from the average cost of the previous row.

⑤ Netting the Quantity Bought/Sold column proves there are 4 items left in inventory.

> **QUESTION 4.** An inventory contains some merchandise at $5, some at $6, and some at $7. What is the weighted average price of the merchandise in inventory?

12.3. FOLLOWING THE TRAIL OF DEBITS

Debits increase assets. In the inventory process, debits start in the cash account, move to inventory, and end up in cost of goods sold. To see these debits move, check Figure 12-4. It shows the VJEs to record all the inventory transactions as shown on the preceding inventory records.

Columns (1) and (3c)—*Purchase of inventory*. Debits move from cash to inventory. In the journal entry for purchased inventory, debit inventory and credit cash. The purchases have been combined for simplification.

Columns (2), (3), and (4)—*Sale of inventory*. Debits move from inventory to cost of goods sold. These VJEs have two parts. The first part (a) records the sale: Credit sales and debit cash or a receivable. The second part (b) removes the debits from the inventory account and moves them to cost of goods sold.

All three of Balloon Party's inventories use the perpetual inventory method.

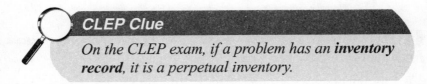

CLEP Clue

*On the CLEP exam, if a problem has an **inventory record**, it is a perpetual inventory.*

12.4. THE PERIODIC INVENTORY METHOD

In a periodic inventory system, purchases of all merchandise go into a single account called Purchases. **Purchases** is not an expense account. It is a cost of goods sold account, used to calculate cost of goods sold on the income statement. Inventory is not increased or decreased throughout the year. It is adjusted a single time at the end of the year.

Figure 12-4. Balloon Party Perpetual Inventory VJEs: Summer 20x2

BALLOON PARTY
Vertical Journal Entries
From August 20x2 to January 20x3

(partial list of accounts)	Start	1 Purchased goods	2 Sold balloons for a profit	3 a & b. Sold booth. c. Made 4 more	4 Sold 1 $3,300 booth for notes	End
ASSETS						
Current Assets						
Cash	25,000	(9,560)		a 10,000 c (12,500)		12,940
Accounts Receivable	15,400		a 3,800			19,200
Allowance for uncollectible accounts	(84)					(84)
Note Receivable					a 20,000	20,000
Balloon Inventory	80	990	b (944)			126
Helium Inventory	25	570	b (537)			58
Booth Inventory		8,000		b (4,000) c 12,500	b (3,300)	13,200
Fixed Assets						
All fixed asset accts	11,063					11,063
LIABILITIES						
All current liabilities	(11,000)					(11,000)
EQUITY						
Lauren—Equity	(3,070)					(3,070)
Lauren—Withdrawal	10,166					10,166
REVENUE						
Balloon Sales	(49,000)		a (3,800)			(52,800)
Booth Sales	(10,000)			a (10,000)	a (20,000)	(40,000)
Interest revenue	(580)					(580)
EXPENSES						
Cost of goods sold exp			b 1,481	b 4,000	b 3,300	8,781
All expense accts	12,000					12,000
TOTALS	—	—	—	—	—	—

1. During the summer, bought $990 of balloons, $570 of helium, and $8,000 for booth.
2a. Sold balloons and helium for $3,800.
2b. Cost of goods sold: $944 for balloons and $537 of helium.
3a. Sold one booth for $10,000.
3b. Cost of the booth sold was $4,000
3c. Made 4 more booths: one for $3,500 and 3 for $3,000 apiece.
4a. Sold one booth for $20,000. Buyers gave $20,000 of 10% notes.
4b. Cost for the booth sold was $3,300.

CLEP Clue

If a CLEP problem shows the inventory account changing only once a year, it is a periodic inventory. In contrast, perpetual inventories change with every purchase and sale.

Figure 12-5 shows the VJEs for a sample periodic inventory for Balloon Party. Note that there is no cost of goods sold account.

Figure 12-5. Balloon Party Periodic Inventory VJEs: Summer 20x2

BALLOON PARTY
Vertical Journal Entries
From August 20x2 to January 20x3

(partial list of accounts)	Start	1	2		3	4		End
ASSETS **Current Assets**								
Cash	25,000	(21,520)	a b	(520) 70	10,000	a	(90)	12,940
Accounts Receivable	15,400				3,800			19,200
Allowance for uncollectible accounts	(84)							(84)
Note Receivable					20,000			20,000
Balloon Inventory	80					b	46	126
Helium Inventory	25					b	33	58
Booth Inventory						b	13,200	13,200
Fixed assets, Liabilities, Equity and Revenue accounts not shown								
Balloon Sales	(49,000)				(3,800)			(52,800)
Booth Sales	(10,000)				(30,000)			(40,000)
Interest revenue	(580)							(580)
EXPENSES **Cost of Goods Sold**								
Purchases		21,520	a	550		b	(13,279)	8,791
Purchases R & A			b	(70)				(70)
Purchases Discount			a	(30)				(30)
Freight In						a	90	90
All expense accts	12,000							12,000
TOTALS	—	—	—		—	—		—

1. During the summer, bought $470 of balloons, $570 of helium, and $8,000 for booth.
2a. Bought $550 of balloons. By paying cash, got a $30 discount.
2b. Some of the balloon supplies were defective. The vendor sent a $70 refund check.
3. Sold $3,800 of balloon sales and $30,000 of booth sales. Received $20,000 of notes, $3,800 of accounts receivable, and the rest cash.
4a. Received $90 freight bill for balloon inventory bought earlier, and paid bill.
4b. On December 31, 20x2, determined that the ending inventories are: balloons, $126; helium, $58; and booths, $13,200.

Column (1)—*Purchasing merchandise*. Debit the purchases account, not inventory. There is no cost of goods sold account. Cost of goods sold is calculated on the income statement.

Column (2a)—*Purchase discount*. If a company vendor gives a discount for paying early, record the discount in a **contra-purchases account** called **purchases discount**.

Column (2b)—*Returns and allowances*. When goods are defective, vendors allow the goods to be returned for a refund (as happened with Balloon Party), or gives them an allowance for a future purchase. **Purchases returns and allowances** is a contra-purchases account.

Column (3)—*Selling merchandise*. Balloon Party decided on two separate sales accounts. Owners can break down sales into any categories they want. This VJE shows the three ways that customers pay for merchandise: with cash ($10,000), on account ($3,800), and with a note ($20,000).

Column (4a)—*Paying freight-in*. Most of the time, vendors include the cost of freight in the price of the merchandise. If buyers pay freight separately to ship merchandise bought, they debit **freight-in**. Freight-in is another cost of goods sold account like the purchases account.

Column (4b)—*Adjusting a periodic inventory*. Beginning periodic inventory accounts never change for an entire year. At the end of the year, businesses physically count the inventory and make the adjustment on the books using the FIFO, LIFO, specific item, or weighted average systems. The balloon inventory computes to $126, and beginning inventory is $80, so the adjustment is $46 (126 − 80). The amount credited to the purchases account is whatever is necessary to make the VJE balance.

12.5. COMPARING THE FOUR INVENTORY SYSTEMS AND TWO METHODS

FIFO is the most common system. It results in fewer layers than LIFO, and computers handle it more easily. In periods of rising prices, the cost of older, cheaper merchandise ends up as cost of goods sold, making it lower. Net income therefore becomes higher.

LIFO is the most complicated system. It may result in scores of layers. The cost of older, cheaper merchandise stays in inventory, making it lower. The newer, more expensive merchandise ends up in cost of goods sold. Businesses switch to *LIFO* for tax reasons because as net income drops, taxes decrease.

Weighted average and *specific unit* methods fall somewhere between FIFO and LIFO.

Accounting Principle

*The **Consistency Principle** requires that businesses not switch back and forth from one inventory system to another. The **Disclosure Principle** requires businesses to reveal the type of inventory system used. Under the **Conservatism Principle** (which requires a business to err on the side of reporting less net income) the **Lower of Cost or Market Principle** requires that businesses lower their inventory accounts if damage or a change in the market makes the inventory less valuable.*

The *perpetual inventory method* requires much more accounting. It is more accurate, but also more expensive. The inventory accounts and cost of goods sold account are always up to date. Modern computer systems make this system more economical.

The *periodic inventory method* is much simpler and cheaper than the perpetual method. Its less-accurate information may be sufficient for small business owners. Under this system, there is no cost of goods sold account. For inventories that do not fluctuate, the purchases account is a fair approximation of cost of goods sold.

The income statement differs under the two inventory methods, as Figure 12-6 shows. The perpetual inventory method keeps an up-to-date cost of goods sold account, so there is no need to calculate it like the periodic inventory method does.

1 Owners break down sales into as many categories as they want.

2 The *cost of goods sold formula* is

Beginning inventory + Net purchases = Goods available for sale
Goods available for sale – Ending inventory = Cost of goods sold,

abbreviated as:

$$BI + NP = GAS$$
$$GAS - EI = CGS$$

Figure 12-6. The Difference Between Perpetual and Periodic Cost of Goods Sold

BALLOON PARTY
Partial Income Statement
For the year ended December 31, 20x2

	Perpetual Method		Periodic Method	
Sales				
Balloon Sales	$52,800		$ 52,800	
Booth Sales	40,000		40,000	
Total Sales	$92,800		$ 92,800	**1**
Less Cost of Goods Sold				
Beginning Inventory			$ 105	**2**
Purchases		$ 22,070		
Less Purchases Returns & Allowances		(70)		**3**
Less Purchases Discounts		(30)		
Plus Freight-in		90		
Net Purchases			22,060	
Goods Available for Sale			$22,165	
Less Ending Inventory		**4**	13,384	
Cost of Goods Sold	8,781		8,781	
Gross Profit	$84,019		$ 84,019	

5 Gross profit percentage: GP/Sales = 84,019 / 92,800 = 91%
6 Average inventory: (105 + 13,384)/2 = $6,744.50
7 Inventory turnover: CGS/Avg Inv = 8,781 / 6,744.50 = 1.3 times per year
8 Days in inventory: 365/Inventory turnover = 365/1.3 = 280.35 days.

CLEP Clue

The CLEP exam will test your knowledge of this formula two ways: (1) finding missing numbers, and (2) calculating the effect of errors.

QUESTION 5. Ending inventory is $6,000, goods available for sale is $56,000, and beginning inventory is $10,000. What is net purchases and cost of goods sold?

QUESTION 6. If beginning inventory was incorrectly overstated, how does that affect the cost of goods sold? Gross profit? Net income?

3 The *net purchases formula* is

Purchases – Purchases returns and allowances –
Purchases discounts + Freight in = Net purchases,

abbreviated as:

Purch – PR&A – PDisc + Fr-in = NP

4 Cost of goods sold is the same under both methods.

12.6. ANALYZING HOW WELL A BUSINESS HANDLES INVENTORY

At the bottom of Figure 12-6 are four tools for analyzing inventory.

5 The *gross profit percentage formula* is

$$\frac{\text{Gross profit}}{\text{Total sales}} = GP\%.$$

In this case, 84,091 / 92,800 = 91%. Balloon Party's GP% is very good. A 91% GP% means the cost of goods sold percentage (CGS%) is 9% (100% – 91% = 9%). These percentages are usually consistent, so Balloon Party can estimate its ending inventory at any time during the year. For example, Balloon Party's beginning inventory for 20x3 is the same as ending inventory for 20x2: $13,384. Assume that sales for the first five months of 20x3 total $50,000, and the Purchases account shows $6,000. Lauren can estimate ending inventory by using the cost of goods sold formula.

BI	+ NP	= GAS	GAS	–	EI	= CGS [Sales × CGS%]
13,384 + 6,000 =		?	?	–	?	= [50,000 × (100% – 91%)]
13,384 + 6,000 =		19,384	19,384 –		? =	4,500
13,384 + 6,000 =		19,384	19,384 – 14,884 =			4,500

So Lauren estimates the ending inventory to be $14,884.

> **QUESTION 7.** Company A had $100,000 of sales, beginning inventory of $20,000, purchases of $60,000, and a gross profit percentage of 30%. Estimate ending inventory using the gross profit percentage method.

6 *Average inventory* = $\dfrac{\text{(beginning inventory + ending inventory)}}{2}$

7 The *inventory turnover* measures the number of times inventory completely sells per year. The formula is:

$$\frac{\text{Cost of goods sold}}{\text{Average inventory}} = \text{Inventory turnover}$$

A turnover of 12 is very good, indicating that inventory completely sells every month. Four is decent. Balloon Party's 1.3 is low. It may mean that too much of the business's money is tied up in inventory that is not selling.

8 *Days in inventory* is similar to inventory turnover. Good is 30 – 90 days, and the lower the better. Balloon Party's 280 days needs improvement. The formula is:

$$\frac{365}{\text{Inventory turnover}} = \text{Days in inventory}$$

QUESTION 8. Suppose beginning inventory is $90,000, ending inventory is $110,000, and cost of goods sold is $400,000. What is the inventory turnover and days in inventory?

CLEP CRAM

A. *VOCABULARY*

Contra-purchases account—An account that is subtracted from Purchases to compute Net Purchases. Examples: *Purchases Discount* and *Purchases Returns and Allowances*.

Cost of goods sold—The cost paid for the merchandise sold.

FIFO—First-in, first-out. The inventory system that assumes the oldest items in inventory are the first ones sold.

Gross margin—See *gross profit formula* in the next section, Accounting Principles and Formulas.

LIFO—Last-in, first-out. The inventory system that assumes the latest items purchased are the first ones sold.

Periodic inventory method—The inventory method that keeps track of merchandise costs in various purchases and contra-purchases accounts and then computes cost of goods sold on the income statement. Inventory on the books is adjusted only at year-end.

Perpetual inventory method—The inventory method that increases the inventory account with every purchase and lowers the inventory account with every sale.

Purchases account—A cost of goods sold account used in the periodic inventory method to keep track of all merchandise bought for resale during the year.

Purchases discount account—A contra-purchases account used under the periodic inventory method to keep track of discounts granted by vendors for paying early.

Purchases returns and allowances—A contra-purchases account used under the periodic inventory method to keep track of refunds a business gets for returning merchandise to vendors, or reductions in price (allowances) the vendors offer to resolve complaints.

Specific unit—The inventory system that keeps track of the actual historic cost of each inventory item. When that item is sold, the cost flows into cost of goods sold.

Weighted average—The inventory system that averages the cost of all items in inventory and assigns that averaged cost to the items sold.

B. *ACCOUNTING PRINCIPLES AND FORMULAS*

Average inventory.

$$\frac{(\text{Beginning inventory} + \text{Ending inventory})}{2} = \text{Average inventory}$$

Consistency Principle—Businesses should use the same accounting system from period to period. For example, there is no switching back and forth from LIFO to FIFO.

Cost of goods sold formula.

> Beginning inventory
> + Net purchases
> = Goods Available for Sale (GAS)
> – Ending inventory
> = Cost of goods sold

Cost of goods sold percent (CGS%). There are two ways to compute CGS%:

- $\dfrac{\text{Cost of goods sold}}{\text{Total sales}} = \text{CGS}\%$

- 100% – Gross profit percent (GP%) = CGS%

Days in inventory formula. Measures the average number of days before merchandise sells.

$$\dfrac{365}{\text{Inventory turnover}} = \text{Days in inventory}$$

Disclosure Principle—Financial statements should disclose enough information to allow outside readers to make intelligent decisions. The information should be relevant, reliable, and comparable. For example, financial statements must disclose the inventory system used.

Gross profit formula.

> Sales – Cost of goods sold = Gross profit, or *gross margin*

Gross profit percent (GP%) **formula**.

$$\dfrac{\text{Gross profit}}{\text{Total sales}} = \text{GP}\%$$

Inventory turnover formula. Measures the number of times inventory completely sells per year.

$$\dfrac{\text{Cost of goods sold}}{\text{Average inventory}} = \text{Inventory turnover}$$

Lower of Cost or Market (LCM) Principle—The company must report inventories at cost or the current market price, whichever is lower.

Net purchases formula.

Purchases − Purchase discounts −
Purchase returns and allowances + Freight-in = Net purchases

C. JOURNAL ENTRIES

Show the journal entry (JE) to record:

Buy merchandise for resale, perpetual method	Inventory 100 Cash 100
Buy merchandise for resale, periodic method	Purchases 100 Cash 100

Sell item for $500 that cost $300, perpetual inventory system	Cash 500
	    Sales 500
	Cost of goods sold 300
	    Inventory 300

Sell item for $500 that cost $300, periodic inventory system	Cash 500 Sales 500 (Do not adjust inventory under the periodic system.)
Return $50 of purchases for a refund	Cash 50 Purchases returns and allowances 50

Pay $98 to buy $100 of merchandise. Vendor discounted $2 for paying quickly.	Purchases 100
	    Cash 98
	    Purchases Discount 2

Adjust a periodic inventory at year end. Inventory account is $1,000, but should be $1,075.	Inventory 75 Purchases 75

ANSWERS TO QUESTIONS FOUND IN THIS CHAPTER

Q1: The Matching Principle. The cost of goods sold expense matches the associated sales revenue.

Q2. Using FIFO, the most current costs end up in inventory as the most recent layer.

Q3: LIFO will normally have more layers. By using LIFO, a business can add several layers to inventory each year. With FIFO, the old layers always get sold, so only the one or two newest layers end up in inventory.

Q4: This is a trick question. It is impossible to answer from the information given. If you answered $6, you fell into a common CLEP exam trap. The weighted average does *not* just average the prices. You need to know the quantity at each price. Review the example.

Q5:

BI	+	NP	= GAS	GAS	–	EI	= CGS
10,000 +		?	= 56,000	56,000	–	6,000 =	?
10,000 +		**46,000**	= 56,000	56,000	–	6,000 =	**50,000**
		(net purchases)					(cost of goods sold)

Q6: The cost of goods sold will be overstated. The surest way to analyze this type of question is to make two very simple examples: first as correct, then as overstated.

Correct: BI + NP = GAS   GAS – EI = CGS
$$1 + 2 = 3 \qquad 3 - 1 = 2$$

Overstated
beginning inventory: **2** + 2 = **4**   **4** – 1 = **3**

The cost of goods sold number in the second example is larger, therefore overstated. If the cost of goods sold is overstated, gross profit, as well as net income, will be smaller (understated).

Q7: Using the cost of goods sold formula:

BI	+	NP	= GAS	GAS	–	EI	= CGS [Sales ×	CGS%]
20,000 +		60,000 =	?	?	–	?	=	[100,000 × (100% – 30%)]
20,000 +		60,000 =	80,000	80,000 –		?	= 70,000	[100,000 × 70%]
20,000 +		60,000 =	80,000	80,000 –		10,000	= 70,000	

So ending inventory is estimated to be $10,000.

Q8: Average inventory is $100,000 [(90,000 + 110,000)/2]. Inventory turnover is 4 (400,000 / 100,000 = 4). Days in inventory is therefore 91 (365 / 4 = 91).

CHAPTER 13

Supplies and Prepaids

Chapter 13

Supplies and Prepaids:
Finishing Out the Current Asset Section

In April 20x3, in order to get a year's lease on the rental space for Balloon Party, Lauren pays $3,000 for three months of rent in advance: the first two months and the last month. To protect herself, Lauren buys a three-year liability insurance policy for $2,400. As part of normal operations, she keeps a shelf-full of miscellaneous supplies which she uses up at the rate of about $100 per month. She spends $1,200 for 12 quarter-page advertisements in *Balloon World*, a monthly magazine.

In this chapter you will learn:

- How to account for prepaid assets.

- Two methods for handling supplies inventory.

13.1. ACCOUNTING FOR PREPAID ASSETS

When Lauren paid in advance for the rent, liability insurance, and advertising, she actually acquired assets that have future value. The rent gives her rights to use the building on into the future. The insurance protects her for three years. The advertising solicits sales for an entire year. How does Lauren show these valuable assets on the balance sheet? How does she use up these assets over time?

Balloon Party's rent is $1,000 per month. When Lauren paid $3,000 for the first, second, and last month's rent, she purchased an asset called "prepaid rent." **Prepaids** are assets that represent expenses paid in advance that provide future benefits to the business. When Lauren bought three years of insurance coverage, she gained an asset called "prepaid insurance." The right to a year's worth of advertising is called "prepaid advertising." Figure 13-1 shows the VJEs to record these purchases.

Figure 13-1. Balloon Party VJEs for prepaids and supplies: 20x3

BALLOON PARTY
Vertical Journal Entries
From April 1, 20x3 to Dec. 31, 20x3

(partial list of accounts)	Start	1 4/1/x3 Prepay rent, ins and adv	2 4/15/x3 Buy $80 of supplies	3 4/31/x3 End of month adj of ppds	4 a. May– Dec ppd adj. b. Buy sup	5 a. 7 mon rent. b. adj supplies	End
ASSETS							
Current Assets							
Cash and cash equivalents	16,400	(6,600)	(80)		b (770)	a (7,000)	1,950
Accounts receivable	15,000						15,000
Allowance for uncollectible accounts	(300)						(300)
Note receivable	20,000						20,000
All merchandise inventory	13,300						13,300
Supplies inventory	100					b 100	200
Prepaid rent		3,000		a (1,000)	a (1,000)		1,000
Prepaid insurance		2,400		b (67)	a (533)		1,800
Prepaid advertising		1,200		c (100)	a (800)		300
Fixed Assets							
All fixed asset accts	12,000						12,000
LIABILITIES							
All current liabilities	(11,000)						(11,000)
EQUITY							
Lauren—Equity	(59,000)						(59,000)
REVENUE							
All revenue accounts	(10,000)						(10,000)
EXPENSES							
Cost of goods sold exp	1,500						1,500
Advertising exp				c 100	a 800		900
Insurance exp				b 67	a 533		600
Rent exp				a 1,000	a 1,000	a 7,000	9,000
Supplies exp			80		b 770	b (100)	750
All other exp accts	2,000						2,000
TOTALS	—	—	—	—	—	—	—

1. Paid $3,000 for 3 months of rent, $2,400 for 3 years of insurance, and $1,200 for a year of advertising.
2. Buy $80 of operating supplies.
3. April 30, 20x3, end of month adjustment of prepaid assets.
4a. May–December adjustments for all prepaid assets.
4b. May–December purchases of operating supplies: $770.
5a. Record June–December payment of rent @ $1,000 per month.
5b. A physical count of supplies inventory shows there are $200 worth of operating supplies left at the end of the year.

Column (1)—*Paying in advance*. Whenever a business pays bills in advance, it buys an asset whose name starts with "prepaid." Prepaids usually get used up within one year, so they are current assets. Consider the prepaid section of the balance sheet like a warehouse that stores debits until the proper time when they can move into expense accounts.

Column (3)—*Adjusting prepaids at end-of-month*. The matching principle requires the expenses to be recognized over time as the asset gets used up. Rather than make April, 20x3 expenses seem outrageously high and expenses for all the following months seem strangely low, the accounting profession requires the expenses to be recognized each period. Here, Balloon Party recognizes $1,000 for April rent. The $67 represents 1/36 of the 3-year insurance policy ($2,400/36 months). The $100 ($1,200/12) advertising expense reflects that the magazine has already performed 1/12 of its obligation and now owes Balloon Party only 11 more months of advertising.

Column (4a)—*Eight months have gone by*. Balloon Party recognizes 8 months of insurance and advertising expense. It adjusts for May rent only. The last month in the prepaid rent account belongs to March 20x4 because that was how the lease was written.

Column (5a)—*Paying 7 months of rent*. For the months of June through December, Balloon Party must make cash rent payments. Since each rent payment has a useful life of only a month, Balloon Party records the payments as expenses, not prepaids.

QUESTION 1. On June 1, 20x8, Company X purchased a 1-year insurance policy for $1,200, debiting the prepaid insurance account. Company X made no financial statements until December 31, 20x8, and therefore had made no monthly adjustments to the prepaid account. On December 31, what single adjusting entry should the company make to bring the books up to date?

13.2. TWO METHODS TO ACCOUNT FOR OPERATING SUPPLIES

The two methods for handling operating supplies are the purchase method and the consumption method. The names of these methods explain when the business recognizes the *expense*. The **purchase method** recognizes supplies expense when the supplies are purchased. The **consumption method** recognizes supplies expense when the supplies are consumed.

QUESTION 2. Look at Figure 13-1 and determine what method of accounting Balloon Party uses for operating supplies.

Figure 13-1 models the purchases method of handling operating supplies.

Column (2)—*Purchasing supplies*. Under the purchase method, Balloon Party recognizes supplies expense when it purchases the supplies.

Column (4b)—*Eight months of buying supplies*. Throughout the entire year, whenever the business buys supplies, it debits supplies expense. Supplies inventory is never touched.

Column (5b)—*Adjust supplies inventory at year-end*. Under the purchase method, supplies inventory is adjusted at year-end only. Here, a physical count shows $200 of supplies in inventory at the end of the year. Since the inventory had $100 in it at the beginning of the year, it needs an additional $100. The credit goes to the supplies expense account.

QUESTION 3. What if the end-of-year count of inventory had shown that ending inventory had gone down to $80. What would the adjusting entry be?

Figure 13-2 shows that the journal entries for supplies would be if Balloon Party used the consumption method.

Column (1) and (2)—*Purchasing supplies*. Under the consumption method, the supplies originally go into inventory. The debits stay in inventory until an inventory adjustment moves the debits into the expense account.

Column 3—*Adjust ending inventory*. A sophisticated supplies inventory might adjust monthly. In this case, the adjustment was made at the end of the year. Lauren calculated that the supplies inventory account had a debit balance of $950 (100 + 80 + 770). Her actual inventory count determined that the balance should be $200. Thus she needed a $750 reduction.

The two methods for handling operating supplies reach the same result. In the purchases method, the debits are stored in supplies expense during the year. In the consumption method, the debits are stored in supplies inventory. Either way, the accounts are corrected whenever an actual inventory count is made.

Figure 13-2. VJEs Using the Consumption Method
of Recording Supplies Inventory

BALLOON PARTY
Vertical Journal Entries
From April 1, 20x3 to Dec. 31, 20x3

(partial list of accounts)	Start	1 4/15/x3 Buy $80 of supplies	2 May–Dec Supplies	3 Adjust ending supplies inv to $200	End
ASSETS					
Current Assets					
Cash and cash equivalents	16,400	(80)	(770)		15,550
Other current assets	77,000				77,000
Supplies inventory	100	80	770	(750)	200
Fixed Assets					
All fixed asset accts	12,000				12,000
LIABILITIES					
All current liabilities	(40,000)				(40,000)
EQUITY					
Lauren—Equity	(59,000)				(59,000)
REVENUE					
All revenue accounts	(10,000)				(10,000)
EXPENSES					
Cost of goods sold exp	1,500				1,500
Supplies exp				750	750
All other exp accts	2,000				2,000
TOTALS	—	—	—	—	—

1. Paid $80 for supplies.
2. Paid for 8 months more of supplies.
3. Determined that ending inventory of supplies is $200.

CLEP CRAM

A. VOCABULARY

Consumption method for supplies—The method of accounting for operating supplies that recognizes supplies as an expense when they are consumed. When supplies are purchased, the debits are stored in supplies inventory. The supplies expense account is not touched until the inventory account is adjusted.

Prepaids—Assets that represent expenses paid in advance that provide future benefits to the business.

Purchase method for supplies—The method of accounting for operating supplies that recognizes supplies as an expense when they are purchased. When supplies are purchased, the debits are stored in supplies expense. The supplies inventory is not touched until the end of the year.

B. JOURNAL ENTRIES

Show the journal entry (JE) to record:

Buy 3 years insurance for $3,600	Prepaid Insurance Cash	3,600	3,600
Use up $100 of prepaid insurance	Insurance Expense Prepaid Insurance	100	100
Purchase $100 supplies, purchases method	Supplies Expense Cash	100	100
Purchase $100 supplies, consumption method	Supplies Inventory Cash	100	100
Adjust supplies inventory at end of year	Supplies Inventory (whatever is necessary to correct inventory account) Supplies Expense	xxx xxx	xxx xxx

ANSWERS TO QUESTIONS FOUND IN THIS CHAPTER

Q1: Company X should adjust the prepaid account for 7 months of insurance expense (June through December) using the following general journal entry:

12/31/x8	Insurance expense	700	
	Prepaid insurance		700

(To adjust the prepaid insurance account for 7 months of expense)

Q2: Balloon Party uses the purchase method for handling operating supplies. It recognizes an expense when the supplies are purchased.

Q3: Balloon Party would need to lower the supplies inventory account by $20 (100 – 80).

12/31/x3	Supplies expense	20	
	Supplies inventory		20

(To adjust supplies inventory to $80 per inventory count)

CHAPTER 14
Buying and Selling Plant Assets

Chapter 14

Buying and Selling Plant Assets:
Investing in Assets that Make Money

As the mobile booths became more and more profitable, Balloon Party switched more to manufacturing. In January 20x3, Lauren bought three machines from a bankrupt business. On July 1, 20x3, she furnished her new business space with $10,000 of used furniture. In 20x4, Lauren offered to buy the building she was in, and her landlord agreed. She paid $180,000 for the building and the land.

In this chapter you will learn:

- How to value assets.

- How to allocate the purchase price among a group of assets.

- How to distinguish between repairs and capital improvements.

- How to dispose of fixed assets.

- How to present fixed asset transactions on the cash flow statement.

14.1. BALLOON PARTY BUYS A GROUP OF MACHINES

On January 1, 20x3, Balloon Party pays $15,000 for three machines. Lauren hires three men to move the machines for $270 plus $30 for their lunches. She lays a concrete pad for the machines, which cost $700. How much does each machine cost?

Accounting Principle

*The **All-Costs-to-Get-Operating Principle** requires a business to capitalize (record as an asset) all costs necessary to get any asset operating. Once an asset is operating, record any further maintenance as repair expense. For example, suppose Company X buys an old house because it wants the land to build a new office. The cost of the land, the old house, the demolition of the old house, and the grading of the land are all part of the land cost.*

The cost of the three machines is $16,000 (15000 + 270 + 30 + 700). In order to allocate the $16,000 to the three machines, Lauren researches the market value of each machine. She discovers that Machine A has a value of $10,000, Machine B has a value of $8,000, and Machine C has a value of $2,000. She then spreads the $16,000 cost among the three machines in proportion to their market values, as shown in Figure 14-1.

**Figure 14-1. Allocation of Purchase Price
in Proportion to Market Value**

	Market	%		Price
Machine A	$10,000	50%		$8,000
Machine B	8,000	40%	× $16,000 =	6,400
Machine C	2,000	10%		1,600
TOTAL	$20,000	100%		$16,000

QUESTION 1. Company X bought 4 machines for $12,000. It determined the market value of the machines as follows: A: $1,000, B: $2,000, C: $3,000, and D: $4,000. What is the purchase price of each machine?

In February 20x4, Balloon Party pays $180,000 for the building it has been renting. There is a question of how much Balloon Party pays for land and how much for the building. If the purchase agreement does not break down the price, Lauren must do so. A realtor tells her the land is worth between $30,000 and $45,000. For tax reasons, Lauren picks the lower price.

QUESTION 2. Why does Lauren pick the lower price?

14.2. REPAIRS OR IMPROVEMENTS

After the machines were installed, Machine C would not work. Lauren hires mechanic Phil to fix it. She pays him $300 for labor plus $800 for parts. While he is there, he installs new belts on Machine B for $200 "just in case." The company car also needs work. Phil installs a new transmission for $1,080. "She'll go another three years now," he says. He also tunes the engine and changes the oil for $50.

Accounting Principle

*The **New-Life Principle** says that if any work on an asset extends the asset's life, the cost of that work should be capitalized. **Capitalized** means to record the cost as an asset. If the work on an asset merely returns an asset back to the condition it was, the cost should be **expensed** as a repair expense.*

QUESTION 3. Which amounts should be capitalized? Which should be expensed?

Cost	Capitalized	Expensed
Labor to fix Machine C	$_____	$_____
Parts to fix Machine C	$_____	$_____
New belts for Machine B	$_____	$_____
The new transmission	$_____	$_____
Oil change and tune-up	$_____	$_____

14.3. DISPOSING OF FIXED ASSETS

Show fixed assets at historical cost. Over time, fixed assets get used up through depreciation expense. (The next chapter discusses depreciation expense in detail.) The sum of all past depreciation expense for each asset accumulates in the accumulated depreciation account. The **book value** (BV) of an asset is the historical cost less accumulated depreciation for that asset.

At the end of 20x4, Balloon Party disposes of Machine B and Machine C. Machine B sells for $5,000. Machine C is scrapped for $100. Just prior to their disposal Machine B was on the books at a historical cost of $6,400 less accumulated depreciation of $1,792, for a book value of $4,608 (6400 − 1792). Machine C was on the books at a historical cost of $2,700 ($1,600 initial cost + $1,100 labor and parts to get it working) less accumulated depreciation of $920, for a book value of $1,780 (2700 − 920).

Balloon Party had a $392 gain when it sold Machine B. The formula for computing the gain or loss on the disposal of an asset is:

Amount received – Book value (BV) given up = Gain or (Loss)

$5,000   – $4,608   = $392 gain

The calculation of the loss on disposal of Machine C is:

Amount received – BV given up = Gain or (Loss)

$100   – $1,780   = ($1,680) loss

14.4. VERTICAL JOURNAL ENTRIES FOR FIXED ASSETS

Figure 14-2 shows the VJEs to record the above transactions.

Column (1)—*Purchasing capital assets.* Balloon Party buys three machines for a bulk price of $15,000. On a separate depreciation schedule, Lauren keeps track of the three machines individually. (More on that in the next chapter.) Because the price of any asset is the total cost to get it operational, the $300 transportation cost and the $700 concrete pad to go under the machines is part of the cost of the machines.

Column (2a)—*Making repairs.* Balloon Party spends $2,350 to work on the equipment. The $1,100 of labor and parts is an additional cost of Machine C because all costs necessary to make equipment operational become part of the cost of the equipment. The $250 ($200 for new belts for Machine B and $50 for an oil change and tune up on the car) is a repair expense because it is part of general upkeep.

Adding new life. The $1,080 for the new transmission for the car adds an extra year to the life of an old asset. Before the work, the car had a historical cost of $2,000 and accumulated depreciation of $1,000 for a book value of $1,000. After adding the $1,080 cost of the transmission, the car will have a book value of $2,080. However, rather than add the $1,080 to the car account, the accounting profession first negates any accumulated depreciation. In general journal format, the journal entry to put in the new transmission is:

Accumulated depreciation (up to balance in A/D acct.)	1000	
Equipment and Furniture—Car		80
Cash		1,080

(To record a new transmission for the car that adds a year more life)

Therefore, the $1,180 debited to Equipment and Furniture includes $1,100 for Machine C and $80 for the car.

Figure 14-2. VJEs for Fixed Assets

BALLOON PARTY
Vertical Journal Entries
Partial for years 20x3 and 20x4

(partial list of accounts)	Start	1		2		3		4		End
ASSETS										
Current Assets										
Cash	50,000	a	(15,000)	a	(2,430)	a	(20,000)	a	5,000	6,670
(BOY: $5,000)		b	(1,000)	b	(10,000)			b	100	
Other current assets	57,800									57,800
Fixed Assets										
Equipment & furniture	2,500	a	15,000	a	1,180			a	(6,400)	20,580
		b	1,000	b	10,000			b	(2,700)	
A/D—Equipment	(1,040)			a	1,000	b	(11,526)	a	1,792	(8,854)
								b	920	
Building						a	150,000			150,000
A/D—Building						b	(3,300)			(3,300)
Land						a	30,000			30,000
LIABILITIES										
All current liabilities	(40,000)									(40,000)
Loans Payable						a	(160,000)			(160,000)
EQUITY										
Lauren—Equity	(24,260)									(24,260)
REVENUE										
All revenue accounts	(60,000)									(60,000)
EXPENSES								Net Inc from ops: $29,924		
Repair expense				a 250						250
Depreciation expense						b	14,826			14,826
All other exp accts	15,000									15,000
NONOPERATING REVENUES AND EXPENSES										
Gain on sale of equip								a	(392)	(392)
Loss on disposal of equip								b	1,680	1,680
TOTALS	—	—		—		—		—		—

1a. Purchased Machine A, Machine B, and Machine C for $15,000 cash.
1b. Paid $300 to move the machines and $700 for a concrete pad to go under them.
2a. Hired Phil to work on machines and car.
2b. Bought $10,000 of furniture, July 1, 20x3
3a. Bought building and land. Paid $20,000 down and got a loan for the rest, Feb 20x4.
3b. Record depreciation expense for 20x3 and 20x4.
4a. Sold Machine B for $5,000.
4b. Scrapped Machine C for $100.

Column (2b)—*New furniture*. Buying furniture is just like buying equipment.

Column (3a)—*Buying a building*. Lauren must allocate the total cost to building (which is depreciable) and land (which is not depreciable). Lauren pays with cash and a loan.

Column (3b)—*Depreciation*. The next chapter will discuss depreciation more fully. Although accountants keep separate accumulated depreciation accounts for equipment and building, there is normally only a single depreciation expense account.

Column (4)—*Gain/loss on disposal of capital asset*. Gains and losses from selling capital assets are not part of ordinary operations. On the income statement they appear in their own section under operational expenses. The amounts of the gains and losses are as calculated in Section 14.3. The easiest way to handle VJEs to sell a capital asset is with three steps:

Step 1. Remove both the asset and the associated accumulated depreciation. Remove a debit from the books by adding a credit of the same amount. Vice versa for removing credits.

Step 2. Add anything the business gets in exchange—in this case, cash.

Step 3. Whatever is necessary to balance the VJE is either a gain (if a credit) or a loss (if a debit).

End column—*Net income from operations*. In the last column, the net income from operations ($29,924) does not include gains and losses from the sale of capital assets. Gains and losses will appear on the income statement after net income from operations.

14.5. THE CASH FLOW STATEMENT AND FIXED ASSETS

Figure 14-3 shows the impact on the cash flow statement of buying and selling fixed assets.

❶ Net income from operating activities combines all the revenues and expenses *except* the gains and losses:

$$60,000 - 250 - 14,826 - 15,000 = 29,924.$$

❷ Because depreciation expense is a non-cash expense, it is added back to net income from operations to get cash flow from operations.

Figure 14-3. Capital Transactions on the Cash Flow Statement

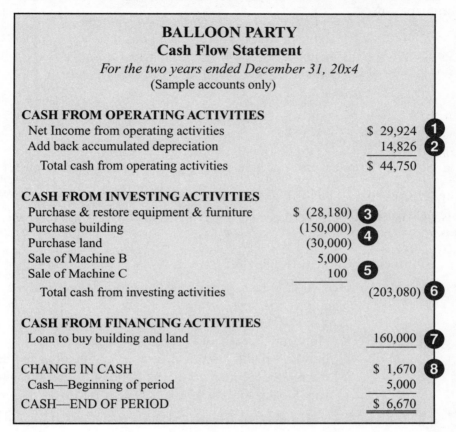

BALLOON PARTY
Cash Flow Statement
For the two years ended December 31, 20x4
(Sample accounts only)

CASH FROM OPERATING ACTIVITIES

Net Income from operating activities	$ 29,924 ❶
Add back accumulated depreciation	14,826 ❷
Total cash from operating activities	$ 44,750

CASH FROM INVESTING ACTIVITIES

Purchase & restore equipment & furniture	$ (28,180) ❸
Purchase building	(150,000)
Purchase land	(30,000) ❹
Sale of Machine B	5,000
Sale of Machine C	100 ❺
Total cash from investing activities	(203,080) ❻

CASH FROM FINANCING ACTIVITIES

Loan to buy building and land	160,000 ❼
CHANGE IN CASH	$ 1,670 ❽
Cash—Beginning of period	5,000
CASH—END OF PERIOD	$ 6,670

❸ Cash spent to purchase and restore equipment and furniture comes from the debits in the equipment and furniture account and the $1,000 debit to accumulated depreciation (from Figure 14-2):

$$15,000 \underset{\text{(purchase)}}{+} \quad 1,000 \quad \underset{\text{(moving and pad)}}{+} 2,180 \underset{\text{(Phil)}}{+} 10,000 = 28,180$$
$$\hspace{4.5cm}\text{(furniture)}$$

❹ The building and the land come from column (3) in the VJEs (Fig. 14-2: 150,000 and 30,000).

❺ The cash flow from the sale of assets ($5,000 and $100) are the amounts Balloon Party received for the two assets.

CLEP Clue

If the CLEP exam gives you the cash received on the sale of capital assets, doing the cash flow statement is easy. More likely, the exam will give you only the book value of the asset and the gain or loss.

Use this formula:

Book value (historical cost – accum. depr.) + gain or – loss = Cash received

For Machine B, the formula yields:

Book value (historical cost – accum. depr.) + gain or – loss = Cash received

(6,400 – 1,792) + 392 = 5,000

For Machine C, the formula yields:

Book value (historical cost – accum. depr.) + gain or – loss = Cash received

(2,700 – 920) – 1,680 = 100

QUESTION 4. How much cash did Company X get for selling a building if the historical cost was $500,000, the accumulated depreciation was $200,000, and the gain was $100,000?

6 The large negative number in the cash flow from investing activities is not a problem. It is good when a business invests in income-producing assets.

7 This is the loan used to buy the land and the building. Financing activities come from borrowing and paying back loans, or from the owners contributing or taking out money. The large borrowing in this case is good because the business used the money to buy fixed assets. Large borrowing to offset negative cash from operations, however, is a warning sign.

8 A positive cash flow for the year is generally good. Add the beginning cash to the cash flow to get the ending cash. Compare this ending cash with the balance in the cash account in the "End" column of your VJEs.

CLEP CRAM

A. *VOCABULARY*

Capital assets—See *plant assets*.

Capitalized—Recorded the cost as an asset.

Expensed—Recorded the cost as an expense.

Fixed assets—See *plant assets*.

Plant assets—Plant assets (or *capital assets* or *fixed assets*) are assets that have a life longer than one year.

B. *ACCOUNTING PRINCIPLES AND FORMULAS*

All-Costs-to-Get-Operating Principle—Requires a business to capitalize all costs necessary to get an asset operating.

Allocate a purchase price among assets—(Memorize this entire format.)

Asset	Market Value	Proportion	×	Purchase Price	= Cost
Machine A	$500	500/1,000 = 50%	×	$1,200	= $600
Machine B	$300	300/1,000 = 30%	×	$1,200	= $360
Machine C	$200	200/1,000 = 20%	×	$1,200	= $240
Total	$1,000				$1,200

Book value of a fixed asset—

Historical cost of an asset

− Asset's accumulated depreciation

= Asset's book value

Cash received on sale of asset—

Book value + Gain (or − Loss) = Cash received

Gain or Loss calculation—

Amount received − Book value (BV) given up = Gain or (− Loss)

New Life Principle—If any work on an asset extends the life of that asset, the cost of that work should be capitalized.

C. *JOURNAL ENTRIES*

Show the journal entry (JE) to record:

Purchase fixed asset	Building or equipment or land	xxx	
	Cash		xxx
Spent $50 on repairs and $1,000 to extend life of Machine A, with $600 in accumulated depr.	Repair Expense	50	
	Accumulated depreciation	600	
	Machines	400	
	Cash		1,050
Spend $700 to make new equipment operational	Equipment	700	
	Cash		700
Sell a $1,000 machine with $300 A/D for $500	Cash 500		
	Accumulated depreciation	300	
	Loss on sale of machine	200	
	Machine		1000
Sell a $1,000 machine with $300 A/D for $800	Cash 800		
	Accumulated depreciation	300	
	Machine		1,000
	Gain on sale of machine		100

ANSWERS TO QUESTIONS FOUND IN THIS CHAPTER

Q1: Figure 14-4 shows the calculation of the purchase price.

Figure 14-4. Answer to Question 1

	Market	%		Price
Machine A	$ 1,000	10%		$1,200
Machine B	2,000	20%	× $12,000 =	2,400
Machine C	3,000	30%		3,600
Machine D	4,000	40%		6,400
TOTAL	$10,000	100%		$12,000

Q2: Land does not depreciate. The lower the price of the land, the more of the price applies to the building. The higher the price of the building, the more the depreciation expense. The more expense, the lower the taxable income. The lower the taxable income, the lower the taxes. Tax-conscious people always want the purchase price applied to land to be as low as possible.

Q3: Capitalized: Machine C parts ($800) and labor ($300) + new transmission ($1,080) that extended the life of the car by one more year.

Expensed: Machine B belts ($200) plus the tune-up and oil change ($50) that are part of normal maintenance and do not add new life.

Q4: $400,000. The formula for calculating the cash received is:

Book value (historical cost − accum. depr.) + gain or − loss = Cash received

(500,000 − 200,000) + 100,000 = 400,000

CHAPTER 15
Depreciation

Chapter 15

Depreciation:
Allocating the Cost of
Long-Lived Assets to Future Periods

Balloon Party has been properly handling depreciation ever since Lauren noticed that she was slowly using up the helium canister and the car. Over the years, every time Balloon Party bought an asset with a life longer than one year, Lauren recorded the transaction on a depreciation schedule, where she keeps a detailed record for each asset.

In this chapter you will learn:

- Why businesses depreciate assets.

- How to prepare a depreciation schedule.

- How to depreciate an asset by using several methods and conventions.

- How to change accounting estimates.

15.1. DEPRECIATION: ALLOCATING THE COST OF PLANT ASSETS

Over the years, Balloon Party bought and sold several assets. Lauren did not record the entire asset cost as an expense in the year purchased. That would have made net income in the year of the purchase unrealistically low and future years improperly high. To prevent that distorted picture, Lauren decided to allocate the cost of the assets over their useful lives. So instead of a $2,000 auto expense in 20x1, there is a $500 depreciation expense for each of the years 20x1 through 20x4.

What depreciation is not. Depreciation is not an attempt to show the decline in the value of assets. Some assets, such as buildings, may actually appreciate during the year. Still, businesses depreciate all fixed assets (except land) every year. Depreciation is not money set aside to replace aging assets. If a business did set aside money equal to depreciation expense, the amount saved would likely not be enough to buy a replacement asset.

QUESTION 1. True or false. Depreciation expense shows that the accounting profession is more concerned about the accuracy of the income statement than that of the balance sheet.

15.2. THE DEPRECIATION EXPENSE FORMULA

The formula for computing depreciation starts out like this:

(Depreciable cost) $\times$ (Depreciation annual rate) = Depreciation for the year

The **depreciable cost** of an asset is the amount of historical cost that gets allocated over the useful life of the asset. When an asset is no longer useful, it is sold or thrown away. The amount received at the end of an asset's life is called the **salvage value** (or **residual value** or **scrap value**.) After consulting with knowledgeable people, accountants estimate the salvage value. The depreciation formula as restated is:

(Cost – Salvage) $\times$ (Depreciation rate) = Depreciation for the year

There are many depreciation methods. The Internal Revenue Service allows several methods for income tax purposes. For accounting purposes, use whichever method best reflects the allocation of cost over the years. In practice, most businesses use one of these four methods:

- Straight-line (SL) method. The simplest method.

$$\text{Rate} = \frac{1}{(\text{Useful life in years})}$$

- Units of production (UP) method. The most accurate method.

$$\text{Rate} = \frac{(\text{Units produced this year})}{(\text{Est. units produced over life})}$$

- Tax method. Use the IRS tables.

- Double declining balance (DDB) method.

$$\text{Rate} = \frac{2}{(\text{Useful life in years})}$$

For the first three methods,[1] the depreciation equation is now:

$$(\text{Cost} - \text{Salvage}) \times \left\{ \begin{array}{c} \text{SL: } 1/(\text{useful life in years}) \\ \text{or} \\ \text{UP: (units this yr)/(total units)} \\ \text{or} \\ \text{Tax: Use tax tables} \end{array} \right\} = \text{Depreciation this year}$$

Straight-Line Method

For the car and the canister, Balloon Party uses the straight-line method. Lauren divided the depreciable cost by an estimated useful life. The depreciation expense stays the same every year during the asset's estimated useful life.

For example, Company X buys a car for $15,000. The company plans to drive the car for 5 years or 200,000 miles. After that time, it estimates it can sell the car for $3,000. The depreciable cost is $12,000 (15,000 − 3,000). The rate is .20 (1/5-year useful life). The depreciation expense is $2,400 (12,000 × .20).

Units of Production Method

The straight-line method does not reflect that equipment may operate more in one year than another. The units of production method solves this problem. Company X planned to keep its car for 200,000 miles. In the first year, the car went 10,000 miles. The formula is:

(cost − salvage) × (units this year)/(total est. units) = depreciation expense

(15,000 − 3,000) × (10,000 / 200,000) = depreciation expense

12,000 × .05 = $600

---

[1] The formula for DDB depreciation is a bit different, as you will see.

Suppose Company X actually kept the car for seven years, with the following mileage:

Year 1: 10,000 miles

Year 2: 30,000 miles

Year 3: 50,000 miles

Year 4: 50,000 miles

Year 5: 40,000 miles

Year 6: 40,000 miles

Year 7: 10,000 miles

Table 15-1 calculates depreciation expense for all seven years.

Table 15-1. Units of Production Method

Year	Miles Driven	Miles Driven / Total Est Miles	Rate	Depreciable Cost	Rate × Cost
1	10,000	10,000 / 200,000	0.05	12,000	$600
2	30,000	30,000 / 200,000	0.15	12,000	1,800
3	50,000	50,000 / 200,000	0.25	12,000	3,000
4	50,000	50,000 / 200,000	0.25	12,000	3,000
5	40,000	40,000 / 200,000	0.20	12,000	2,400
*6	40,000	40,000 / 200,000	*0.10	12,000	*1,200
7	10,000	10,000 / 200,000		12,000	0
Total	230,000		1.00		$12,000

* In order to not depreciate more than the depreciable cost, in the 6th year the maximum depreciation is $1,200. If the car is used more years, there is no further depreciation expense.

The car ran 30,000 miles over the 200,000-mile estimate. In order to not depreciate more than the depreciable cost, the maximum depreciation for year 6 is only $1,200. After the depreciable cost has been fully allocated, there is no further depreciation no matter how much longer the asset lasts. The asset is said to be **fully depreciated**, or **depreciated out**.

QUESTION 2. A fully depreciated asset will have a book value equal to _____?

CLEP Clue

The CLEP exam often gives you information you do not need. If you get a units-of-production question with information about the useful life in years, just ignore the years.

Double Declining Balance Method (DDB)

The DDB method records more depreciation expense in the early years than in the later years. It is an **accelerated depreciation method**.

The formula for DDB method is different from the other methods:

$$\left(\begin{array}{c} \text{Book value of} \\ \text{the asset at} \\ \text{the beginning} \\ \text{of the year} \end{array} \right) \times \frac{2}{\text{(Useful life)}} = \text{Depreciation expense for the year}$$

Remember these differences between DDB and other methods:

- Depreciation rate = 2/useful life, or twice that of the straight line rate.

- The DDB rate multiplies against the book value (historical cost – accumulated depreciation), not depreciable cost (historical cost – residual value).

- Use salvage value to know when to stop depreciating the asset. Never depreciate an asset below the salvage value, even when using DDB method.

Table 15-2 shows Company X's car depreciated under the DDB method.

Table 15-2. Double Declining Balance Method

Year	Book Value at Beginning of Year	Rate (2 / Life) (2 / 5)	Depreciation for the Year	Accumulated Depreciation
1	15,000	0.4	6,000	6,000
2	9,000	0.4	3,600	9,600
3	5,400	0.4	2,160	11,760
4	3,240	0.4	240	12,000
5	3,000	0.4	0	12,000

The depreciation in Year 4 is only $240 instead of $1,296 (3,240 x .40). At the beginning of Year 4, the book value was $3,240, only $240 above the residual value. Assets never depreciate below the estimated residual value, so the depreciation in the final year is whatever is necessary to bring the book value down to the residual value. Once the asset is fully depreciated, there is no further depreciation expense even if the business still uses the asset. Therefore, depreciation in Year 5 is zero.

QUESTION 3. Company Z buys a $5,000 machine with a useful life of five years. How much DDB depreciation is there in the first year? Second year?

Tax Method

The Internal Revenue Service (IRS) of the United States federal government requires you to pay an income tax on the net income of your business. As you can imagine, people want to lower their net income, because the lower the net income, the less tax they pay. To standardize depreciation expense, the IRS developed its own method—the **Modified Accelerated Cost Recovery System**, or **MACRS**. It is an accelerated depreciation method, like the double declining balance method. IRS tables tell you what rate to use.

CLEP Clue

The CLEP exam will not require you to memorize the many IRS tables. Learn to use Table 15-3 and you will be able to handle all the IRS depreciation tables.

Table 15-3. MACRS Depreciation Method

Year	5-Year Property	7-Year Property	10-Year Property
1	0.2	0.1429	0.1
2	0.32	0.2449	0.18
3	0.192	0.1749	0.144
4	0.1152	0.1249	0.1152
5	0.1152	0.0892	0.0922
6	0.0576	0.0892	0.0737
7		0.0892	0.0655
8		0.0446	0.0655
9			0.0655
10			0.0655
11			0.0328
Total	1.000	1.000	1.000

To use the MACRS table, first determine whether the asset is 3-year property, 5-year property, 7-year property, 10-year property, or something else. The years are roughly equivalent to estimated useful life. The IRS has tables that classify all assets.

CLEP Clue

The CLEP test will most probably tell you what type of property the asset is. If not, guess 5-years for equipment, 7-years for furniture.

After determining the type of property, determine the year of the asset's life and find the decimal in the proper column. For example, Table 15-3 shows that if Company A has 5-year property with a historical cost of $10,000 that is in its third year of use, the decimal is .192. Plug the decimal into the following formula:

Historical cost × Decimal = Depreciation this year

$$\$10,000 \times .192 = \$1,920$$

Note that when using MACRS, the residual value is always $0.

QUESTION 4. When an asset is fully depreciated for tax purposes, what is its book value?

15.3. DEPRECIATION CONVENTIONS

Table 15-3 shows that 5-year property depreciates over 6 years, 7-year property depreciates over 8 years, and 10-year property depreciates over 11 years. This is because the IRS assumes you bought the property in the middle of the first year. Thus they give only a half-year of depreciation for the first year. They make up for it by giving another half-year of depreciation for an extra year. This is called the **mid-year convention**. Conventions are assumptions about the purchase dates of fixed assets. They simplify the depreciation process. Table 15-4 shows of some of the more prominent conventions.

Table 15-4. Depreciation Conventions

Convention	Abbrv	Assumptions	Computed	Comments
Mid-year	½ yr	All assets were purchased on the exact middle of the year.	Full year × ½	Used by IRS
Mid-month	½ mo	All assets were purchased in the middle of the month. Depreciate fraction of year remaining.	If bought in April: Full year × 8½/12	More accurate monthly financial statements for small companies
Nearest Year	NY	Assets were purchased on the nearest first day of the year.	If bought in 1st half, full year. If bought in 2nd half, none this year.	Allowed by IRS; avoids bothering with fraction of years
Nearest month	NMo	Assets were purchased on nearest first day of month.	Bought by April 10: Full year × 9/12. Bought April 16: Full year × 8/12	Avoids ½ month issue; requires partial year depreciation in first year
Beginning of year	BOY	All assets were purchased on first day of the year	All assets get full year depr for first year	Not allowed by IRS

QUESTION 5. Which depreciation conventions will always result in a full year of depreciation in the first year?

15.4. THE DEPRECIATION SCHEDULE

Lauren recorded all purchases and sales of fixed assets on the depreciation schedule shown in Figure 15-1.

Figure 15-1. Balloon Party Depreciation Schedule

BALLOON PARTY
Depreciation Schedule

#	Date	Item	Cost	Residual Value	Life in yrs or hrs	Meth	Convention	20x1	20x2	20x3	20x4	20x5	Book Value
								DEPRECIATION EXPENSE					
1	4/x1	Car	2,080 **(1)**	0	4	SL	Full Yr	500	500	693	693	694	—
		—Accum Depr	1,000										
2	4/x1	Canister	500	0	25	SL	FY	20	20	20	20	20	400
3	1/x3	Machine A	8,000	0	10	DDB	½ yr			800	1,440 **(3)**	1,152	4,608
4	1/x3	Machine B	6,400	0	10	DDB	½ yr **(4)**			640	1,152	Sold	4,608
5	1/x3	Machine C	1,600	400 **(5)**	10000 hrs	UP	n/a **(6)**			230 1000hr	690 3000hr	Sold **(9)**	1,780
		—improvements	1,100										
6	7/x3	Office Furniture	10,000	0	7 **(7)**	Tax	Tax			1,429	2,449	1,749	4,373
7	1/22/x4	Building	150,000	9,600	39	SL	NMo				3,300 **(8)**	3,600	143,100
8	1/22/x4	Land	30,000										30,000
			210,680										

Circle markers: (2) near Meth column, (10) near Accumulated Depr—Bldg.

	20x1	20x2	20x3	20x4	20x5	
Depreciation Exp:	520	520	3,812	9,744	7,215	188,869
Accumulated Depr—Equip:	(520)	(520)	(3,812)	(6,444)	(3,615)	
Accumulated Depr—Bldg:				(3,300)	(3,600)	

1 The car originally cost $2,000. After two years, Balloon Party added the new $1,080 transmission to the car. The first $1,000 of the cost lowered accumulated depreciation to zero, and the remaining $80 was added to the car account.

2 The car and canister use the straight line (SL) method of depreciation.

3 After depreciating the car $500 per year for two years, the book value of the car was reduced to $1,000 (2,000 – 500 – 500). The transmission increased the book value to $2,080 (1,000 BV + 1080 transmission). The estimated useful life at this time was 3 more years. Thus, the depreciation expense for the last three years is $693 (2,080 / 3).

4 Machines A and B use double declining balance with a half-year convention. The calculation of the depreciation of Machine A is:

- Year 1: [BV (8,000 cost) × 2 (double) / 10 years] × ½ year for first year = $800
- Year 2: BV (8,000 – 800) × 2/10 = $1,440
- Year 3: BV (8,000 – 800 – 1,440) × 2/10 = $1,152

The calculation of the depreciation of Machine B is:

- Year 1: BV [(6,400 cost) × 2 (double) / 10 years] × ½ year = $640
- Year 2: BV (6,400 – 640) × 2/10 = $1152
- Year 3: Machine B was sold at the end of Year 2.

5 The cost of Machine C is $2,700, including the cost to get it operational.

6 Machine C used the units of production method. It had an estimated useful life of 10,000 hours of operation. In the first year, the machine ran 1,000 hours, and the second year it ran 3,000 hours, after which it was sold. There is no need for any depreciation convention for the units of production method because the use of hours automatically handles any fraction-of-year issues. The calculation of depreciation for Machine C is:

- Year 1: depreciable cost (2,700 – 400 salvage) × 1,000 / 10,000 = $230
- Year 2: (2,700 – 400) × 3,000 / 10,000 = $690
- Machine C was sold at the end of Year 2.

7 The office furniture is depreciated by using the tax method, so its salvage value is $0. The 7 under "life" means this furniture is 7-year property according to the IRS tables. The depreciation for the furniture is:

- Year 1: $10,000 cost × .1429 (yr1 decimal) = $1,429

- Year 2: $10,000 × .2449 (yr2 decimal) = $2,449

- Year 3: $10,000 × .1749 (yr3 decimal) = $1,749

8 Balloon Party bought the building and land on January 22, 20x4. Using the nearest month convention, Balloon Party assumes the building was purchased on February 1, 20x4. Therefore, Balloon Party depreciates the building for only 11/12 of a year in the first year. Using the straight-line method, the computation for depreciation of the building is:

- Year 1: (150,000 cost − 9,600 salvage) / 39 years × 11/12 = $3,300

- Year 2 and future years: (150,000 − 9,600) / 39 = $3,600

9 When assets are sold, stop depreciating them. Thus, total 20x5 depreciation is less than total 20x4 depreciation. The depreciation schedule also is a handy way to calculate book value. The book values for Machines B ($4,608) and C ($1,780) were used to calculate gain or loss on the sale of assets in Section 14.3.

10 At the bottom, the depreciation schedule computes the debits to depreciation expense and the credits to accumulated depreciation for equipment and building.

15.5. CHANGING ACCOUNTING ESTIMATES

Accounting is not exact; it involves estimates. In the computation of depreciation expenses, businesses estimate salvage value and useful life. What happens if the estimates change? For example, after installing the new transmission in the car, the estimated useful life changed from 2 more years remaining to 3 more years.

Accounting Principle

*The **Change-in-Accounting-Estimates Principle** allows businesses to change estimates (such as useful life or salvage value) as more accurate information becomes available. This principle allows no **retroactive** changes to past financial statements. Instead, a business merely uses the new estimates in the current and all future years.*

CLEP Clue

*CLEP test-takers often confuse the Change-in-Accounting-Estimates Principle, which allows changing estimates, and the Consistency Principle, which forbids changing accounting methods. For example, a business **may** change a machine's useful life from 5 years to 7 years, but **may not** change the depreciation method from straight line method to double declining balance method.*

QUESTION 6. You decided that your estimates of uncollectible accounts receivable is too uncertain. You have been estimating that 2% of accounts receivable was uncollectible. Now you think it is more like 5%. You are considering either counting revenue only when the money comes in, or increasing your allowance for uncollectible accounts to 5%. Which of these options should you select?

CLEP CRAM

A. VOCABULARY

Accelerated depreciation method—A depreciation method that results in higher depreciation expense in an asset's early years.

Depreciable cost—The amount of the historical cost of an asset that gets allocated over the useful life of the asset.

Depreciated out—Same as *fully depreciated*.

Depreciation convention—Conventions are assumptions about the purchase dates of fixed assets in order to simplify the depreciation process.

- **Beginning of year.** Assume all assets purchased during the year were purchased on the first day of the year.

- **Nearest month.** Assume all assets purchased within the first 15 days of the month are purchased on the first day of the month. Assume all assets purchased after the 15th of the month are purchased on the first day of the following month.

- **Nearest year.** Assume all assets purchased within the first 6 months of the fiscal year are purchased on the first day of the year. Assume all assets purchased within the last 6 months of the fiscal year are purchased on the first day of the following year.

- **Mid year:** Assume all assets are purchased on the first day of the 7th month of the fiscal year.

- **Mid month:** Assume all assets are purchased on the 15th of the month.

Depreciation schedule—A list of all fixed assets in the company, their purchase dates, their depreciation methods, and their depreciation each year.

Fully depreciated—An asset is said to be fully depreciated when its book value equals its salvage value.

MACRS—Modified Accelerated Cost Recovery System, for which IRS tables tell the rate by which to multiply an asset's historical cost.

Residual value—Same as *salvage value*.

Salvage value—The estimated amount received for an asset at the end of its useful life. Also called *residual value* and *scrap value*.

Scrap value—Same as *salvage value*.

B. *ACCOUNTING PRINCIPLES AND FORMULAS*

Change-in-Accounting-Estimates Principle—Allows businesses to change *estimates* when more accurate information becomes available. Changes are made for the current and all future years, but not retroactively.

Consistency Principle—Forbids businesses to change accounting *methods* from year to year.

Double declining balance depreciation—

$$\frac{\text{Book value at beginning of year} \times 2}{\text{Estimated life}} = \begin{array}{l}\text{Depreciation expense for year until} \\ \text{book value reaches salvage value}\end{array}$$

MACRS depreciation—

Historical cost $\times$ IRS decimal = Depreciation for year.

Salvage value = \$0

Straight-line depreciation—

$$\frac{(\text{Historical cost} - \text{Salvage value})}{\text{Estimated life}} = \text{Depreciation for all years}$$

Units of production method—

$$\frac{(\text{Historical cost} - \text{Salvage value}) \times \text{Units this year}}{\text{Total estimated units (hours or miles)}} = \frac{\text{This year's}}{\text{depreciation}}$$

C. *JOURNAL ENTRIES*

Show the journal entry (JE) to record:

Depreciate $3,000 on buildings and $1,000 on equipment	Depreciation expense 4,000
	      Accumulated depreciation—building
	      Accumulated depreciation—equipment
		
		 3,000
		 1,000

ANSWERS TO QUESTIONS FOUND IN THIS CHAPTER

Q1: True. The accounting profession prefers to sacrifice balance sheet perfection in order to make the income statement more accurate. It is more important to match the cost of an asset with all the income it produces over the years than to show that asset at its current value.

Q2: Its residual value or salvage value. It is tempting to say $0 because businesses commonly use a salvage value of $0, but $0 would earn you one mistake on the CLEP test.

Q3: First year: (5000 cost − 0 A/D) × 2/5 years = $2,000.
Second year: (5000 − 2,000) × 2/5 = $1,200.

The problem does not mention a salvage value. Salvage value is unlikely to come into play in the early years.

Q4: Zero. An asset that is fully depreciated has reached its residual value. Residual value is always $0 for tax purposes, so a fully depreciated asset has a book value of $0.

Q5: Nearest-year and beginning-of-year methods. The nearest-year method sometimes results in no depreciation for the asset in the year purchased. The beginning-of-year method always gives a full year of depreciation for each asset no matter when purchased. This is the least accurate method.

Q6: Change your estimate from 2% to 5%. You may not change your accounting method from the accrual method (which uses accounts receivable) to a cash basis method (which recognizes revenue when you get the money) because of the Consistency Principle.

CHAPTER 16

Land, Natural Resources, and Intangible Assets

Chapter 16

Land, Natural Resources, and Intangible Assets:
Rounding Out the Long-Lived Assets

When Balloon Party bought the land and building in February 20x4, there was enough extra land on which it could build a small factory. Lauren surveyed the land, paid back taxes, cut down three trees and bulldozed the land smooth. For security, she built a fence around the land and put in a driveway. To beautify the office building, she added landscaping and trees. After doing quite a bit of research and development, Balloon Party's mobile balloon sales booths became so effective and so well known that Lauren had the name registered as a trademark.

In this chapter you will learn:

- What makes up the cost of an intangible asset.

- How to allocate the cost of intangible assets over future years.

- How to distinguish between land and land improvements.

- What to do when an intangible asset goes bad.

16.1. LAND OR LAND IMPROVEMENT?

All costs to get the land ready for use are considered to be part of the cost of the land. If working on the land creates something with a limited life, it is land improvement. Some regular costs, such as watering, planting annual flowers, and installing mulch, have a value that lasts less than one year, and so are expensed. Lauren needs to know which of Balloon Party's expenditures are for land and which are for something else.

> **QUESTION 1.** Allocate the following expenditures between land, land improvements, and regular maintenance expense.

Expenditure	Land	Land Improvements	Regular Maintenance Expense
$400 land survey	$_____	$_____	$_____
$2,000 fence	$_____	$_____	$_____
$1,500 back taxes	$_____	$_____	$_____
$5,000 driveway	$_____	$_____	$_____
$250 trees along property line	$_____	$_____	$_____
$100 Mowing lawn	$_____	$_____	$_____
$350 shrubs around office	$_____	$_____	$_____
$200 pruning trees	$_____	$_____	$_____
$900 grading land	$_____	$_____	$_____
$700 cutting trees	$_____	$_____	$_____

16.2. ASSETS YOU CANNOT GRAB HOLD OF

Intangible assets have no physical form, yet they offer value to the business for a long time. The total cost of an intangible asset is everything necessary to make it useful. Examples of types of costs that often end up in intangible assets are legal fees, design, artwork, engineering, software, franchise contracts, and marketing programs.

If the life of an intangible asset is known, such as a franchise term or a copyright limit, then the cost of the intangible asset is spread over the useful life (not *legal* life) using the straight-line method without salvage value. For example, if Company X spent $40,000 designing a gizmo and paid its lawyer $10,000 to get the patent, the journal entry would be:

12/31/xx   Patent ($40,000 + $10,000) $50,000

          Cash $50,000

          (To record getting a patent on the gizmo)

If the patent has a useful life of 5 years and a legal life of 15 years, each year Company X will have the following general journal entry each year:

12/31/xx   Amortization Expense $10,000

          Patent (50,000 / 5 years) $10,000

          (To amortize 1/5 of the patent)

Amortization expense is the amount of an intangible asset used up during the period. Think of it as depreciation expense for intangible assets. There is no accumulated amortization account. The credit directly lowers the patent account year after year until the patent account reaches zero. Then the patent will be **fully amortized**.

Some intangible assets have indefinite lives. They are not amortized. In the future, if these intangible assets are impaired (lose their value), they are written down. They are never written up. For example, if Company X paid $5,000,000 extra to buy out another company, the general journal entry will be:

6/5/xx	Goodwill	$5,000,000	
	Cash		$5,000,000

(To record paying goodwill for Company Y)

If 10 years later, the goodwill of Company Y is worth $7,000,000, Company X will make no adjustment. However, if the goodwill of Company Y drops to $3,000,000, Company X will make this general journal entry:

12/31/xx	Loss on goodwill	$2,000,000	
	Goodwill		$2,000,000

(To record that Company Y goodwill has dropped in value)

Common types of intangible assets are:

- **Patents.** The exclusive right to produce and sell an invention. The legal right may be 20 years, but the useful life may be shorter.

- **Copyrights.** The exclusive right to publish, perform, or reproduce music, art, film, books, or software. Legal life can be more than 100 years, but the opportunity to make money from the copyright may be 3 to 5 years.

- **Trademarks** and **trade names.** Special identifications that are protected against infringement. Many have indefinite lives.

- **Goodwill.** The extra cost a business pays for another business as recognition for being unusually profitable. It has an indefinite life.

- **Franchises** and **licenses.** Contracts or government grants that give the owner special rights. Many have indefinite lives.

Research and development, the cost a company pays to create and develop a product, although intangible, is treated differently. Although drug companies spend many millions of dollars developing new drugs, the accounting profession requires that these costs be expensed in the year they are incurred.

QUESTION 2. Mr. Smith developed a machine. It cost $3,000 to make a working model (as required by the patent office) and $1,000 for a patent lawyer. Mr. Jones offered $1,000,000 for the patent, but the word is that he would pay $1,500,000. On the books, at what value does Mr. Smith show the patent?

16.3. NATURAL RESOURCES

The land next to Balloon Party's new office has an oil well on it. The minerals under the land commonly go with the land, but many times they do not. Balloon Party owns the oil rights to its land. Company X, the next-door neighbor, paid $200,000 for their mineral rights. Geologists have estimated that there are 40,000 barrels of oil under that land. Therefore, Company X estimates that it paid $5 a barrel for the underground oil (200,000/40,000 = 5). When Company X bought the mineral rights, it made this general journal entry:

5/5/xx	Oil Mineral Rights	$200,000	
	Cash		$200,000

(To record purchase of mineral rights of surrounding land)

Whenever Company X pumps oil out of the ground, those mineral rights are used up. **Depletion expense** is the name of the account that records natural resources being used up. If Company X pumps 5,000 barrels of oil from the ground this year, it will record $25,000 ($5/barrel x 5,000 barrels) of depletion expense.

12/31/xx	Depletion Exp (5000 barrels $\times$ $5) $25,000	
	Accumulated Depletion—Oil	$25,000

(To record depletion for 5,000 barrels of oil at $5/barrel)

QUESTION 3. Company X paid $120,000 for land that contains 600 black walnut trees. It estimated that the trees are one-fourth of the value of the land, or $30,000. When Company X cut down and sold 40 trees, what is the general journal entry?

16.4. VERTICAL JOURNAL ENTRIES FOR INTANGIBLE ASSETS

Figure 16-1 shows VJEs assuming that Balloon Party has transactions involving all the types of intangible assets discussed in the previous section.

Figure 16-1. VJEs for Intangible Assets

BALLOON PARTY
Vertical Journal Entries
For the year ended December 31, 20x5

	Start	1	2	3	4	End
ASSETS						
Current Assets						
Cash	150,000	a (11,400) b (60,000)	a (56,000) b (18,000)			4,600
All other current assets	40,000					40,000
Fixed Assets						
Equipment	21,580					21,580
A/D—Equipment	(10,333)					(10,333)
Building	150,000	a 350				150,350
A/D—Building	(6,900)				a (10)	(6,910)
Land Improvements		a 7,000				7,000
A/D—Land Improvements					a (200)	(200)
Oil mineral rights		b 60,000				60,000
Accumulated Depletion—Oil				b (12,000)		(12,000)
Land	30,000	a 3,750				33,750
Patent			a 50,000	a (10,000)		40,000
Goodwill	50,000				b (40,000)	10,000
Trade name			a 6,000			6,000
LIABILITIES						
All liability accounts	(220,000)					(220,000)
EQUITY						
All equity accounts	(91,562)					(91,562)
OPERATING REVENUE						
All operating rev accts	(150,000)					(150,000)
OPERATING EXPENSES						
Amortization Expense				a 10,000		10,000
Depletion Expense				b 12,000		12,000
Depreciation Expense	7,215				a 210	7,425
Maintenance Expense		a 300				300
Research and Development Exp			b 18,000			18,000
Other operating expenses	30,000					30,000
OTHER REVENUES AND EXPENSES						
Loss in value of goodwill					b 40,000	40,000
TOTALS	—	—	—	—	—	—

1a. Record all the cash out in Question 1: Land = $3,750, Land Improvements = $7,000, Building (landscaping around the office) = $350, Maintenance = $300.

1b. Pay $60,000 for mineral rights

2a. Developed the traveling booth design for $40,000, and paid the patent lawyer $10,000. Paid $6,000 to register the trade name, "Balloon Party."

2b. Spent $18,000 on researching new balloon materials.

3a. Amortize the patent over 5 years. ($50,000 / 5 years = $10,000/year.)

3b. Pumped 6,000 barrels of oil out of an estimated 30,000 barrels. ($60,000 × 6/30)

4a. Extra depr exp on the building ($350/35yrs = $10), land improvements ($7000/35yrs = $200)

4b. The value of goodwill paid for a competing business has dropped in value to $10,000.

Start column—These VJEs assume that Balloon Party bought out a competitor by paying $50,000 more for the business than the fair market value of the assets. That extra purchase price is called goodwill.

Column (1)—*Buying intangible assets*. The transactions in (1a) come from Question 1 above, answered at the end of this chapter. Debit land $3,750 ($400 survey + $1,500 back taxes + $250 trees along property line + $900 grading + $700 cutting down trees); debit land improvements $7,000 ($2,000 fence + $5,000 driveway); debit building $350 for plantings close to the building; and debit regular maintenance expense $300 ($100 mowing + $200 pruning). In (1b) Balloon Party bought the mineral rights under their land for $60,000. An estimated 30,000 barrels of oil are under their land, at an estimated cost of $2/barrel (60,000/30,000).

Column (2)—*Creating intangible assets*. The patent and the trade name are intangible assets with a historical cost equal to whatever was necessary to bring those assets into existence. In contrast, research and development costs are expensed and never capitalized.

Column (3)—*Amortization and depletion*. The difference between these two VJEs is that the credit for amortization directly lowers the intangible asset, whereas the credit for depletion is a contra-asset called "accumulated depletion."

CLEP Clue

The reason there is no "accumulated amortization" account for intangible assets is not very logical. Just remember this difference because the CLEP test will almost certainly check your knowledge of it.

Column (4)—*Depreciation and adjustment*. Depreciate the additions to the building and land improvements. Goodwill is adjusted only in the year the value is impaired. In this year, the value went down $40,000.

CLEP Clue

Table 16-1 lists types of fixed assets and how their costs eventually become expenses affecting the income statement.

Table 16-1. Types of Expenses for Fixed Assets

Type of asset	Expense	Method
Equipment, furniture, buildings, and land improvements	Depreciation	4 basic methods (Chapter 15) Straight-line Units of production Tax Double declining balance
Natural resources	Depletion	Units of production method
Intangible assets	Amortization	Straight-line, no salvage value
Indefinite life intangible assets	Adjustment	Lower in year value impaired
Land	Never expensed	

CLEP CRAM

A. *VOCABULARY*

Amortization expense—The amount of an intangible asset used up during the period.

Depletion expense—The amount of a natural resource used up during the period.

Fully amortized—When an intangible asset is fully amortized, all of its cost will have been allocated to past fiscal periods, and its book value will be zero.

Intangible assets—Assets with no physical form, yet they offer value to a business for more than one year. Common types are:

- **Patents.** The exclusive right to produce and sell an invention.

- **Copyrights.** The exclusive right to publish, perform, or reproduce music, art, film, books or software.

- **Trademarks** and **trade names.** Special identifications that are protected against infringement.

- **Goodwill.** The extra cost a business pays for another business for being unusually profitable.

- **Franchises** and **licenses.** Contracts or government grants that give the owner special rights.

Research and Development—The cost a company pays to create and develop a product. It is never an intangible asset, but instead is expensed each year.

B. JOURNAL ENTRIES

Show the journal entry (JE) to record:

Develop a patent	Patent (design and legal)	xx,xxx	
	Cash		xx,xxx
Put in a $4,000 driveway and $3,000 fence	Land improvements	7,000	
	Cash		7,000
Spend $50,000 on research and development of a new drug	Research and development expense	50,000	
	Cash		50,000
Amortize a patent $500	Amortization expense	500	
	Patent		500
Deplete mineral rights $10,000	Depletion expense	10,000	
	Accumulated depletion		10,000
Report that a franchise with an indefinite life has gone up in value	(No journal entry. Do not increase the book value of intangible assets when they go up in value.)		
Report that a franchise with an indefinite life has gone down in value	Loss on franchise	xx,xxx	
	Franchise (an intangible asset)		xx,xxx

ANSWERS TO QUESTIONS FOUND IN THIS CHAPTER

Q1:

Expenditure	Land	Land Improvements	Regular Maintenance Expense
$400 land survey	$400	$_____	$_____
$2,000 fence	$_____	$2,000	$_____
$1,500 back taxes	$1,500	$_____	$_____
$5,000 driveway	$_____	$5,000	$_____
$250 trees along property line	$250	$_____	$_____
$100 mowing lawn	$_____	$_____	$100
$350 shrubs around office	$_____	$350[1]	$_____
$200 pruning trees	$_____	$_____	$200
$900 grading land	$900	$_____	$_____
$700 cutting trees	$700	$_____	$_____

Trees are part of the land unless you know they have a shorter life. Landscaping close to a building has a life equal to that of the building. Cutting down trees to get the land ready to build on is part of the cost of the land. The fence and driveway have limited lives and are capitalized and depreciated. The pruning and mowing is normal upkeep and is expensed.

Q2: $4,000 (3,000 for the working model + 1,000 for the patent cost). Patents and other intangible assets are recorded on the books at historical cost necessary to get the patent. The Historical Cost Principle requires that intangible assets not be increased to their fair market values.

Q3: Depletion Expense (30,000/600 trees × 40)   2,000

　　　Accumulated Depletion—trees   2,000

(To record depletion of 40 trees at $50)

---

[1] This asset is considered part of the building

CHAPTER 17
Current Liabilities

Chapter 17

Current Liabilities:
Discovering More Debts
That Are Due Within One Year

Balloon Party often gets bills in one period but pays them in another period. Lauren wants to make sure expenses of December 20x5, get counted in 20x5 even though they are paid in January 20x6. For example, at the end of December, Balloon Party owes wages to its employees, but it will not pay those employees until January. Balloon Party offers a warranty on the mobile booths that it sells. How can it match the estimated warranty expense with the revenue that those warranties generated?

In this chapter you will learn:

- How to make sure expenses get counted in the right period.

- How to estimate future liabilities.

- How to accrue interest expense on outstanding loans.

- How to calculate the current portion of a loan.

- How reversing entries make accounting easier.

17.1. WHAT DOES IT MEAN TO "ACCRUE" A LIABILITY?

Accrue means to recognize something on the accounting books even though no cash changes hands. In previous chapters, Lauren accrued revenue (credit) when it was earned. Instead of debiting cash, Balloon Party debited another asset, such as accounts receivable or notes receivable.

In this chapter, Balloon Party is going to accrue an expense (debit) when it is incurred. Instead of crediting cash, Balloon Party will credit a liability account, such as accounts payable (A/P), wages payable (W/P), or interest payable (I/P).

Figure 17-1 shows the VJEs for Balloon Party's current liabilities. In the start column that reflects conditions at the start of 20x5, Balloon Party has a current liability account called accounts payable with a credit balance of ($60,000). That means there is a stack of invoices in Balloon Party's office that the company has not yet paid. Those invoices total exactly $60,000. In the previous month, December 20x4, Balloon Party recorded those bills by making this general journal entry:

12/31/20x4 Various expense accounts   60,000

             Accounts payable   60,000

(To accrue expenses not paid at the end of the year)

This journal entry recognized $60,000 additional operating expenses in 20x4. The expenses and the liability were **accrued**. Once an expense has been accrued, make sure not to count it again when the business pays. Instead, debit accounts payable.

1/11/20x5 Accounts payable   60,000

             Cash   60,000

(To pay last year's expenses)

Note that if Balloon Party debits the various expense accounts again when it pays the cash, it would count the expenses twice.

CLEP Clue

*The CLEP exam will test your knowledge of accrual expenses by suggesting that you debit an expense account when you pay the bills. BEWARE! The exam may also ask about cash basis accounting which **does** recognize the expense when you pay the cash. Table 17-1 will help you to keep things straight.*

Table 17-1. Cash Basis versus Accrual Basis

Transaction	Cash Basis	Accrual Basis
Order a product	No journal entry	No journal entry.
Receive the product and bill	No journal entry	Debit exp., credit A/P
Pay the bill	Debit exp., credit cash	Debit A/P, credit cash

The time to accrue an expense is when:

- the business legally owes the money, and
- the amount owed is reasonably estimable.

Figure 17-1. VJEs for Balloon Party's Current Liabilities

BALLOON PARTY
Vertical Journal Entries (partial)
For the year ended December 31, 20x5

	Start	1	2	3	4	End
ASSETS						
Current Assets						
Cash	60,000	b 20,000	a (58,000)	a (17,627)	c (400)	3,973
All other current assets	40,000					40,000
Fixed Assets						
All fixed assets	300,000					300,000
LIABILITIES						
Current Liabilities						
Accounts payable	(60,000)	a (10,000)	a 58,000			(12,000)
Interest payable					b (1,305)	(1,305)
Wages payable				b (6,400)		(6,400)
Warranties payable			b (1,000)		c 400	(600)
Loan payable—current portion	(1,789)				a (180)	(1,969)
Long-term Debt						
Loan payable—LT portion	(156,584)			a 1,790	a 180	(154,615)
EQUITY						
All equity accounts	(181,627)					(181,627)
OPERATING REVENUE						
All operating revenue accts		b (20,000)				(20,000)
OPERATING EXPENSES						
Interest expenses				a 15,837	b 1,305	17,142
Wages expenses				b 6,400		6,400
Warranty expenses			b 1,000			1,000
Other operating expenses		a 10,000				10,000
TOTALS	—	—	—	—	—	—

1a. Received bills totaling $10,000 that were for operating expenses.
1b. Sold a balloon sales booth for $20,000 cash. The sale included a five-year warranty.
2a. Paid $58,000 of the bills on account.
2b. The company estimates that they will pay $1,000 of warranty repairs over the next five years.
3a. Made a $17,627 loan payment. Interest = $15,837 (see loan amortization schedule).
3b. At the end of the year, the business owed $6,400 to employees for wages. Paid in January.
4a. Adjusted the current portion of loan payable to $1,969.
4b. Accrued one month's interest (Dec.) on loan (156,584 x 10% $\times$ 1/12 = $1,305)
4c. Spent $400 to replace a wheel on booth that was under warranty.

Do *not* accrue an expense when you order goods, or when you accept a bid, or when you sign a purchase contract. *Do* accrue the expense after the goods and invoice arrive, or when the contractor has performed services and bills the company.

QUESTION 1. Under accrual basis accounting, when do you debit accounts payable?

QUESTION 2. Under the cash basis accounting, when do you debit accounts payable?

17.2. ADJUSTING ENTRIES AT THE END OF THE PERIOD

Accounts payable transactions have events that trigger them: A/P goes up when the business gets an invoice; A/P goes down when the business pays the invoice. Many other current liabilities have no triggering event. The business keeps a list of non-cash adjustments, which are called **adjusting entries**. Included in those adjustments are items such as:

- Accruing interest expense on debts
- Accruing wages expense for unpaid wages at the end of the period
- Estimating the amount of warranty expense from the current period's warranties
- Recalculating the current portion of loans payable

All the above adjusting entries involve current liabilities and expenses. This chapter discusses them further. Refer to previous chapters for other adjusting entries:

- Depreciation, amortization, depletion (Chapter 15)
- Adjust A/R allowance for uncollectible accounts (Chapter 10)
- Recognize some of the prepaid assets as expense (Chapter 13)
- Accrue interest income on investments made (Chapter 9)

QUESTION 3. Without a doubt, the one account that you will never use in any adjusting entry is _____.

17.3. MAKE SURE WAGES GET COUNTED AT THE END OF THE PERIOD

Payment for wages commonly comes a week or two after employees earn those wages. Suppose Balloon Party pays its employees every week after a one-week delay, as illustrated in Figure 17-2.

Figure 17-2. Calculating Balloon Party's Payroll Delay

20x5					Eight days of delay				20x6					
	M	T	W	Th	F	M	T	W	Th	F	M	T	W→
Dec	22	23	24	25	26	29	30	31	Jan 1	2	5	6	7

x Payday for
Dec 15–19

x Payday for
Dec 22–26

Figure 17-2 shows that at the end of the year, Balloon Party employees still had not been paid for work from December 22 through December 31. If employees' earnings total an average of $800 per day, then on December 31, Balloon Party owes $6,400 ($800 × 8 days) of wages. The general journal entry to record this liability is:

12/31/20x5	Wages expense	6,400	
	Wages payable		6,400

(To accrue unpaid wages expense as of December 31, 20x4)

On the next payroll date, January 2, employees receive wages earned in December. The journal entry is:

1/2/20x6	Wages payable ($800 × 5 days)	4,000	
	Cash		4,000

(To pay wages earned in December 20x4)

The next payday pays for three December workdays and two January workdays. The journal entry is:

1/9/20x6	Wages payable ($800 × 3 days)	2,400	
	Wages expense ($800 × 2 days)	1,600	
	Cash		4,000

(To pay some 20x5 wages and some 20x6 wages)

The reason wages payable (and not wages expense) was debited in these two entries is that wages expense had already been recognized in 20x5 through the adjusting entry on December 31. Figure 17-1 column (3b) shows Balloon Party's year-end adjustment for wages payable.

QUESTION 4. Company X pays its administrators a salary. Each month's salary gets paid on the 15th and the last day of that month. On December 31, at the end of the fiscal year, how many days of salary expense must Company X accrue for its administrators?

17.4. ESTIMATING WARRANTY EXPENSE

Balloon Party is successful selling its mobile balloon sales booths because it offers a five-year warranty. Lauren estimates that Balloon Party will spend $1,000 per booth making warranty repairs. (Of course, over time, experience will make these estimates more accurate.) The Matching Principle requires that a business match expenses with its associated revenue. Because Balloon Party recognizes the sales in the period the booths sell, it must also recognize the $1,000 warranty expense in the same period. The general journal entry to recognize this expense is:

12/31/x5	Warranty expense	1,000	
	Warranties payable		1,000

   (To accrue 5-year warranty expense for
     the booths sold this year)

Years later, when something goes wrong with the booth and Balloon Party must spend $400 to repair it, the journal entry will be:

5/14/x8	Warranties payable	400	
	Cash		400

   (To repair a booth under warranty)

Suppose the $1,000 estimate was too low. The Change-In-Accounting-Estimates Principle requires recording the effect of the change in the year the business discovers that the first estimate was off. If Balloon Party must make another repair to the booth later for $800, the general journal entry would be:

9/22/x8	Warranties payable (1000 – 400 earlier)	600	
	Warranty expense (800 – 600)	200	
	Cash (amount spent for repairs)		800

   (To repair a booth under warranty that was
     estimated $200 too low)

Figure 17-1, column (2b), shows Balloon Party's VJE to estimate warranty expense.

QUESTION 5. Suppose Company X overestimated its warranty expense. Five years later, it shows a warranties payable of $100,000. The accountant is positive that the company will never spend more than $70,000 on these warranties. What should the accountant do and when should she do it?

17.5. LOAN AMORTIZATION SCHEDULES

When loans require periodic payments, some of those payments will be current liabilities (due within 12 months) and some will be long-term liabilities. Part of every payment is interest and part is principal. The **principal** of a loan is that part of the original money borrowed that has not yet been paid. After each payment, the balance of principal due on the loan decreases by the amount of the principal paid. Figure 17-3 shows the loan amortization for the 25-year $160,000 loan that Balloon Party borrowed on December 1, 20x3. The company will pay off the loan with 25 annual payments of $17,627. The first payment was paid on December 1, 20x4, after which Balloon Party owed $158,373.

How to tell the current portion of the loan

The liability section of the balance sheet breaks down into current liabilities and long-term debt. The **Current Portion Principle** requires reporting the current and non-current portions of all debt. Where the current portion cannot easily be estimated, this principle requires reporting the entire debt as current. The loan amortization schedule reveals the amount of principal due within the next year. If the loan has monthly payments, total the principal of the next 12 payments. If the payments are quarterly, total the principal of the next 4 payments. Because Balloon Party's loan has annual payments, look only at the next payment. Payment #2 pays $1,790 of the principal. That is the current portion of the loan. The balance due after that payment ($156,584) is the long-term portion. The Start column of Figure 17-1 shows those amounts as the current and long-term portions of the loan at the beginning of the year.

Figure 17-3. Balloon Party Loan Amortization Schedule

BALLOON PARTY
Loan Amortization Schedule
For Year 20x4 through 20x8

Loan Date	Dec 1, 20x3	
Loan Amount	$160,000	
Interest rate	10%	/year
Term of loan	25	years
Number of pmts/yr	1	payment per year
Payment	$17,627	per year

Pmt #	Year	Payment	Principal	Interest	Balance
					160,000
1	20x4	17,627	1,627	16,000	158,373 Paid
2	20x5	17,627	1,790	15,837	156,584

Step 2	Step 1	Step 3
$17,627	$158,373	$158,373
− 15,837	× 10%	− 1,790
= $1,790	= $15,837	= $156,584

Pmt #	Year	Payment	Principal	Interest	Balance
3	20x6	17,627	1,969	15,658	154,615
4	20x7	17,627	2,165	15,461	152,450
5	20x8	17,627	2,382	15,245	150,068
6	20x9	17,627	2,620	15,007	147,448
7	20y0	17,627	2,882	14,745	144,565
21	20z4	17,627	10,945	6,682	55,875
22	20z5	17,627	12,039	5,587	43,835
23	20z6	17,627	13,243	4,384	30,592
24	20z7	17,627	14,568	3,059	16,024
25	20z8	17,627	16,024	1,602	0

Current portion of loan at the beginning of 20x5
Long-term portion of the loan at beginning of 20x5

Interest payable on loan for December, 20x5

Loan Payable on 12/1/20x5:	156,584
Times annual interest rate	× 10%
Times fraction of a year (1 month = 1/12 of year)	1/12
	1,305

How to calculate an amortization schedule

Follow the three steps to calculate each row of the loan amortization schedule:

Step 1: *Calculate the interest.* The formula to calculate interest is:

Principal x Rate% $\times$ Time in years = Interest

The loan balance at the end of the previous row is the principal. The rate and time stay the same:

$158,373 $\times$ 10% $\times$ 1 year = $15,837.

Step 2: *Calculate the principal paid.* The formula is:

Payment – Interest = Principal

$17,627 – 15,837 = $1,790.

Step 3: *Calculate the new balance due.* The formula is:

Previous balance – Principal paid = New balance

$158,373   – $1,790   = $156,584.[1]

After payment #2, the loan balance is $156,584. The principal of payment #3 ($1,969) is the new current portion of the loan.

Figure 17-1, column (3a), shows the journal entry to make the payment. Loan payments always involve three accounts.

12/1/x5	Interest expense	15,837	
	Loan Payable (non-current)	1,790	
	Cash		17,627
	(To record loan payment #2)		

After the loan payment #2, the current principal portion of the loan increases by $179 to $1,969. Figure 17-1 column 4a adjusts the current portion of loans payable by that amount.[2]

QUESTION 6. That $179 increase happens to be exactly 10% of the amount of principal paid ($1,790) in payment #2. Is this a coincidence?

---

[1] Because, for simplicity, the figures round to the nearest dollar, there is a $1 rounding error.
[2] The VJEs show a $180 adjustment due to the same $1 rounding error.

QUESTION 7. The interest paid on each payment is (greater/less) than the interest of the payment before. The principal paid on each payment is (greater/less) than the principal of the payment before.

17.6. ACCRUING INTEREST EXPENSE

Balloon Party made a loan payment on December 1, 20x5. The next payment will be December 1, 20x6. However, by the end of the year, on December 31, 20x5, the loan will have accrued one month of interest expense that will not be paid until 11 months later. Since that interest expense is part of 20x5, Balloon Party should accrue it on December 31, 20x5.

Principal × Rate% × Time in years = Interest

$156,584 × 10% × 1/12 of a year = $1,305

The general journal entry to accrue the interest expense is:

| 12/31/x5 | Interest expense | 1,305 | |
| | Interest Payable | | 1,305 |

(To accrue one month of interest on the loan)

When the payment is made in 20x6, the journal entry takes into consideration that $1,305 of the interest has already been counted as an expense in 20x5:

12/1/x6	Interest Payable (counted in 20x5)	1,305	
	Interest expense (for 20x6 15,658 — 1,305)	14,353	
	Loan Payable (the amount of principal)	1,969	
	Cash		17,627

(To record the loan payment with 1 month of
interest accrued in 20x5)

Figure 17-1 column 4b shows Balloon Party accruing one month of interest expense.

QUESTION 8. Company Y's loan has a balance of $240,000 on September 30. The interest rate is 10%. The annual payment is due on September 30 each year. How many months of interest should Company X accrue at the end of their fiscal year on December 31? What will be the amount?

17.7. REVERSING ENTRIES—MAKING ADJUSTING ENTRIES EASIER

One of the problems of adjusting entries is that they break the routine. For example, when you pay bills, you usually debit expenses and credit cash. How are you supposed to remember which bills you accrued as an expense the previous period? You make 51 regular weekly payroll accounting entries. Then, at the end of the year, you accrue wages payable. On the next payroll, how are you supposed to remember not to count wages expense twice? Likewise, when you pay for warranty repairs, how are you supposed to know how much expense you have already counted?

Reversing entries solve that problem. Suppose these are the adjusting entries you make on December 31, 20x5:

12/31/20x5	Various expense accounts	60,000	
	Accounts payable (liability)		60,000
	(To accrue expenses not paid at the end of the year)		
12/31/20x5	Warranty expense	1,000	
	Warranties payable		1,000
	(To accrue 5-year warranty expense for the booths sold this year)		
12/31/20x5	Wages expense	6,400	
	Wages payable		6,400
	(To accrue wages expense as of December 31, 20x4)		

When the accountant pays the bills or pays for warranty repairs, or pays wages, must he change his normal routine and look up the amount of these expenses already recognized in the previous year? No. Reversing entries are the answer.

First, remember that at the end of the year, all income and expense accounts are closed out to the equity account. After closing entries, all the revenue and expense accounts will have a zero balance. Then, on the first day of the next fiscal year, reverse the adjusting entries.

1/1/20x6	Accounts payable	60,000	
	Various expense accounts		60,000
	Warranties payable	1,000	
	Warranty expense		1,000
	Wages payable	6,400	
	Wages expense		6,400
	(Reversing entries)		

These entries will have the effect of removing all the liabilities and placing a credit in all these expense accounts! Because expense accounts normally have a debit balance, these credits will make the accounts start out in the hole, with a negative balance. That negative balance will be exactly the amount necessary to prevent the business from counting expenses twice when the company accountant follows the standard routine.

> ## CLEP Clue
>
> *Accounting students usually struggle to visualize how reversing entries actually work. For the CLEP test, you should keep in mind the following four basics and leave the conceptualizing for another time:*

1. Reversing entries happen immediately after the closing entries of the previous year.

2. Reversing entries are always made on the first day of the new period.

3. Reversing entries are the reverse of the adjusting entries—that is, they switch the debits and credits.

4. When a business uses reversing entries, the bookkeepers never need to change their routine to watch out for prior adjusting entries.

CLEP CRAM

A. *VOCABULARY*

Accrue—Recognize revenues or expenses on the accounting books even though no cash changes hands.

Adjusting entry—A non-cash journal entry at the end of a period that adjusts a balance sheet account.

Amortization schedule—A schedule showing the principal, interest, and remaining balance for each payment on a loan.

Interest payable—The account that reflects interest accrued on business debts.

Principal—The amount borrowed; this is the non-interest portion paid back when making loan payments.

Reversing entries—Entries made on the first day of a new period that switch the debits and credits of the adjusting entries made on the last day of the previous period.

Wages payable—The account that reflects wages earned as of the end of the period but not yet paid.

Warranty—A promise by a business to pay for future expenses of a product sold.

Warranties payable—An account that shows the estimated amount owed on the warranties a business offers.

B. *ACCOUNTING PRINCIPLES AND FORMULAS*

Current Portion Principle—The accounting principle that requires a reporting of the current and non-current portions of all debt. Where the current portion cannot easily be estimated, this principle requires reporting the entire debt as current.

Loan amortization schedule—A schedule that shows key information about all payments of a loan. The first entry of a loan amortization schedule would appear as follows:

Payment				10%/yr	Balance
#	Year	Payment	Principal	Interest	160,000
1	20x4	17,627	1,627	16,000	158,373

The entries for this schedule are calculated as follows:

- Previous balance × Rate% × Time in years = Interest

  $160,000 × 10% × 1 year = $16,000

- Payment – Interest = Principal

  $17,627 – $16,000 = $1,627

- Previous balance – Principal = New balance

  $160,000 – $1,627 = $158,373

- Payment never varies

C. *JOURNAL ENTRIES*

Show the journal entry (JE) to record:

Get a $290 invoice for utilities	Utilities expense	290	
	Accounts payable		290
Pay a $290 bill in our accounts payable	Accounts payable	290	
	Cash		290
Company owes $1,000 of wages	Wages expense	1,000	
	Wages payable		1,000
Pay $1,000 of wages accrued last period	Wages payable	1,000	
	Cash		1,000
Estimate cost of warranties: $6,000	Warranties expense	6,000	
	Warranties payable		6,000
Pay $3,000 on products covered by warranty	Warranties payable	3,000	
	Cash		3,000
Make a loan payment	Interest expense (decreases each period)	xxx	
	Loan payable (principal portion)	xxx	
	Cash		x,xxx
Accrue $500 of interest owed on a loan	Interest expense	500	
	Interest payable		500
Reverse this entry: Interest expense 500, Interest payable (500)	Interest payable	500	
	Interest expense		500
	(Reversing entries switch the debits and credits)		

ANSWERS TO QUESTIONS FOUND IN THIS CHAPTER

Q1: When a business pays bills. Debits make accounts payable go down.

Q2: Never. Under cash basis accounting, the accounts payable account does not exist because the business never accrues the liability.

Q3: Cash. The entire purpose of adjusting entries is to recognize an expense or a revenue when there is no cash transaction to trigger the recognition.

Q4: None. The cash payment on the last day of the month fully pays for all the salary expense for that month, so there is nothing to accrue.

Q5: The accountant should change the warranties payable account to $70,000 in the period she decides that the prior estimate was incorrect. The journal entry would include a debit to warranties payable for $30,000 and a credit to warranty expense for $30,000.

Q6: No coincidence. Payment #2 paid off $1,790 of principal, so the company no longer owes interest on that amount. Because interest on the loan is 10%, that is a $179 savings. With less interest paid, more of the loan payment applies to the principal.

Q7: With each payment, the interest expense becomes less and the principal payment becomes more.

Q8: Three months—October, November, and December. The interest is $240,000 \times 10\% \times 3/12$ of a year $= \$6,000$.

CHAPTER 18
Long-Term Liabilities

Chapter 18

Long-Term Liabilities:
Financing the Business for the Long Haul

It's time for Balloon Party to go really big. Lauren decides to incorporate the business. (Chapter 19 discusses incorporation in detail.) After incorporating, Balloon Party, Inc. (BPI) borrows $3,000,000 to begin large-scale manufacturing. When buyers buy the movable sales booths, they pay for a warranty. They give BPI cash immediately in exchange for services provided years in the future.

In this chapter you will learn:

- How to issue bonds.

- How to record a bond's periodic cash payments.

- How to defer recognition of income until a future period.

18.1. WHAT ARE BONDS?

Bonds are a way to borrow large amounts of money from a large number of people. The normal four-step process is as follows:

Step 1.   A corporation (or a government) prints up a number of paper bond certificates. These certificates are actually a contract between the corporation and the lenders/investors. The back of the bond certificate contains the detailed contract terms. The **face of the bond**, or the front of the bond certificate, contains key information: (1) the **maturity date**, which is the final date of the loan contract; (2) the **face amount** of the bond, which is the amount that the corporation promises to pay on the maturity date; (3) the **face rate**, which is used to calculate the periodic cash payment that the corporation promises to regularly pay; and (4) the **payment dates** of those payments. Most bonds pay interest semiannually.

Step 2. The corporation sells the bonds. Commonly a bond under-writer buys all the bonds. A **bond underwriter** is a company with plenty of cash that hopes to resell the bonds at a profit. The price the corporation gets for the bonds depends on the market interest rate. The **market interest rate** is the interest rate that most lenders can immediately get for their money. The market interest rate fluctuates constantly. The face interest rate is printed on the face of the bond and cannot change. If the face rate is greater than the market rate, lenders pay a **premium** to get the bonds—that is they loan more than the face amount. When the face rate is less than the market rate, the corporation will have to sell the bonds at a **discount**—meaning lenders loan less than the face amount. When the face rate and the market rate are the same, lenders will pay the face amount for the bonds.

Step 3. The corporation makes regular cash payments on the payment dates. Unlike a note, for which the accrued interest keeps in-creasing until the note is paid off, corporations pay the interest on the bonds several times a year. For example, if the bonds mature in 10 years and have quarterly payments, the corpora-tion will make 40 (10 years × 4 payments per year) periodic cash payments.

Step 4. On the maturity date, the corporation pays the **bondholder** the face amount. The bondholder is the current investor in the bond. Because bond certificates are freely negotiable, the bondholder at the maturity date will most likely be someone different than the lender who first bought the bonds.

18.2. RECORDING THE MONEY RECEIVED WHEN ISSUING BONDS

On July 1, 20x6, Balloon Party, Inc. issued $1,000,000 worth of bonds. It printed up one thousand of the $1,000 bond certificates shown in Figure 18-1.

Figure 18-1. Balloon Party Bond #1

BALLOON PARTY, INC.
Corporate Bond

$1,000

Interest of 6% payable semiannually on
June 30 and December 31 each year until
June 30, 20z6, when the principal is repaid.

QUESTION 1. What can you tell from the face of the bond?

Face amount of the bond: $_____

Total amount of bonds issued: $_____

Face interest rate: _____%

Market interest rate: _____%

Maturity date: ____/____/_____

Frequency of the interest payments: _____ per year

Periodic cash payment: $_____

Because the market interest rate fluctuates, it usually has changed by the time the company sells the bonds. In BPI's case, the market rate is 7%. Because the market rate is greater than the face rate, BPI receives only $893,225. Lenders receive a $106,775 discount. In addition, companies commonly pay a bond issuance cost for expenses such as printing up the bond certificates. The general journal entry to record Bond #1 is:

07/01/20x6	Cash	888,225	
	Discount on bonds payable—Bond #1	106,775	
	Bond issuance expense	5,000	
	Bonds payable—Bond #1		1,000,000

(To record issuing $1,000,000 of 6% bonds at a discount)

CLEP Clue

Good news: CLEP test-takers will not need to crunch bond math. Questions involving bonds provide the key information. However, you will need to understand the relationships among all of these numbers. A simple way to remember whether lenders pay a premium or a discount: People pay more for something better. If your bond has a higher than market interest rate, people will pay a premium for it.

QUESTION 2. Company X issued $1,000,000 of 8% bonds at a price of $918,000. What can you say about the market interest rate?

On December 31 of the same year, BPI issued $2,000,000 more in bonds, this time with 8.5% interest printed on the face of the bond, as shown in Figure 18-2.

Figure 18-2. Balloon Party Bond #2

BALLOON PARTY, INC.
Corporate Bond

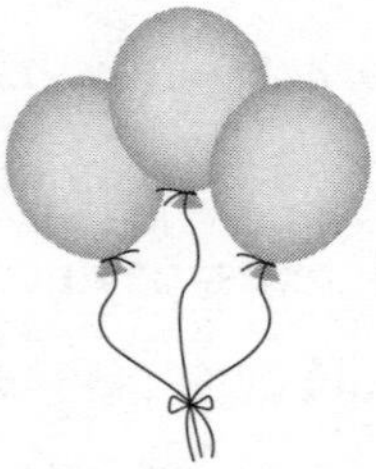

$1,000

Interest of 8.5% payable semiannually on June 30 and December 31 each year until June 30, 20z1, when the principal is repaid.

QUESTION 3. If the market interest is still 7%, will these bonds sell at a discount or a premium?

BPI received $2,275,881 for these bonds, less $10,000 of bond issuance costs. The general journal entry to record these bonds is:

12/31/20x5	Cash	2,265,881	
	Bond issuance expense	10,000	
	Premium on bonds payable		275,881
	Bonds payable		2,000,000

(To record issuing $2,000,000 of 8.5% bonds at a premium)

Figure 18-3 shows BPI's vertical journal entries.

In column (1b), BPI issues Bonds #1. The bond payable account and the discount on bonds payable are both in the long-term debt section of the balance sheet. A discount has a debit normal balance because it is a **contra-liability account**. It represents a reduction of the bond liability. The $1,000,000 bond payable less the $106,775 discount represents the **bond book value**, or the true liability of $893,225 (100,0000 − 106,775). If the company wanted to eliminate this debt, it could buy the bonds back for the same price of $893,225.

The **formula for the book value of a bond** is:

Face amount of bond + Premium (or − Discount) = Book value of bond

In column (2a), BPI issues Bonds #2. Both the bond payable and the premium on bonds payable are liability accounts, and their total ($2,275,881) represents the bond book value.

Note that the bond issuance cost of both these transactions is expensed in the year the bonds are issued.

CLEP Clue

The CLEP test will try to trick you into thinking that the bond issuance costs should reduce the premium or increase the discount and thus spread over the life of the bond. However, the bond issuance cost is always expensed in the year the bonds are issued.

Bond prices are quoted as a percentage of face amount without the percent sign. For example, if $30,000 of bonds sell at 100, they will sell for $30,000 (100% × 30,000). If $30,000 of bonds sell at 105, they will sell for $31,500 (105% × 30,000), or if they sell at 95, they will sell for $28,500 (95% × 30,000). The formula to calculate the bond price is:

Figure 18-3. VJEs for Balloon Party's LT Debt

BALLOON PARTY, INC.
Vertical Journal Entries (partial)
For the years 20x6 and 20x7

	Start	1. 7/1/x6	2. 12/31/x6	3. 6/30/x7	4	End
ASSETS						
Current Assets						
Cash	4,000	a 10,000 b 888,225	a 2,265,881 b (30,000)	a (85,000) b (30,000)		3,023,106
Other current assets	40,000					40,000
Fixed Assets						
All fixed assets	300,000					300,000
LIABILITIES						
Current Liabilities						
Other current liabilities	(30,000)					(30,000)
Deferred warranty revenue—current		a (2,000)				(2,000)
Loan Pay—current	(2,165)					(2,165)
Long-term Debt						
Deferred warranty rev—LT		a (8,000)	c 2,000		2,000	(4,000)
Loan Payable—LT	(152,450)					(152,450)
Bond Payable #1		b (1,000,000)				(1,000,000)
Discount on B/P #1		b 106,775	b (1,263)	b (1,307)		104,205
Bond Payable #2			a (2,000,000)			(2,000,000)
Premium on B/P #2			a (275,881)	a 5,344		(270,537)
EQUITY						
All equity accounts	(59,385)					(59,385)
OPERATING REVENUE						
Warranty revenue			c (2,000)		(2,000)	(4,000)
All operating rev accts	(200,000)					(200,000)
OPERATING EXPENSES						
Interest exp			b 31,263	a 79,656 b 31,307		142,226
Bond issuance exp		b 5,000	a 10,000			15,000
Other operating exp	100,000					100,000
TOTALS	—	—	—	—	—	—

1a. 7/1/x6: BPI sold extended (5-year) warranties for $10,000.

1b. 7/1/x6: BPI issued $1,000,000 of 6% Bonds #1 at a discount of $106,775 with a $5,000 issuance cost.

2a. 12/31/x6: BPI issued $2,000,000 of 8.5% Bonds #2 at a premium of $275,881.

2b. 12/31/x6: BPI makes its first $30,000 interest payment on Bonds #1: $31,263 of interest expense.

2c. 12/31/x6: BPI recognizes $2,000 of warranty revenue for the first year.

3a. 6/30/x7: BPI makes its first $85,000 interest payment on Bonds #2: $79,656 of interest expense.

3b. 6/30/x7: BPI makes its second $30,000 interest payment on Bonds #1: $31,307 of interest expense.

4. 12/31/x7: BPI recognizes another $2,000 of warranty revenue for the second year.

$$\frac{\text{Amount paid}}{\text{Face amount}} = \text{\textbf{Quoted bond price} stated as a percent without the percent sign.}$$

For example, the quoted price of Bond #1 is:

$$\frac{\$893,225}{\$1,000,000} = 89.32\%, \text{ or restated without the percent sign: } 89.32$$

18.3. MAKING THE PERIODIC CASH PAYMENTS FOR BONDS

From the face of the bonds, lenders can determine the amount of cash BPI will periodically pay. The **formula to compute the periodic cash payment** is:

Face amt. of bond × *Face* rate of bond × Fraction of year = Cash payment

For Bond #1, this computes to:

$$\$1,000,000 \times 6\% \times \tfrac{1}{2} \text{ year} = \$30,000$$

For Bond #2, this computes to:

$$\$2,000,000 \times 8.5\% \times \tfrac{1}{2} \text{ year} = \$85,000$$

There is a reason this is called periodic cash payment instead of an interest payment. The actual economic "Interest expense" is calculated differently. The **formula to compute bond periodic interest expense** is:

Book value of the bond × *Market* rate × Fraction of year = Interest expense

For the first payment of Bond #1, this computes to:

$$\$893,225 \times 7\% \times \tfrac{1}{2} \text{ year} = \$31,263$$

For the first payment of Bond #2, this computes to:

$$\$2,275,881 \times 7\% \times \tfrac{1}{2} \text{ year} = \$79,656$$

The periodic cash payment is a contractual amount written on the face of the bond. The interest expense is an economic amount involving the true liability (book value of the bond) and the market interest rate. To make up the difference between the periodic cash payment and the interest expense, a portion of the discount or premium is used up. Here are the general journal entries to record these payments.

12/31/20x6	Interest expense (893,225 × 7% × ½)	31,263	
	Discount on bond payable #1		1,263
	Cash (never changes)		30,000
	(To record the first periodic cash payment on Bond #1)		
6/30/20x7	Interest expense (2,275,881 × 7% × ½)	79,656	
	Premium on bond payable #2	5,344	
	Cash (never changes)		85,000
	(To record the first periodic cash payment on Bond #2)		

The cash payment never changes. The face of the bond contractually defines the amount. The other numbers do change because the book value of each bond changes after each payment. For example, after the first payment for Bond #1, the discount on bonds payable changes. It started out as a debit of $106,775 and received a credit of $1,263 after the first payment. Therefore, after the first payment the discount has a debit balance of $105,512 (106,775 − 1,263), and the book value of the bonds increases to $894,488 (1,000,000 − 105,512). Since the book value increases, the interest expense for the second payment also increases to $31,307 (894,488 × 7% × ½).

CLEP Clue

More good news: The CLEP exam will probably not ask you to calculate these amounts. It will, however, expect you to understand the relationships among these amounts. Here is a single concept that will help you answer most bond discount and premium questions: Over the life of the bonds, the book value gradually approaches the face amount. This is logical because, on the maturity date, the company owes the face amount whether the bonds were issued at a discount or a premium. So the book value (and interest expense) of bonds issued at a premium gradually goes down, and the book value (and interest expense) of bonds issued at a discount gradually goes up.

QUESTION 4. Company Y issued $1,000,000 of 10% bonds at $890,000 that mature in 10 years. Five years after issuing the bonds, will the book value of the bonds be greater or lesser than it is now? If so, will the interest expense be greater or lesser 5 years later than it is now? Will the periodic cash payment be greater or lesser 5 years from now?

CLEP Clue

*The CLEP exam may refer to the periodic cash payment as an "interest payment." Beware! Remember that this "interest payment" does **not** represent interest expense.*

Figure 18-3 shows BPI's periodic cash payments. Column 2b shows the first payment for Bond #1 on 12/31/20x6. The interest expense of $31,263 is greater than the periodic cash payment of $30,000, so the discount is credited for the difference. Directly to the right in column 3 is the interest expense for the second payment for Bond #1. It has increased, and will continue to increase over the life of the bond. Column 3a shows the first payment for Bond #2. The $79,656 interest expense is less than the $85,000 periodic cash payment, so the difference is debited to the premium. Both the premium and the discount gradually decrease to zero over the life of the bonds, causing the book value of both bonds to gradually approach their face values.

CLEP Clue

Bonds are one of the most difficult parts of the CLEP accounting exam. To help you understand the workings of discounts and premiums, study Figure 18-4, which shows the impact of periodic payments for both Bond #1 and Bond #2. You will probably not need to reproduce this schedule on the CLEP exam.

Figure 18-4. Amortization Schedule of BPI's Bonds

BOND #1

Period	Date	Periodic Payment	Debit Interest	Credit Discount	Discount Bal	Book Value
					106,775	893,225
1	12/31/x6	30,000	31,263	(1,263)	105,512	894,488
2	6/30/x7	30,000	31,307	(1,307)	104,205	895,795
3	12/31/x7	30,000	31,353	(1,353)	102,853	897,147
4	6/30/x8	30,000	31,400	(1,400)	101,452	898,548
5	12/31/x8	30,000	31,449	(1,449)	100,003	899,997
6	6/30/x9	30,000	31,500	(1,500)	98,503	901,497
7	12/31/x9	30,000	31,552	(1,552)	96,951	903,049
8	6/30/y0	30,000	31,607	(1,607)	95,344	904,656
38	6/30/z5	30,000	34,510	(4,510)	9,498	990,502
39	12/31/z5	30,000	34,668	(4,668)	4,831	995,169
40	6/30/z6	30,000	34,831	(4,831)	0	1,000,000
		1,200,000	1,306,775	106,775		

BOND #2

Period	Date	Periodic Payment	Debit Interest	Debit Premium	Premium Bal	Book Value
					275,881	2,275,881
1	12/31/x6	85,000	79,656	5,344	270,537	2,270,537
2	6/30/x7	85,000	79,469	5,531	265,005	2,265,005
3	12/31/x7	85,000	79,275	5,725	259,280	2,259,280
4	6/30/x8	85,000	79,075	5,925	253,355	2,253,355
5	12/31/x8	85,000	78,867	6,133	247,223	2,247,223
6	6/30/x9	85,000	78,653	6,347	240,876	2,240,876
7	12/31/x9	85,001	78,431	6,570	234,305	2,234,305
28	12/31/z0	85,000	71,471	13,529	28,495	2,028,495
29	6/30/z1	85,000	70,997	14,003	14,493	2,014,493
30	12/31/z1	85,000	70,507	14,493	0	2,000,000
		2,550,000	2,274,119	(275,881)		

18.4. DEFERRING THE RECOGNITION OF REVENUES

The final part of the liability section includes accounts called deferred credits. **Deferred credits** or **deferred revenues** are liabilities that result from receiving cash prior to earning the income. The business in effect owes future service. If it does not provide the service, it will be required to return the money. Think of the deferred credit section of the balance sheet as a warehouse to store these credits until it is time to recognize them as revenues. Examples of situations that result in deferred credits are:

- A magazine company gets subscriptions in advance
- A research company receives a grant
- An insurance company receives premiums in advance
- A landlord receives rent in advance

BPI sold five-year special warranties for an additional $10,000. BPI must now be ready to provide the warranty services for five years. It earns the warranty income as the years pass. BPI estimates that it will earn $2,000 of the warranty revenue each calendar year.

Figure 18-3 shows BPI's warranty entries. In column (1a), BPI records the $10,000 sale of the extended warranty. BPI stores the $10,000 credit in the liability section, breaking it into two accounts: deferred warranty revenues—current and deferred warranty revenue—long-term. The $10,000 credit thus waits until a later period when it will move to the revenue section.

> ### CLEP Clue
> *The CLEP exam will most likely use the account name "deferred warranty [or something] revenue." The final word "revenue" in the name confuses test-takers into thinking this is a revenue account. Remember that every account beginning with the word "deferred" is a liability account.*

In columns (2c) and (4) BPI removes the credits from their storage in the liability section and transfers them to a revenue account. The company estimates that it earned $2,000 of the warranty revenue in each of the years 20x6 and 20x7. The balance in the liability account deferred warranties payable—long-term reduces to $4,000. The current portion of the liability stays at $2,000, the amount of service that BPI needs to provide within the coming 12 months.

QUESTION 5. On March 1, 20x1, Company Z receives an advance of $36,000 from a renter for three years of rent. Its fiscal year ends on December 31. On March 1, 20x1, how much of the $36,000 is a current liability and how much is long-term? On December 31, 20x1, assuming Company Z has made no adjustment all year to the deferred rent income account, what is the journal entry to recognize the rent income?

CLEP CRAM

A. *VOCABULARY*

Bonds—Certificates that corporations (and governments) issue to borrow large amounts of money from a large number of people. The certificates call for periodic cash payments each year with a lump sum payment on the maturity date.

Bond book value—The true value of the bond liability. See the next section for the formula.

Bondholder—The investor who currently owns the bond certificate.

Contra-liability account—A negative liability, such as a bond discount.

Deferred credit or **deferred revenue**—A section of the liability section of the balance sheet. These liabilities result from receiving cash before earning it.

Discount—When lenders pay less for a bond than the face amount, the difference between what the lenders pay and the face amount is the discount.

Face (of a bond)—The front side of the bond certificate

Face amount—The amount written on the face of a bond that represents the lump sum payment the borrowing corporation promises to pay on the maturity date.

Face rate—The percentage written on the face of a bond used to calculate the periodic cash payment.

Interest payment dates—The dates (usually semiannual or quarterly) each year on which the borrowing corporation promises to make the periodic cash payments.

Market interest rate—The rate that most lenders can immediately get for their money.

Maturity date—The day the borrowing corporation promises to pay the lump sum payment required by the bond.

Periodic cash payments—The semiannual or quarterly payments a bond requires the borrowing corporation to make.

Premium—The amount that lenders pay for a bond in excess of the face amount.

Underwriter—A company with plenty of cash that buys an entire offering of bonds with the hope of reselling them for a profit.

B. *ACCOUNTING PRINCIPLES AND FORMULAS*

Bond book value.

Face amount of bond + Premium (or − Discount) = Bond book value

Periodic cash payment.

Face amt. of bond × *Face* rate of bond × Fraction of year = Cash payment

Periodic interest expense.

Book value of the bond × *Market* rate × Fraction of year = Interest expense

Quoted price of a bond.

$$\frac{\text{Amount investors pay for bond}}{\text{Face amount of bond}} = \begin{array}{l}\text{Quoted price stated as a}\\ \text{percent, but without the \% sign.}\end{array}$$

C. JOURNAL ENTRIES

Show the journal entry (JE) to record:

Issue $10,000 of bonds at a price of 110	Cash ($10,000 × 110%) Premium on bonds payable Bonds payable	11,000	1,000 10,000
Issue $10,000 of bonds at a price of 90	Cash ($10,000 × 90%) Discount on bonds payable Bonds payable	9,000 1,000	10,000
Bond periodic cash payment of $10,000 with an interest expense of $9,000	Interest expense Premium on bond payable Cash	9,000 1,000	10,000
Bond periodic cash payment of $10,000 with an interest expense of $11,000	Interest expense Discount on bond payable Cash	11,000	1,000 10,000
Receive $24,000 in advance for 4 years of rent	Cash Deferred rent revenue—current Deferred rent revenue—long-term	24,000	6,000 18,000
Earn $10,000 of rent income received in advance	Deferred rent revenue Rent revenue	10,000	10,000

ANSWERS TO QUESTIONS FOUND IN THIS CHAPTER

Q1: You can determine all the following:

Face amount of the bond: $1,000

Total amount of bonds issued: Cannot tell from one bond

Face interest rate: 6%

Market interest rate: Cannot tell from face of bond

Maturity date: June 30, 20z6

How frequent are the interest payments: 2 per year

Periodic cash payment: $30 per bond[1]

Q2: The market rate was greater than 8%. If people pay more for something better, they also pay less for something worse.

Q3: At a premium. The face interest rate is greater than the market rate.

Q4: If the bonds were issued at $890,000, then there is a $110,000 discount and the book value is $890,000. *Over time the book value always approaches the face value.* So the book value will eventually increase to $1,000,000. Five years from now the book value will be greater. Since the interest expense is calculated by using the book value, it, too, will be greater five years from now. The periodic cash payments, however, never change.

Q5: The rent is $1,000 per month ($36,000 / 36 months). The definition of current liability is that which is due within the coming year. Company Z thus has a current liability of $12,000 (12 months × $1,000/month). The journal entry on March 1, 20x1, to record the cash is:

3/1/x1	Cash		36,000
	Deferred rent revenue—current		12,000
	Deferred rent revenue—long-term		24,000
	(To record 3 years of rent received in advance.)		
12/31/x1	Deferred rent revenue—long-term	10,000	
	Rent revenue		10,000
	(To record 10 months of rent income [March – Dec] in 20x1)		

---

[1] $1,000 face amount x 6% x ½ year = $30.

CHAPTER 19

The Equity Section

Chapter 19

The Equity Section:
Keeping Track of How Much Belongs to the Owners

During 20x6 and 20x7, Balloon Party went through many changes. Cousin Lou entered the business as a partner. The year was very profitable, but Lou withdrew a lot of money from the business. They decided to incorporate the business as Balloon Party, Inc. (BPI). Uncle Ned was willing to invest $300,000, provided he would get regular dividends. The business went well, but Lauren and Lou had a falling out. They agreed that BPI would buy Lou out.

In this chapter you will learn:

- Why partnerships are the most complicated form of business arrangements.

- The best way to split partnership profits.

- When to issue common stock and when to issue preferred stock.

- The hows and the whys of paying dividends.

- The value of having treasury stock.

19.1. THE SOLE PROPRIETORSHIP BECOMES A PARTNERSHIP

On January 1, 20x6, Lauren invited Cousin Lou to join her as a partner. When partners join, the accounting is the same as when a sole proprietor contributes money. In Figure 19-1, column (1a), Lou contributes $100,000. Lou contributed for a 50% partnership. In a partnership, partners have their own equity and withdrawal accounts in order to keep track of how much of the net assets each partner can claim.

Figure 19-1. BPI's Equity Transactions

BALLOON PARTY, INC.
Vertical Journal Entries (partial)
For the years 20x6 and 20x7

	Start	1	2	3	4	End
ASSETS						
Current Assets						
Cash	15,000	a 100,000 b 70,000	b 300,000	b 100,000	a (90,000) c (30,000)	465,000
All other current assets	40,000					40,000
Fixed Assets						
All fixed assets	280,000					280,000
LIABILITIES						
Current Liabilities						
Dividends payable				c (30,000)	c 30,000	—
All other current liab accts	(80,000)					(80,000)
Long-term Debt						
All other LT debt accounts	(155,000)					(155,000)
EQUITY						
Lauren Equity	(100,000)		a (89,000)	a 189,000		—
Lauren—Withdrawal		b 20,000	a (20,000)			—
Partner Lou Equity		a (100,000)	a 19,000	a 81,000		—
Ptr Lou—Withdrawal		b 110,000	a (110,000)			—
Common Stock (3,000 shares issued @ $10 par)				a (30,000)		(30,000)
Addl Paid-in Capital—Com Stk				a (240,000)		(240,000)
Treasury stock—common stk (900 shares @ $100/share)					a 90,000	90,000
Preferred Stock (3,000 shares @ $100 par)			b (300,000)			(300,000)
Retained Earnings					b (70,000)	(70,000)
Dividends				c 30,000	b (30,000)	—
OPERATING REVENUE						
Sales		b (300,000)	a 300,000	b (500,000)	b 500,000	—
OPERATING EXPENSES						
Officers' salary exp				b 200,000	b (200,000)	—
Other operating expenses		b 100,000	a (100,000)	b 200,000	b (200,000)	—
TOTALS	—	—	—	—	—	—

1a. 1/1/x6: Lauren asks Lou to go into a partnership with her. Lou contributes $100,000 for a 50% ownership.

1b. Feb. thru 12/31/x6: The partnership makes $200,000 profit ($300,000 sales – $100,000 expenses). Of that profit, Cousin Lou takes home $110,000 and Lauren takes home $20,000.

2a. 12/31/x6: The partnership decides to incorporate. They close the accounts. The revenue and expense accounts result in a net income of $200,000, which splits $109,000 to Lauren and $91,000 to Lou. The withdrawal accounts also get closed to their respective equity accounts.

2b. 1/1/x7: Uncle Ned is willing to be an investor in the corporation, but he wants preferred stock. He pays $300,000 for 3,000 shares of preferred stock at a par of $100.

3a. 1/1/x7: Lauren and Lou change equity into shares. Lauren has $189,000 of equity and Lou $81,000 of equity. They decide that Lauren will buy 2,100 shares and Lou 900 shares of $10 par stock for $90 a share.

3b. Jan.–Dec. 20x7: The corporation makes $300,000 profit. Lauren and Lou each take a $100,000 salary.

3c. 10/21/x7: The corporation declares a 10% dividend ($300,000 x 10% = $30,000) on preferred stock.

4a. 11/26/x7: Lou and Lauren end their business relationship. The corporation buys Lou's stock at a price of $100/share.

4b. 12/31/x7: The corporation closes the revenue, expense, and dividend accounts to retained earnings.

4c. 12/31/x7: The corporation pays Uncle Lou his $30,000 dividend.

Partnership law allows partnerships to organize any way the partners choose. Following the advice of her CPA advisor, Lauren arranged with Lou to divide profits in three steps:

Step 1. Pay partners 10% of average equity for the year in order to reward them for keeping money in the partnership.

Step 2. Pay partners $10/hour worked in order to reward them for working to make the partnership successful.

Step 3. Divide any remaining profit (or loss) evenly.

In Figure 19-1, column (1b), the partnership earned net income of $200,000 ($300,000 of revenue – $100,000 of operating expenses). Cousin Lou took home $110,000 of withdrawals and Lauren only $20,000 (revealing one of the common pitfalls of a partnership).

According to the three-step process mentioned above, $109,000 of that $200,000 partnership net income belongs to Lauren and $91,000 belongs to Lou. Figure 19-2 shows the calculation.

Figure 19-2. Allocation of Partnership Net Income

BALLOON PARTY PARTNERSHIP
Allocation of Partnership Net Income
For the year ended December 31, 20x6

	Lauren	Lou	Total
❶ Partnership net income			200,000
Allocate 10% of average equity			
Lauren [(100,000 + 80,000)/2] × 10%	9,000		(9,000)
❷ Lou [(100,000 – 10,000)/2] × 10%		4,500	(4,500)
Allocate $10/hour worked			
❸ Lauren (2,100 hours × $10)	21,000		(21,000)
Lou (750 hours x $10)		7,500	(7,500)
Balance			158,000
❹ Divide the balance 50/50	79,000	79,000	(158,000)
Allocation of Partnership Income	109,000	91,000	—

❶ The partnership net income comes from a netting together of the revenue and expense accounts.

❷ The partnership agreements grants partners a 10% return on their average investment. Lauren started with $100,000 in her equity account and ended with $80,000 after taking home $20,000 of withdrawals. The average is $90,000 [(100,000 + 80,000)/2]. Accordingly, Lauren gets $9,000 (90,000 × 10%) of partnership profits for her return on average investment.

Lou started with $100,000 in his equity account and ended with a negative $10,000 after taking home $110,000. His average is $45,000 [(100,000 – 10,000)/2]. Accordingly, Lou gets $4,500 (45,000 × 10%) of partnership profits for his return on average investment.

❸ The partnership agreement grants partners $10/hour for working in the partnership. Lauren worked 2,100 hours and Lou worked 750 hours. Accordingly, Lauren gets $21,000 (2,100 hours x $10) and Lou gets $7,500 (750 hours × $10).

The division of partnership profits for return on average investment and pay per hour is collectively called the partnership **guaranteed payment**. A guaranteed payment is any amount partners get for any reason other than splitting the profits by some ratio.

❹ The partnership calls for the remaining profit (or loss if the balance at this step is a negative number) by a **sharing ratio**. Partners are free to select any sharing ratio they negotiate. In this case, the remaining $158,000 gets split evenly between Lauren and Lou. The total for the partners represents their share of the partnership profits.

Figure 19-1, column (2a), is the closing entry for the partnership. The revenue and expense accounts, which net to a ($200,000) credit, are divided according to the computation in Figure 19-2 into a ($109,000) credit to Lauren and ($91,000) credit to Lou. The $20,000 debit in Lauren's withdrawal account also gets closed out to her equity account. The net result is Lauren's account goes up $89,000 ($109,000 share of profit – $20,000 withdrawal). Lou's equity account goes down $19,000 ($91,000 share of profit – $110,000 withdrawal). In general journal format, the entry looks like this;

12/31/x6	Sales	300,000	
	Lou equity (91,000 – 110,000)	19,000	
	Lauren equity (109,000 – 20,000)		89,000
	Lauren withdrawal		20,000
	Lou withdrawal		110,000
	All expense accounts		100,000

(To close out revenue, expense and withdrawal accounts to partner equity according to the sharing formula.)

QUESTION 1. Partnership AB earned $50,000 of net income. The guaranteed payments were $30,000 to Partner A and $24,000 to Partner B. The partners split any remaining profits 75% to A and 25% to B. How did the two partners split the $50,000 of net income?

19.2. WHAT IS A CORPORATION?

A **corporation** is an artificial person, created by the laws of a state and allowed to do business. Each state has laws regulating corporations. Unlike a partnership, corporation management is very structured. The laws that dictate running a corporation are very good for handling thousands of individual stockholders.

When a business **incorporates** (that is, becomes a corporation), individuals contribute net assets (assets less liabilities) in exchange for **stock certificates**. Stock certificates contain certain key information. For example, here is the stock certificate that Balloon Party, Inc. issued to Lauren.

Figure 19-3. BPI Stock Certificate

BALLOON PARTY, INC.
Common Stock Certificate

2,100 shares of common stock

$10 par

This stock certificate contains:

- The name of the corporation
- The type of stock, in this case common stock
- The number of shares represented by the stock certificate, in this case 2,100
- Either par value, stated value, or the statement "no par stock"

It is not possible to tell from a stock certificate:

- What the stock is worth
- What portion of ownership the shares represent
- What the stock owner paid for the stock

19.2.1. Type of Stock

Every corporation must have **common stock**. Common stock represents the basic ownership of a corporation. Corporation law grants to common stockholders certain rights:

- Right to vote
- Right to share in dividends
- Right to a certain percentage of the corporation upon liquidation
- The **preemptive right**—the right to buy a portion of each new issuance of stock in order to maintain the same ownership percentage

Corporations may wish to attract more cautious investors by issuing preferred stock. **Preferred stock** is stock with special privileges. Corporations have total freedom to mix and match these privileges to suit investors. Preferred stock commonly has a steady price; it does not go up when the corporation does well, nor does it drop much when the company does poorly. Preferred stockholders usually do not get to vote in stockholder meetings. Examples of privileges for preferred stockholders are:

- The first right to cash dividends before common stockholders
- The right to participate in corporate profits the same as common stockholders
- The right to be paid dividends in arrears if years go by without paying a dividend
- The right to convert preferred stock into common stock

Sometimes corporations issue a second class of common stock (normally called Class B Common Stock) with different rights than Class A Common Stock.

19.2.2. The Number of Shares Issued

Accounting students are often shocked by how much flexibility there is in issuing stock. If a corporation wants to sell $1,000,000 of stock, it can sell a single share for $1,000,000, or it can sell 100,000,000 shares at a penny each. Many corporations like to keep their stock prices between $10 and $99. The balance sheet gives a lot of information about the stock. For example, the Balloon Party, Inc. balance sheet contains the following line:

Common Stock (100,000 authorized, 3,000 issued, 2,100 outstanding)

Authorized shares are the number of shares that the corporate articles of incorporation allow the corporation to issue. **Issued** shares are those that the corporation has sold to investors in exchange for cash or other net assets. Sometimes corporations reacquire their own shares. When that happens fewer shares are outstanding than were originally issued. **Outstanding** shares are those currently held by investors, who can vote and receive dividends. With this information, Lauren can tell that her stock certificate for 2,100 shares, as shown in Figure 19-3, represents 100% of the voting shares outstanding.

19.2.3. Par Value, Stated Value, or No-Par Stock

Par value is often confusing to accounting students. **Par value** stock has a par value printed on the stock certificate. The BPI stock in Figure 19-3 is $10 par value stock. Some states do not allow no-par stock. For these states, if there is no par value written on the stock certificate, those stocks nevertheless have a stated value. **Stated value** is the same as par value for stock with no value printed on the certificates.

CLEP Clue

*Par value does **not** have anything to do with the value of the stock or the original sales price. It is most useful for reasons usually not discussed in an introductory accounting class. Therefore, you need not spend time wondering why par value exists. Instead, just learn how par affects journal entries.*

For financial accounting students, there are only three things to remember about par:

- Most states make it illegal to originally issue stock at less than par value.

- The common stock account contains a dollar amount equal to the number of shares issued × par value per share.

- Sometimes corporations declare dividends as a percent of par. For example, a 5% dividend for $8 par common stock is 40¢/share.

Normally, stock issues for much more than par. When that happens, any money paid for issuing stock over par value goes into an account called "additional paid-in capital," or "paid-in capital in excess of par." For example, if Lauren buys 2,100 shares of $10-par common stock at a price of $90 per share, the general journal entry will be:

1/1/x7	Cash & various other assets & liabilities	189,000	
	Common stock (2100 shares × $10 par)		21,000
	Additional paid-in capital (2,100 shares × $80)		168,000
	(To issue 2,100 shares in exchange for assets and liabilities at a value of $90 per share)		

Suppose BPI had no par value written on the stock certificate. Suppose also that BPI was incorporated in a state that did not allow no-par stock. The state would require BPI to elect a stated value for the stock. If BPI defined the stated value as $10 per share, the journal entry would be the same.

If, however, there was no par value written on the stock and the state allowed no-par stock, the journal entry would be:

1/1/x7	Cash & various other assets & liabilities	189,000	
	Common stock (2,100 shares × $90)		189,000
	(To issue 2,100 shares in exchange for assets and liabilities at a value of $90 per share)		

QUESTION 2. X Corp. has authorized 1,000,000 shares of $1 par common stock. It issued 10,000 shares at a price of $5 per share. What is the balance in the common stock account? Is it a debit or a credit? What is the balance in the paid-in capital in excess of par account?

19.3. BALLOON PARTY PARTNERSHIP INCORPORATES

On January 1, 20x7, Balloon Party Partnership is ready to incorporate. Lauren goes to the Internet and sets up the corporation authorizing the corporation to issue 100,000 shares of common stock and 10,000 shares of preferred stock. She simply made those numbers up after consulting with her CPA.

The partnership's $505,000 of assets minus its $235,000 of liabilities equals net assets of $270,000. According to the partner equity accounts, Lauren owns $189,000 of those net assets and Lou owns $81,000. Lauren decided to issue 3,000 shares of common stock. She divided $270,000 by 3,000 shares and arrived at $90 per share. Figure 19-4 shows that Lauren purchased 2,100 shares and Lou purchased 900 shares with their partnership equity.

Figure 19-4. Calculation of Number of Shares Purchased

BALLOON PARTY PARTNERSHIP Calculation of Number of Shares Purchased *January 1, 20x7*	
Lauren's equity in partnership	$189,000
Lou's equity in partnership	81,000
Total equity in partnership	$270,000
Divided by 3,000 shares	÷ 3,000
Cost per share	$ 90.00
Number of shares bought by Lauren (189,000 / 90)	2,100 shares
Number of shares bought by Lou (81,000 / 90)	900 shares

In Figure 19-1, column (3a), the partners use their equity accounts to purchase stock. The $189,000 debit to Lauren's equity account and the $81,000 debit to Lou's equity account bring those accounts to zero. The corresponding credits are to the common stock account and the additional paid-in capital account.

Lauren and Lou needed more cash, so they convinced Uncle Ned to purchase 3,000 shares of $100 par preferred stock for a total price of $300,000. Figure 19-1 column 2b shows that transaction.

That next year, the corporation operates very profitably. Its $500,000 of sales less $200,000 of operating expense means that it earned a profit of $300,000. Lauren and Lou decided to give themselves a salary of $100,000 each. Figure 19-1, column (3b), records the income and salary.

> ### CLEP Clue
>
> *The CLEP test will tempt you to give the stockholder-owners a withdrawal such as is done in a sole proprietorship or a partnership. That cannot happen with a corporation. Lauren and Lou are now employees of BPI. If they want to get money from their corporation, the best way is with a salary.*

QUESTION 3. A sole proprietor had $100,000 of assets and $30,000 of liabilities. The owner wanted to incorporate. How many shares should he issue to himself? What should be the par value of those shares? (This is a trick question.)

19.4. PAYING A DIVIDEND

To keep Uncle Ned happy, BPI authorized a 10% dividend. Since the preferred stock is $100 par, that means a dividend of $10 per share. Uncle Ned owns 3,000 shares, so the total preferred stock dividend is $30,000. A **dividend** is a distribution of the profits of a corporation to its stockholders. A corporation never has to pay a dividend. The corporate board of directors must authorize a dividend by vote. In a **cash dividend**, the corporation distributes cash to the stockholders. The amount of the dividend is either stated as a dollar amount or as a percentage of par. The formula for computing the total dividend under each method is:

Dollar amount per share:

Dollar amount per share × Number of shares = Total dividend

$10 × 3,000 = $30,000

Percent of par:

Dividend% × CS (or PS) account = Total dividend

10% × $300,000 (PS) = $30,000

There are three important dates for dividends, as the BPI example illustrates.

- *Declaration date*. There is no liability for a dividend until the board of directors authorizes the dividend. On the **declaration date**, the corporation records the dividend and the dividend payable. BPI recorded their dividend in Figure 19-1, column (3)c. The dividends account is a contra-equity account. It is the corporate equivalent of the withdrawal account. Dividends payable is a liability account.

- *Date of record*. To make it extremely clear who gets the dividend, corporations declare a date of record. Whoever owns the stock on the **date of record** gets the dividend. There is no journal entry on this date. It commonly is a couple weeks after the declaration date.

- *Payment date*. Figure 19-1, column (4c), shows BPI paying Uncle Ned his preferred stock dividend. The **payment date** common follows the date of record by one or two weeks.

QUESTION 4. X Corp. has $2-par common stock. The common stock account has a credit balance of $100,000, and the additional paid-in capital account has a credit balance of $900,000. X Corp. declares a 10% cash dividend. How many shares of common stock are issued? What is the total dividend?

- *Stock dividends*. A **stock dividend** is a distribution of a small amount of stock proportionally to all stockholders. In a stock dividend, the common stock account goes up by the amount of par value of the newly issued stock. The credits come out of the additional paid-in capital account.

4/4/x4 Additional paid-in capital	5,000	
Common stock (500 shares @ $10 par)		5,000
(To record a stock dividend of 500 shares of $10 par stock)		

Stock Split

A **stock split** is a large distribution of stock to stockholders that at least doubles the amount of issued stock. Stock splits are commonly two or three new shares issued for every one share already existing. In a stock split, stockholders are asked to turn in all their existing stock certificates in exchange for newer stock certificates. The par value is likewise split. For example, suppose BPI has a 4-to-1 stock split. Lauren would submit her single certificate showing 2,100 shares of $10 par stock, and she would get in return a certificate showing 8,400 shares of $2.50 par stock. There is no accounting entry for a stock split because the total amount of par in the common stock account does not change.

> **QUESTION 5.** Why would a corporation pay a stock dividend or a stock split?

19.5. TREASURY STOCK

Treasury stock is a corporation's investment in its own stock. Sometimes it buys its own stock on the open market to keep the price high. Sometimes it buys stock from employees who leave. If a corporation were to buy any other stock as an investment, the investment would appear as an asset. However, treasury stock appears in the equity section as a contra-equity account.

In BPI's case, when Lauren and Lou had a falling out and agreed to have BPI buy out Lou's stock, the VJE is as shown in Figure 19-1, (column 4a). On the balance sheet, BPI's equity section will include the treasury stock account as a negative number. The common stock account will now have different amounts for shares issued and outstanding.

EQUITY

Common stock (100,000 $10-par authorized, 3,000 issued, 2,100 outstanding)	$ 30,000
Additional paid-in capital	240,000
Treasury stock (900 shares purchased @ 100)	(90,000)
Preferred stock (10,000 $100-par shares authorized, 3,000 issued and outstanding)	300,000
Retained earnings	70,000
TOTAL EQUITY	$550,000

When a corporation resells its treasury stock, it is possible to make a profit. However, the accounting profession does not approve of a corporation showing income from the sale of its own stock. Accordingly, when a corporation resells its treasury stock, the "profit" goes into additional paid-in-capital.

4/4/x8	Cash	110,000	
	Additional paid-in capital[1]		10,000
	Treasury stock		100,000
	(To record the sale for $110,000 of treasury stock purchased at $100,000)		

If BPI sells its treasury stock at a price less than what it paid for it, the "loss" comes out of retained earnings.

4/4/x8	Cash	80,000	
	Retained earnings	10,000	
	Treasury stock		90,000
	(To record the sale for $80,000 of treasury stock purchased at $90,000)		

19.6. CLOSING ENTRIES FOR A CORPORATION

In partnerships and sole proprietorships, all the revenue and expense accounts get closed out to the individual equity accounts. In corporations, **retained earnings** is the account that keeps a running total of all profit that the corporation has made and not distributed as dividends. Figure 19-1, column (4b), shows the corporate closing entries. All the revenue accounts, expense accounts, and the dividend account close out to zero, with retained earnings getting whatever is necessary to balance the debits and credits.

---

[1] Or a specialized account name like, "Paid-in capital from sale of treasury stock."

CLEP CRAM

A. VOCABULARY

Authorized shares—Maximum shares that a corporation may legally issue.

Cash dividend—A share of the profits distributed to stockholders in the form of cash.

Common stock—The type of stock that represents the basic ownership of a corporation.

Corporation—An artificial "person" created by the laws of a state that has the right to do business.

Date of record—Usually a week or two after the declaration date. Whoever owns corporate stock on the date of record gets the dividend.

Declaration date—The date on which the corporate board of directors declares a dividend.

Guaranteed payment—Money partners receive for some reason other than splitting profits by some ratio.

Incorporate—To become a corporation.

Issued shares—The number of shares of a corporation that the corporation has issued to investors.

No-par stock—Corporate shares with no dollar amount written on the stock certificate.

Outstanding shares—The number of issued shares of a corporation less any treasury stock repurchased.

Par value—A dollar amount written on a stock certificate.

Preemptive right—The right to buy a portion of each new issuance of stock in order to maintain the same ownership percentage.

Preferred stock—Stock in a corporation with certain special privileges.

Retained earnings—The equity account in a corporation that contains all the earnings the corporation has ever earned but not yet distributed to stockholders.

Sharing ratio—The method of splitting partnership profits after making guaranteed payments.

Stated value—An accounting value, the equivalent to par value, given to stock with no par value written on the stock certificate.

Stock certificate—A document evidencing ownership in a corporation.

Stock dividend—A distribution of a small amount of stock proportionally to all stockholders.

Stock split—A large distribution (2-for-1 or larger) of new stock in which stockholders turn in old certificates and receive new stock certificates.

Treasury stock—A corporation's investment in its own stock.

B. *ACCOUNTING PRINCIPLES AND FORMULAS*

Partnership profit-splitting plan.

Step 1. Pay partners a certain percentage of their average equity.

Step 2. Pay partners a certain $/hour for their time.

Step 3. Divide the remaining profit or loss by a sharing ratio.

Calculate a dividend—Corporate dividends are declared either as a dollar per share or a percent of par.

- *Dollar per share.* $/share $\times$ # of shares = Total dividend
- *Percent of par.* There are two valuable formulas.
  - Dividend% $\times$ Par value of 1 share = $Dividend/share
  - Dividend% $\times$ CS (or PS) = Total CS (or PS) dividend

C. JOURNAL ENTRIES

Show the journal entry (JE) to record:

Admit Partner B, who contributes $1,000	Cash 1,000 Equity–Partner B 1,000

Purchase 1,000 shares of 50¢ par stock for $1,000 cash and $2,000 of equipment	Cash 1,000
	Equipment 2,000
	  Common stock (1000 sh × 50¢ par) 500
	  Additional paid-in capital 2,500

Purchase 1,000 shares of no par stock for $1,000	Cash 1,000 Common stock 1,000
Corporation **declares** a $3,000 dividend	Dividend 3,000 Dividend payable 3,000
The dividend date of record arrives	(No entry required)
Corporation pays a $3,000 dividend	Dividend payable 3,000 Cash 3,000
Corporation buys $1,000 of treasury stock	Treasury stock (contra-equity account) 1,000 Cash 1,000

Corporation sells $1,000 of treasury stock for $2,000	Cash 2,000
	  Treasury stock 1,000
	  Additional paid-in capital 1,000

Corporation issues 100 shares in a common stock dividend, $10 par	Additional paid-in capital (100 × $10) 1,000 Common stock 1,000
Distribute a 4:1 stock split	(No journal entry.) Make a notation that the par value is reduced to ¼ the original value.

Closing entry for a corporation	Revenue accounts xxx,xxx
	  Expense accounts xxx,xxx
	  Dividends xx,xxx
	  Retained earnings (either dr or cr) xx,xxx xx,xxx

ANSWERS TO QUESTIONS FOUND IN THIS CHAPTER

Q1: Partner A got $27,000 and Partner B got $23,000. After allocating the guaranteed payments of $54,000 (30,000 + 24000), there remains a partnership loss of ($4,000). This negative number went ($3,000) to Partner A (–4,000 × 75%) and ($1,000) to Partner B (–4000 × 25%). Partner A's portion is $27,000 (30000 guaranteed payment – 3000 share of remaining loss), and Partner B's portion is $23,000 (24,000 guaranteed payment – 1,000 share of remaining loss).

Q2: $10,000 credit (10,000 shares × $1 par). The paid-in capital account will have a $40,000 credit.

Q3: Whatever the owner wants. The owner's business is worth $70,000 (100,000 – 30,000). So the only limitation is that the total par value of the stock issued to the owner must be less than $70,000 because most states do not allow stock to be sold for less than the par value.

Q4: There are 50,000 shares ($100,000 in the common stock account / $2 par), and the total dividend is $10,000 ($100,000 in the common stock account × 10%). Another way to calculate the total dividend is: 20¢ dividend per share ($2 par × 10%) x 50,000 shares = $10,000.

Q5: Although a stock dividend gives stockholders no real economic value, it makes stockholders feel appreciated. It lets stockholders sell their new shares on the open market and get some cash. Its benefit is mostly psychological. Corporations orchestrate a stock split to lower the price of their stock. Corporations have found that investors are more likely to buy stock between the value of $10 and $99.

CHAPTER 20

The Final Word on
Financial Statements

Chapter 20

The Final Word
on Financial Statements:
The Complete Reporting and
Analyzing of Business Operations
and Financial Condition

Lauren has operated her business, Balloon Party, Inc. (BPI), as a corporation now for several years. At the end of each year, she produces a complete set of annual financial statements.

In this chapter you will learn:

- The final word on reporting special items on the income statement.

- How to make the statement of stockholders' equity.

- Where all the balance sheet accounts go.

- What a complete cash flow statement looks like.

- How to do a thorough analysis of the company.

On the following pages, Figure 20-1 shows BPI's General Ledger as of 12/31/20x9. From this complete set of accounts, BPI can produce the four basic financial statements later in this chapter. When studying the financial statements, you may want to refer back to the general ledger.

20.1. THE COMPLETE INCOME STATEMENT

Figure 20-2 shows BPI's income statement. It contains several new sections.

1 *Operating Revenue*. Balloon Party's operating income includes its sales and rent revenue. Although Balloon Party has used **operating revenue** on its income statement before, the phrase now has extra meaning for what it does not include. Operating revenue does not include these six items:

Figure 20-1. Balloon Party, Inc. General Ledger: 12/31/20x9

BALLOON PARTY, INC.
General Ledger
For the year ended December 31, 20x9

	A Beginning of Year	B End of Year	C Difference
ASSETS			
Current Assets			**A – B**
Cash	20,200	87,000	(66,800)
Petty cash	200	200	—
Investments in securities	45,000	200,000	(155,000)
Available for sale investments	200,000	230,000	(30,000)
Accounts receivable	525,000	630,000	(105,000)
Allowance for doubtful accounts	(25,000)	(40,000)	15,000
Notes receivable	—	30,000	(30,000)
Interest receivable	2,000	2,500	(500)
Loan receivable	500	—	500
Prepaid lease—16-wheeler	—	20,000	(20,000)
Prepaid insurance	3,200	4,000	(800)
Supplies inventory	240,000	260,000	(20,000)
Fixed Assets			
Equipment (Bought $90,000; Sold $50,000)	1,280,000	1,320,000	(40,000)
Accum depr—equip (Sold –$10,000; 20x9 depr: +$158,000)	(512,000)	(660,000)	148,000
Building	1,945,000	1,945,000	—
Accumulated depreciation—building	(389,000)	(437,600)	48,600
Land improvements	130,000	230,000	(100,000)
Accumulated depreciation—land improvements	(32,500)	(69,000)	36,500
Oil and mineral rights	60,000	60,000	—
Accumulated depletion—oil rights	(48,000)	(60,000)	12,000
Land	40,000	10,000	30,000
Intangible Assets			
Patent	20,000	10,000	10,000
Trade name	3,000	2,000	1,000
Goodwill	10,000	—	10,000
LIABILITIES			
Current Liabilities			**A – B**
Accounts payable	(120,000)	(150,000)	30,000
Wages payable	(6,000)	(4,000)	(2,000)
Dividends payable	(30,000)	(30,000)	—
Warranties payable	(100,000)	(120,000)	20,000
Taxes payable	(11,000)	(14,000)	3,000
Loan payable—current portion	(2,600)	(2,900)	300
Deferred warranty revenue	(30,000)	(33,000)	3,000
Deferred rent revenue	—	(6,000)	6,000

(Continued)

Figure 20-1. *(continued)*

BALLOON PARTY, INC.
General Ledger
For the year ended December 31, 20x9

	A Beginning of Year	B End of Year	C Difference
Long-term Debt			
Loan payable—long-term portion	(147,700)	(144,800)	(2,900)
Warranties payable—long-term	(120,000)	(150,000)	30,000
Bond payable #2	(2,000,000)	(2,000,000)	—
Premium on bond payable #2	(247,200)	(236,100)	(11,100)
EQUITY			
Common stock	(30,000)	(40,000)	10,000
Additional paid-in capital—common stock	(240,000)	(349,000)	109,000
Treasury stock	90,000	45,000	45,000
Preferred stock	(300,000)	(300,000)	—
Retained earnings	(223,100)	(223,100)	—
Accumulated other comprehensive income			—
Dividends—preferred stock		30,000	(30,000)
OPERATING REVENUE			
Sales revenue		(990,000)	
Rent revenue		(30,000)	
OPERATING EXPENSES			
Cost of Goods Sold			
Direct materials		150,000	
Direct labor		80,000	
Manufacturing overhead		40,000	
Operating Expenses			
Amortization expense		21,000	
Depreciation expense		243,100	
Income tax expense		6,700	
Interest expense (Bond: $157,000 + Loan: $15,000)		172,000	
Marketing expenses		30,000	
Office expenses		12,000	
Officers' salaries expense		200,000	
Lease expense—16-wheeler		4,000	
Transportation expense		15,000	
Travel expense		10,000	
Miscellaneous expenses		6,000	
Other Income and Expenses			
Gain on sale of equipment		(5,000)	
Oil lease revenue		(15,000)	
Depletion expense (oil lease)		12,000	
Tornado loss		22,000	
Unrealized gains on available-for-sale investments		(30,000)	
TOTALS	—	—	(46,200)

Figure 20-2. Balloon Party, Inc. Income Statement: 20x9

BALLOON PARTY, INC.
Income Statement
For the year ended December 31, 20x9

OPERATING REVENUE			
Sales		$990,000	100%
Less cost of goods sold			
Direct materials	$ 150,000		15%
Direct labor	80,000		8%
Manufacturing overhead	40,000		4%
Total cost of goods sold		270,000	27%
Gross profit		$ 720,000	73%
Rent revenue		30,000	3%
TOTAL REVENUE		$ 750,000	76%
OPERATING EXPENSES			
Amortization expense	$ 21,000		2%
Depreciation expense	243,100		25%
Interest expense (Bond: $157,000 + Loan: $15,000)	172,000		17%
Marketing expenses	30,000		3%
Office expenses	12,000		1%
Officers' salaries expense	200,000		20%
Lease expense—16-wheeler	4,000		0%
Transportation expense	15,000		2%
Travel expense	10,000		1%
Miscellaneous expenses	6,000		1%
Total operating expenses		713,100	72%
Operating income		$ 36,900	4%
Other gains and losses:			
Gain on sale of equipment		5,000	1%
Income from continuing operations before income tax		$ 41,900	4%
Less income taxes on continuing operations		(5,400)	−1%
Income from continuing operations		$ 36,500	4%
Discontinued oil lease net of $300 tax		2,700	0%
Income before extraordinary item and cumulative effect		$ 39,200	4%
of change in accounting method			
Extraordinary tornado loss (less $2,000 of tax savings)		(20,000)	−2%
Cumulative effect of a change in accounting method.		0	0%
NET INCOME		**$ 19,200**	2%
Other comprehensive income			
Foreign currency adjustments		0	0%
Unrealized gain on investments (less $3,000 income tax)		27,000	3%
COMPREHENSIVE INCOME		$ 46,200	5%

Earnings per share of common stock, 4,000 shares issued, 3,550 outstanding

Income from continuing ops (less preferred	$	1.83
dividends) [(36,500 − 30,000) / 3,550]		
Income from discontinued operations [2,700 / 3,550]		0.76
Income before extraordinary loss [1.83 + 0.76]	$	2.59
Extraordinary tornado loss [−20,000 / 3,550]		(5.63)
NET INCOME [2.59 − 5.63]	$	(3.04)

Continuing Operations (side label spanning the operating section)

Margin markers: 1, 2, 3, 4, 5, 6, 7, 8, 9, 10, 11, 12, 13, 14, 15

- Gains and losses from the sale of business assets or investments
- Income from discontinued business segments
- Extraordinary gains and losses that are unusual and infrequent
- The cumulative effect of changes in accounting method
- Unrealized gains and losses from available-for-sale investments
- Foreign currency translation adjustments

2 The cost of goods sold calculation for retail and service companies is still the same:

Sales − Cost of goods sold = Gross profit or Gross margin.

The three basic costs in manufacturing cost of goods sold are direct labor, direct materials, and overhead.

CLEP Clue

Remember three ways to calculate cost of goods sold. In Chapter 12, Figure 12-6 shows two methods: the perpetual method and the periodic method. The third method, shown in Figure 20-2, is for manufacturing companies. Although there is much more to know about manufacturing costs, for the CLEP exam, you need to remember these three costs.

3 *Rent revenue* is not one of the six types of income excluded from operating revenue in note 1. Therefore, include it below gross profit.

4 *Amortization and depreciation* go under operating expenses. Depletion expense would also have been in this section if it had not been associated with a discontinued operation (see note 10).

5 *Officers' salaries.* Officer-stockholders are free to set their own salaries. It is preferable to pass corporate profit to stockholders via salaries instead of dividends.

QUESTION 1. Why is it preferable to pass corporate profit to stockholders via salaries instead of dividends?

6 The *lease expense* goes with the prepaid lease found on the balance sheet (Figure 20-4). BPI paid $24,000 on November 1 for a one-year lease on their 16-wheeler, or $2,000 per month. Two months later, on December

31, BPI has $4,000 of lease expense and $20,000 (24,000 – 4,000) of pre-paid lease.

7 *Operating income* now has a specific meaning:

Total operating revenue – Operating expenses =
Operating income or Net operating income.

Operating income reflects how much the basic continuing business earned.

> ### CLEP Clue
>
> *Practice writing out this income statement exactly as it is printed from this point on down to comprehensive income, including parenthetical remarks. That will help you to remember it.*

8 *Other gains and losses* is a special section for gains from the normal process of selling assets and investments. BPI is not in the business of selling its assets for a profit, so these gains and losses are not part of operating income. However, because these gains and losses are an ordinary part of business, they do not go under extraordinary gains and losses (see note 11); they get their own line.

9 *Income tax.* Because businesses must compute income before they can compute income tax, the income statement first computes "income from continuing operations before income tax." Every word in this phrase is important.

Income from "continuing operations" specifically excludes three events that rarely happen: (1) discontinued operations, (2) extraordinary events, and (3) major changes in accounting method. Business owners calculate income without these three items in order to predict future income. The phrase "before income tax" notifies the reader that income tax is *not* included with all the other operating expenses.

The income statement places income tax under "income from continuing operations before income tax." The amount will be the income tax on operating income only. The income tax expense account in the general ledger (Figure 20-1) shows $6,700 of income tax, but the amount on the income statement for "less income taxes on continuing operations" (Figure 20-2) is $5,400. The rest of the income tax is reported separately with the discontinued oil lease income ($300, note 10), the tornado loss (–$2,000, note 11), and the unrealized gain ($3,000, note 14).

10 *Discontinued operations.* Both the income and expenses from discontinued operations are netted into a single number, then reduced by income tax expense or income tax savings. A **discontinued operation** must be large enough to amount to a business segment.

11 *Extraordinary gains and losses* are events that are both unusual and infrequent. Do not include in this section gains and losses on business equipment (see note 8) or results of lawsuits. Losses lower income taxes—if not now, then in the future—so even the $22,000 tornado damage is shown net of a $2,000 tax savings (22,000 – 2,000 = 20,000).

12 *Cumulative effect.* When businesses change accounting methods, the Consistency Principle requires that the business go back to the beginning and calculate the **cumulative effect of a change in accounting method**. The cumulative effect is reported as a single number net of income tax. A common change is the switch from FIFO to LIFO inventory. The sudden decrease in inventory produces a large one-time tax benefit.

CLEP Clue

The CLEP exam will not ask you to calculate the cumulative effect of such a change. If a company does change an accounting method, you should know:

- *If prior year financial statements are presented, they are restated as if the new method had been used from day one.*

- *Where the cumulative effect goes on the income statement.*

- *The cumulative effect is shown net of tax.*

In this case, BPI has no such change. The line is included on the income statement only so you can see where it goes.

13 *Net income* now carries a new meaning. It reflects all the corporation's income *except* two special types of income (see notes 14) that get reported after net income. Net income is the only income from which dividends may be paid.

14 *Other comprehensive income.* In an attempt to agree with international accounting authorities, Generally Accepted Accounting Principles recognize two types of income that most people might not think is true income. **Foreign currency adjustments** are gains and losses resulting only from earning income in one currency but reporting the results in dollars.

In Section 9.3, you read about three types of investments: trading investments, available-for-sale investments, and hold-to-maturity investments. Each is accounted for differently. Unrealized gain in trading investments is reported as an operating revenue. Income from held-to-maturity investments is recognized in the same way interest income is recognized for a note receivable (Section 11.2). Only **unrealized gains on available-for-sale investments** get reported under other comprehensive income.

15 *Comprehensive Income* is the final number on the income statement.

16 *Earnings per share* computations. To help common stock investors understand the value of a single share, corporations are required to calculate earnings per common share for every number from income from continuing operations to net income. To calculate earnings for common stockholders, subtract preferred stock (PS) dividends. The formula is:

(Earnings – PS dividends) / Outstanding shares = Earnings per share (EPS)
(36,500 – 30,000) / 3,550 = $1.83

QUESTION 2. Which account(s) will you *not* see under operating expenses: depreciation expense, income tax expense, flood loss, or payroll tax expense?

20.2. THE COMPLETE STATEMENT OF STOCKHOLDERS' EQUITY

Figure 20-3 shows the Balloon Party, Inc. statement of stockholders' equity.

1 *Beginning of the year (BOY).* The statement of stockholders' equity starts at the beginning of the year, explains all the changes, and ends with the balance at the end of the year (EOY).

2 *Net income* comes directly from the income statement. It does not include the other comprehensive income figures. Net income goes into retained earnings.

Figure 20-3. Balloon Party, Inc.
Statement of Stockholders' Equity: 20x9

BALLOON PARTY, INC.
Statement of Stockholders' Equity
For the year ended December 31, 20x9

	1 Beginning of year balance	**2** Net Income − Dividends	**3** Issue 1000 CS shares @ $110	**4** Reissue 450 shares of TS @ $120	Unrealized gain on investments	End of year balance
Common Stock $10 par	30,000		10,000			40,000
Add'l paid-in capital	240,000		100,000	9,000		349,000
Preferred stock	300,000					300,000
Retained earnings	223,100	19,200 (30,000)				212,300
Treasury stock	(90,000)			45,000		(45,000)
Accumulated other comprehensive income						
Unrealized gain on investments					27,000	27,000
Foreign currency adj						—
Total Equity	$ 703,100	$(10,800)	$ 110,000	$ 54,000	$ 27,000	$ 883,300

287

QUESTION 3. Corporation is to retained earnings, as sole proprietorship is to _____?

3 Issuing new stock. To raise more money, BPI issued 1,000 shares of stock at a price of $110. The general journal entry was:

5/5/x9	Cash (1,000 shares × $110)	110,000	
	Common stock (1,000 shares × $10 par)		10,000
	Additional paid-in capital		100,000
	(To issue 1,000 shares @ $110 per share)		

4 BPI also sold half the treasury stock to another investor at a price of $120 per share. Even though BPI bought the stock at $100 and sold it for a $20/share gain, the accounting profession does not permit a corporation to reflect a profit from selling its own stock. The extra money is simply more paid-in capital. The general journal entry is:

5/5/x9	Cash (450 shares × $120 sale price)	54,000	
	Treasury stock (450 shares @ $100 orig. price)		45,000
	Additional paid-in capital		9,000
	(To resell 450 shares of treasury stock @ $120/share)		

5 Paying a dividend lowers retained earnings, just like taking a draw lowers a sole proprietor's equity account.

QUESTION 4. Corporation is to dividend, as sole proprietor is to

_____.

6 The other comprehensive income accounts do not close out to retained earnings. They close to their own equity accounts that accumulate the effect of these two types of "income."

CLEP Clue

The workings of these two special types of comprehensive income is the subject of a more advanced accounting class. Do not worry if you do not understand these items. If you see these items at all on the CLEP exam, it should simply be about where to report them on the income statement and in the corporate equity section.

20.3. THE COMPREHENSIVE BALANCE SHEET

Figure 20-4 shows a comprehensive balance sheet. Besides having more accounts, there is not much new from previous balance sheets for BPI.

1 The *asset section* now has three sections: current assets, fixed assets, and intangible assets.

2 *Deferred credits* go at the end of the current liabilities section. Some deferred credits may represent long-term liabilities. For example, BPI's warranty liability is part current (representing warranty work coming up in the next 12 months) and part long-term liability (representing warranty work probably due two to five years in the future).

> **CLEP Clue**
>
> *Expect questions on the CLEP exam that will explain a liability and expect you to break it down into current and long-term portions for the balance sheet.*

3 Report the *book value of bonds* on the balance sheet. Remember to add premiums to bond payable (as in BPI's case), but subtract discounts.

4 The *equity section* amounts come from the last column of the statement of stockholders' equity (Figure 20-3).

Figure 20-4. Balloon Party, Inc. Balance Sheet: 12/31/20x9

BALLOON PARTY, INC.
Balance Sheet
December 31, 20x9

ASSETS

Current assets

Cash			$ 87,000
Petty cash			200
Investments in securities			200,000
Available for sale investments			230,000
Accounts receivable		$ 630,000	
Allowance for doubtful accounts		(40,000)	590,000
Notes receivable			30,000
Interest receivable			2,500
Loan receivable			—
Prepaid lease—16-wheeler			20,000
Prepaid insurance			4,000
Supplies inventory			260,000
Total current assets			$1,423,700

Fixed assets

Equipment	$1,320,000		
Less accumulated depreciation—equipment	(660,000)	$ 660,000	
Building	$1,945,000		
Less accumulated depreciation—building	(437,600)	1,507,400	
Land improvements	$ 230,000		
Less accumulated depreciation—land impr	(69,000)	161,000	
Oil mineral rights	60,000	—	
Less accumulated depletion—oil rights	(60,000)	—	
Land		10,000	
Total fixed assets			2,338,400

Intangible assets

Patent		$ 10,000	
Trade name		2,000	
Goodwill		—	
Total intangible assets			12,000
TOTAL ASSETS			$3,774,100

(Continued)

Figure 20-4. *(continued)*

BALLOON PARTY, INC.
Balance Sheet
December 31, 20x9

LIABILITIES
Current liabilities

Accounts payable		$ 150,000
Wages payable		4,000
Dividends payable		30,000
Warranties payable		120,000
Taxes payable		14,000
Loan payable—current portion		2,900
Deferred warranty revenue		33,000
Deferred rent revenue		6,000
Total current liabilities		$ 359,900

Long-Term Debt

Loan payable—long term portion	$ 144,800	
Warranties payable—LT	150,000	
Bond payable #2	$2,000,000	
Plus premium on bond payable #2	236,100	2,236,100
Total Long-Term Debt		2,530,900
TOTAL LIABILITIES		$2,890,800

EQUITY

Common Stock (100,000 $10 par shares authorized, 4,000 shares issued, 3,550 shares outstanding)		$ 40,000
Additional paid-in capital—common stock		349,000
Treasury stock		(45,000)
Preferred stock		300,000
Retained earnings		212,300
Accumulated other comprehensive income		27,000
TOTAL EQUITY		883,300
TOTAL LIABILITIES AND EQUITY		$3,774,100

20.4. THE COMPLETE CASH FLOW STATEMENT

Does a balance-sheet change increase or decrease cash? Column C of Figure 20-1 calculates the change in all of BPI's accounts. The cash flow statement (Figure 20-5) uses all those changes. Many times, CLEP test-takers will be confused about whether a change in an account represents a positive or negative adjustment to cash. The following five guidelines should help you with this problem:

- Add back non-cash expenses.

- When assets go down, assume the business got cash for them—positive adjustment.

- When assets go up, assume the business paid cash to buy them—negative adjustment.

- When liabilities or equity go down, assume they were paid with cash—negative adjustment.

- When liabilities or equity go up, assume it was because the business received the cash—positive adjustment.

CLEP Clue

Quick trick: If BOY – EOY produces a number in parentheses, it will also go in parentheses on the cash flow statement, meaning a negative adjustment. Examples: Prepaid insurance went from $3,200 BOY to $4,000 EOY, producing a change of ($800) [3,200 – 4,000 = (800)], a negative adjustment. Patent went from $20,000 BOY to $10,000 EOY producing a change of $10,000 (20,000 – 10,000 = 10,000), a positive adjustment.

QUESTION 5. Accounts payable went up from $10,000 to $20,000. Will this be a positive or a negative adjustment on the cash flow statement? Where?

1 These are all the non-cash expenses that have already reduced net income but did not lower cash. Always a positive adjustment.

2 These assets went up. Assume the company paid cash for them. Accounts receivable went up because BPI recorded revenue but never got the cash. All the others are assets the company purchased. These are all negative adjustments.

Figure 20-5. Balloon Party, Inc. Cash Flow Statement: 20x9

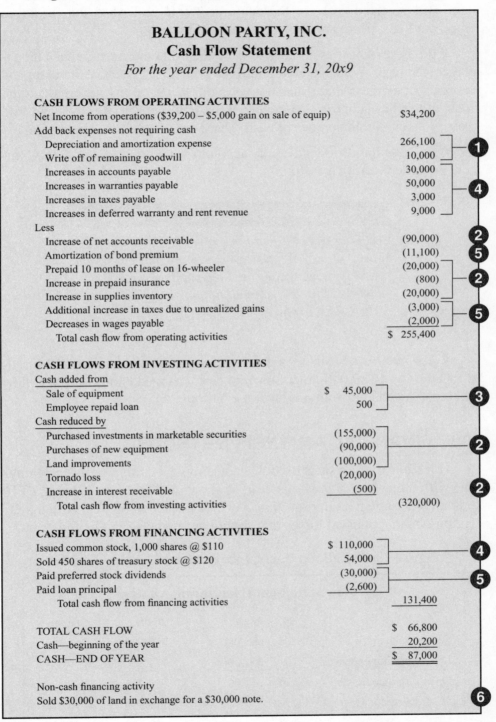

BALLOON PARTY, INC.
Cash Flow Statement
For the year ended December 31, 20x9

CASH FLOWS FROM OPERATING ACTIVITIES

Net Income from operations ($39,200 – $5,000 gain on sale of equip)	$34,200
Add back expenses not requiring cash	
Depreciation and amortization expense	266,100
Write off of remaining goodwill	10,000
Increases in accounts payable	30,000
Increases in warranties payable	50,000
Increases in taxes payable	3,000
Increases in deferred warranty and rent revenue	9,000
Less	
Increase of net accounts receivable	(90,000)
Amortization of bond premium	(11,100)
Prepaid 10 months of lease on 16-wheeler	(20,000)
Increase in prepaid insurance	(800)
Increase in supplies inventory	(20,000)
Additional increase in taxes due to unrealized gains	(3,000)
Decreases in wages payable	(2,000)
Total cash flow from operating activities	$ 255,400

CASH FLOWS FROM INVESTING ACTIVITIES

Cash added from		
Sale of equipment	$ 45,000	
Employee repaid loan	500	
Cash reduced by		
Purchased investments in marketable securities	(155,000)	
Purchases of new equipment	(90,000)	
Land improvements	(100,000)	
Tornado loss	(20,000)	
Increase in interest receivable	(500)	
Total cash flow from investing activities		(320,000)

CASH FLOWS FROM FINANCING ACTIVITIES

Issued common stock, 1,000 shares @ $110	$ 110,000	
Sold 450 shares of treasury stock @ $120	54,000	
Paid preferred stock dividends	(30,000)	
Paid loan principal	(2,600)	
Total cash flow from financing activities		131,400

TOTAL CASH FLOW	$ 66,800
Cash—beginning of the year	20,200
CASH—END OF YEAR	$ 87,000

Non-cash financing activity
Sold $30,000 of land in exchange for a $30,000 note.

3 These assets went down. Assume the company received cash for them. BPI received cash for the equipment sold and when the employee repaid the loan. These are all positive adjustments.

4 These liabilities and equity accounts went up. Assume the company received cash. When current liabilities go up, it is because the company recorded an expense that it has not yet paid. When equity accounts go up, stockholders have contributed money. Here, BPI issued more stock and sold treasury stock—both sources of cash. These are all positive adjustments.

5 These liabilities and equity accounts went down. Assume the company paid them off with cash.

> ### CLEP Clue
>
> *Do not worry about the income tax account. It went up $3,000; however, that amount got spread over several places on the cash flow statement using a process you will not need to know for the CLEP exam.*

6 Sometimes businesses make trades that involve no cash. BPI traded its land for a $30,000 note. Since no cash changed hands, the cash flow statement reports this transaction at the bottom.

20.5. FINANCIAL ANALYSIS METHODS

Horizontal analysis is used when a company compares its current results with those from a previous year, as shown in Figure 20-6. Here, BPI's 20x9 income statement improved in every way over that of 20x8 with the exception of some unusual losses that should not reappear in coming years.

Figure 20-6. Balloon Party, Inc. Horizontal Analysis: 20x9

Income Statement (Horizontal Analysis)			
	20x8	20x9	Change
Total revenue	$ 685,000	$ 750,000	9.5%
Less operating expenses	654,000	713,100	9.0%
Operating income	$ 31,000	$ 36,900	19.0%
Other gains and (losses)	3,000	(17,700)	–690.0%
NET INCOME	$ 34,000	$ 19,200	–43.5%

Vertical analysis is used when a company compares all the numbers of a financial report with a key number from the report. The key number in the income statement is always sales. The key number in the balance sheet is always total assets. Figure 20-7 shows a vertical analysis of BPI's income statement.

Figure 20-7. Balloon Party, Inc.
Vertical Analysis with Benchmark: 20x9

Income Statement (Vertical Analysis with Benchmark)			
	BPI	Percent	Competitor
Sales and other income	$1,020,000	100.0%	100.0%
Less cost of goods sold	(270,000)	–26.5%	34.0%
Total revenue	$ 750,000	73.5%	66.0%
Less operating expenses	713,100	69.9%	62.0%
Operating income	$36,900	3.6%	4.0%
Other gains and (losses)	(17,700)	–1.7%	0.0%
NET INCOME	$ 19,200	1.9%	4.0%

Benchmarking is used when a company compares its financial statements with those of similar companies. Figure 20-7 compares BPI's income statement vertical analysis with that of its major competitor. Here, BPI's Total revenue percent (73.5%) is better than the 66% of the competitor, but BPI has trouble with its expenses (69.9% compared to 62% for the competitor). A company's financial statement shown in percentages only, without dollar amounts (as the competitor's is), is called a **common size statement**.

Ratio analysis is used when a company computes a ratio from various numbers on the financial statements. Figure 20-8 shows a comprehensive list of ratios and their application to BPI's 20x9 financial statements. Some ratios you have already seen, and the figure shows which sections of this book you should use to review. The other ratios are discussed further below.

Figure 20-8. Balloon Party, Inc. Ratio Analysis: 20x9

BALLOON PARTY, INC.
Ratio Analysis
For the year ended December 31, 20x9

Ratio	See Section	Formula	20x9 Calculation	Answer	Analysis
Ability to pay bills in the coming year					
Current Ratio	2.4	$\dfrac{\text{current assets}}{\text{current liabilities}}$	$\dfrac{1,423,700}{359,900}$	396%	Good shape 100% is good
Quick Ratio	11.5	$\dfrac{\text{Cash + ST Investment + Net receivables}}{\text{Current Liabilities}}$	$\dfrac{(8,700 + 200,000 + 590,000)}{359,900}$	244%	Very good. 50% is good
Ability to turn inventory into cash					
Inventory turnover	12.7	$\dfrac{\text{Cost of goods sold}}{\text{Average inventory}}$	$\dfrac{270,000}{250,000}$	1.08	Too low. S/B 4–12 ①
Accounts receivable turnover	11.5	$\dfrac{\text{Net credit sales}}{\text{Average net A/R}}$	$\dfrac{990,000}{577,500}$	1.71	Collection too slow
Days' sales in A/R	11.5	$\dfrac{\text{Average net A/R}}{\text{One day's sales}}$	$\dfrac{577,700}{(990,000 \, / \, 365)}$	213 days	Too many days
Ability to pay debts in the future					
Debt Ratio	2.4	$\dfrac{\text{Total liabilities}}{\text{Total assets}}$	$\dfrac{2,890,800}{3,774,100}$	77%	Getting risky
Times-interest-earned ratio		$\dfrac{\text{Income from operations}}{\text{Interest expense}}$	$\dfrac{36,900}{172,000}$	21%	Looking for > 200% ②
Ability to make a profit					
Rate of return on net sales		$\dfrac{\text{Net income}}{\text{Net sales}}$	$\dfrac{19,200}{990,000}$	1.9%	Not bad after paying salaries ③
Rate of return on total assets		$\dfrac{\text{Net inc + Int exp}}{\text{Average total assets}}$	$\dfrac{19,200 + 172,000}{3,645,850}$	5.2%	Would like 15%–20% ④
Rate of return on common stockholders' equity		$\dfrac{\text{Net income – Preferred dividends}}{\text{Avg. common stock equity}}$	$\dfrac{19,200 - 30,000}{493,200}$	-2.2%	Not good for common stockholders unless officers ⑤
Earnings per share of common stock	20.1	$\dfrac{\text{Net income – Preferred dividends}}{\text{Number of CS shares outstanding}}$	$\dfrac{19,200 - 30,000}{3,550}$	$(3.04)	Each share of common stock lost $3.04
Are the company's shares a good investment?					
Price-earnings ratio		$\dfrac{\text{Market price per common share}}{\text{Earnings per share}}$	$\dfrac{\$110}{(\$3.04)}$	n/a	Meaningless if a net loss ⑥
Equity Ratio	2.4	$\dfrac{\text{Total Equity}}{\text{Total Assets}}$	$\dfrac{883,300}{3,774,100}$	23%	Low. Min = 33%
Dividend yield		$\dfrac{\text{Dividend per share}}{\text{Market price/share}}$	$\dfrac{0}{110}$	0	This co. pays no CS div. ⑦
Book value per share of common stock		$\dfrac{\text{Total equity – PS equity}}{\text{Number of CS shares outstanding}}$	$\dfrac{883,300 - 300,000}{3,550}$	$164	So price of $110 may be good bargain ⑧

1 Several of the formulas ask for an average balance sheet number. To calculate the average, add the beginning of year (BOY) amount with the end of year (EOY) amount and divide by 2. For example, the calculation of average inventory is:

(BOY inventory + EOY inventory) / 2 = Average inventory

($240,000   + $260,000   ) / 2 = $250,000

2 The **times-interest-earned ratio** tells BPI how much interest one year's income could pay. Balloon Party, Inc.'s interest expense is significantly high. The 21% tells Lauren that one year's income can pay 21% of a year's interest expense. With a little downturn, the company may not be able to pay the interest on its debt!

3 The 1.9% **rate of return on net sales** tells owners that they get to keep less than two pennies for every dollar of sales. This might be a problem for a corporation with publicly traded stock. However, in **closely held corporations** (one with fewer than 10 stockholders) such as BPI, this ratio is not that valuable. Stockholder/officers often take the extra corporate profit as a bonus at the end of the year in order to drop taxable income close to zero.

4 The 5.2% **rate of return on total assets** tells investors that every dollar spent on assets earns 5.2¢. This is low. BPI has too many assets (such as $200,000 of short-term investments, $230,000 available-for-sale investments, and $590,000 of accounts receivable) not working for the company. The calculation for average total assets is:

(BOY total assets + EOY total assets) / 2 = Average total assets

(3,517,600   +   3,774,100   ) / 2 =   3,645,850

CLEP Clue

Accounting students often forget to add interest expense to net income in this calculation. Remember this logic: Creditors are another type of investor in the business, and interest is the equivalent of "dividends" to these investors. Adding back interest expense to net income comes up with the total profit the company earned from its assets for all investors, including creditors.

5 The –2.2% **rate of return on common stockholder's equity** tells investors that for every dollar they invested, they lost 2.2¢ in 20x9. This warns new investors that the company profit is going elsewhere (preferred stockholders and officers) rather than to common stockholders. BPI will have to do better if it seeks to attract more investors. Common stockholders own all the equity except what goes to preferred stockholders in case of a liquidation, which is defined by the preferred stock certificate. BPI's preferred stock certificate says the preferred stockholders will get par for their shares upon liquidation. Average common stock equity in BPI's case is calculated as:

[(BOY equity – PS par) + (EOY equity – PS par)] / 2 = Avg CS equity

[(703,100 – 300,000) + (883,300 – 300,000)] / 2 =   493,200

6 The **price-earnings ratio** (P/E) is commonly reported in newspaper stock sections. When investors pay $70/share for popular stock that earns $1/share, the P/E is 70 (70/1). A less popular stock may sell at $25 even though it earns $1.15 per share, for a P/E of 22 (25/1.15). Lower is better. Where there is a loss, as in BPI's case, the P/E ratio is meaningless.

QUESTION 6. What is the price-earnings ratio for a company whose stock sells at $80 and the earnings per share is $2?

7 The **dividend yield** is for investors who are interested in a regular income from the stock. If the price of the stock is $50 and it pays $4 of dividends each year, the dividend yield will be 8% (4/50). Investors compare this percentage with what they can get at a bank or with other investments. In small corporations, such as BPI that pay no dividends, this ratio is not important.

8 The **book value per share of common stock** tells investors what they might get if the corporation would dissolve. The equity section gives the book value for all stockholders. If the corporation were to dissolve, the preferred stockholders would get their equity first ($300,000). The $164 per share of common stock is good news for the new investors who paid $110 and $120 per share.

CLEP CRAM

A. *VOCABULARY*

Benchmarking—Used when a company compares its financial statements with those of similar companies.

Closely held corporation—A corporation with few (usually less than 10) stockholders.

Continuing operations—Income from normal operations that are expected to continue in the coming years. Normal operations + Gains and losses from sale of business assets or investments.

Cumulative effect of a change in accounting method—A single number on an income statement, net of tax, which shows the total effect of a change in accounting method as if the method had been used since day one of the business.

Discontinued operations—If a business segment has discontinued or been sold, all the associated income, expenses, gains, and losses are combined, net of tax, and reported as a single number on the income statement.

Extraordinary gains and losses—Those which are both unusual and infrequent.

Horizontal analysis—Used when a company compares its current results with those from a previous year.

Net income—In a corporation, net income equals all revenues minus all expenses *except* "other comprehensive income."

Net of tax—The number shown represents income or loss after a reduction for income taxes.

Other comprehensive income—Two final types of income shown at the bottom of an income statement. Rather than be closed out into retained income, these two types of income have their own cumulative equity accounts. They are:

- Foreign currency adjustments, and
- Unrealized gains on available-for-sale investments.

Operating revenue—Corporate net income from all sources *except* six specific items. (See Section 20.1, note 1.)

Other gains and losses. A section on the income statement showing gains from the normal process of selling assets and investments.

Ratio analysis—Used when a company computes a ratio from various numbers on the financial statements in order to analyze results. (See Figure 20-8 for a CLEP-comprehensive list.)

Vertical analysis—Used when a company compares all the numbers of a financial report with a key number from the report.

B. *ACCOUNTING PRINCIPLES AND FORMULAS*

Manufacturing cost of goods sold.

Direct labor + Direct materials + Overhead = Manufacturing cost
of goods sold

Operating net income or **operating income.**

Operating revenue – Operating expenses = Operating net income

Ratio analysis—See Figure 20-8 for a CLEP-comprehensive list of formulas. (Make a memory card for each formula.)

ANSWERS TO QUESTIONS FOUND IN THIS CHAPTER

Q1: Salaries avoid double taxation. Both corporations and individuals pay tax on income. Individuals pay tax on salaries and dividends. Corporations, however, get to deduct salary expenses to lower their income tax, but they cannot deduct dividends.

Q2: Income tax expense and flood loss.

Q3: Owner's equity.

Q4: Withdrawal or draw.

Q5: It will be a positive adjustment. Treat credits inside parentheses as negative numbers. Subtracting a negative number is the same as adding. For example,

$$BOY - EOY = (10,000) - (20,000) = -10,000 + 20,000 = 10,000$$

The adjustment will be in the section on cash flows from operating activities.

Q6: P/E = Price / Earnings per share = $80 / $2 = $40.

PRACTICE
TEST 1

CLEP FINANCIAL ACCOUNTING

PRACTICE TEST 1

(Answer sheets appear in the back of this book.)

TIME: 90 Minutes
75 Questions

DIRECTIONS: Each of the questions or incomplete statements below is followed by five possible answers or completions. Select the best choice in each case and fill in the corresponding oval on the answer sheet.

---

1. What does "double entry accounting" mean?

    (A) Record all transactions in the asset section and in the equity section.

    (B) Record transactions upon paying and receiving cash.

    (C) Record where the money came from and where it went.

    (D) Record transactions in the general ledger and the general journal.

    (E) Record debts we owe and debts others owe us.

2. Which of the following is NOT an asset?

    (A) A car

    (B) Loans we owe

    (C) Cash

    (D) Inventory

    (E) Real estate

3. Which of the following are parts of a heading for a balance sheet?

    I.   A date

    II. The name of the business

    III. The name of the owner

    IV. A period of time

    (A) I, II, and III only

    (B) I, II, and IV only

    (C) II and III only

    (D) I and II only

    (E) I, II, III, and IV

4. If Company A has $10,000 of assets and $6,000 of liabilities, what is the equity ratio?

    (A) 2:1   (D) $4,000

    (B) 60%   (E) 40%

    (C) 166%

5. Which statement below about expenses is FALSE?

    (A) Expenses always make owner's equity go down.

    (B) Expenses always involve cash leaving the business.

    (C) Expenses always lower net income.

    (D) Borrowing money is not an expense.

    (E) Expenses usually happen as a result of normal business operations.

6. Depreciation expense

    (A) represents the cash spent this period for asset upkeep

    (B) measures the amount of asset appreciation during a year

    (C) for an asset happens the year that asset is purchased

    (D) for an asset happens the year that asset is sold

    (E) estimates the amount of the asset used up during the year

7. If the cost of goods sold = $6,000, total expenses = $4,000, and gross profit = $3,000, what amount is sales?

(A) $13,000

(D) $2,000

(B) $10,000

(E) $1,000 loss

(C) $9,000

8. At the end of the year, Bob's Bargains' financial statements show these amounts: net income = $10,000, owner's equity at the beginning of the year = $2,000, depreciation expense = $4,000, and withdrawals = $1,000. What is the balance of the owner's equity account at the end of the year?

(A) $3,000

(D) $11,000

(B) $7,000

(E) $12,000

(C) $9,000

9. Which is the best reason for creating a cash flow statement?

(A) It is the easiest financial statement to create.

(B) Net income reflects cash received from operations.

(C) Bankers want to see how quickly business assets depreciate.

(D) Owners need to know how much money they can safely take out of the business.

(E) The balance sheet does not contain information useful in determining what has happened to cash.

10. Where does one find the information to create a cash flow statement?

(A) On a special worksheet showing the changes in balance sheet accounts

(B) On a special worksheet showing the increase in the income statement accounts for the year

(C) The amounts in the balance sheet accounts

(D) The balances in the income and expense accounts

(E) The amounts in the cash flow statement accounts

11. Which of the following is NOT part of the cash flow statement?

    (A) Cash from operations

    (B) Cash from investing activities

    (C) Cash from financing activities

    (D) Cash from marketing activities

    (E) Calculation of cash—end of period

12. During 20x1, a business borrowed $10,000, paid back $2,000 of the loan with an additional $100 of interest, bought an $8,000 machine, and paid the owner a $500 withdrawal. Assuming this is all the relevant information, what is the cash flow from financing activities?

    (A) (600)   (D) $7,500

    (B) (100)   (E) $8,000

    (C) $7,400

13. Who is/are LEAST likely to see your sole proprietorship financial statements?

    (A) Your business banker

    (B) Your business partners

    (C) The Internal Revenue Service

    (D) Your employees

    (E) Potential investors

14. If there is uncertainty about the amount of a liability, which accounting principle would require you to present your financial statements showing the larger estimate of the liability?

    (A) The Creditor Preference Principle

    (B) The Conservative Principle

    (C) The Historical Cost Principle

    (D) The Going Concern Principle

    (E) The Objectivity Principle

15. If in this year the inflation rate is 10%, and your business net income increases by 8%, how would you report this year's income compared to last year's income?

    (A) You would restate last year's income to current year dollars, showing that this year you earned 2% less than last year.

    (B) You would restate this year's income in terms of last year's dollars, showing that this year you earned 2% less than last year.

    (C) You would show both years' financial statements in terms of the standard 1952 dollar.

    (D) You would ignore inflation for your income statement, but your balance sheet would reflect current year dollars.

    (E) You would ignore inflation, showing this year you did 8% better than last year.

16. Company A bought a building in 20x1 for $1,000,000. In 20x3, because of an unusual increase in the population, the demand for real estate increased the value of the building to $1,200,000. Depreciation expense for the building since it was purchased totals $50,000. What is the balance in the building account, and why?

    (A) $1,000,000 because the Historical Cost Principle prevents Company A from showing the building at its current fair value.

    (B) $1,000,000 because the Stable Monetary Unit Principle does not permit restating the building for inflation.

    (C) $1,200,000 because the Going-concern Principle requires showing assets at their current fair values.

    (D) $1,150,000, for the same reason in (C) above, with a reduction for depreciation expense.

    (E) $950,000 because several accounting principles prohibit recognizing the increase in value, but depreciation reduces the building account.

17. Which accounts get closed out to zero at the end of the year?

      I.   Asset accounts

      II. Liability accounts

      III. Withdrawal account

      IV. Income accounts

      V.   Expense accounts

(A) I, II, and III only

(B) IV and V only

(C) III, IV, and V only

(D) V only

(E) I only

18. When a business owner writes a check from the business checking account to pay for personal groceries, the proper journal entry will include

(A) a debit to the withdrawal account

(B) a credit to an income account

(C) a credit to the owner's equity account

(D) a debit to the cash account

(E) a debit to the groceries expense account

19. Bill mistakenly charged Jill $100 too much for plumbing services. When Bill returns the money to Jill, Bill will most probably correct his books by debiting

(A) the cash account

(B) the withdrawal account

(C) the overcharges contra-sales account

(D) the mistakes expense account

(E) the plumbing income account

20. Which accounts normally have a debit balance?

    I. Assets

    II. Liabilities

    III. Equity

    IV. Income

    V. Expense

    (A) I and V only

    (B) II, III, and IV only

    (C) I and IV only

    (D) I, II, and III only

    (E) IV and V only

21. Which of the following is NOT part of a general journal entry?

    (A) The date of the entry

    (B) A debit entry with a number in the debit column

    (C) A credit entry with a number in the credit column

    (D) An explanation, commonly placed inside parentheses

    (E) The current balance of the affected accounts

22. Company A is only six months old. Which of the following is NOT part of any general ledger account on the second-to-last day of the year?

    (A) An account number and/or an account name

    (B) The date of the transaction

    (C) All the increases and decreases in the account

    (D) A closing entry bringing the account balance to zero

    (E) The source of the information

23. The general journal entry to record a loan payment of $670, of which $70 is interest expense, includes

    (A) a debit to loans payable

    (B) a credit to interest expense

(C) a debit to cash

(D) a debit to income summary

(E) a credit to owner's equity

24. The journal entry to buy a $20,000 machine by paying $8,000 in cash and borrowing the remainder from a bank includes

(A) a debit to cash

(B) a debit to machines

(C) a debit to loans payable

(D) a credit to interest expense

(E) a debit to interest expense

25. Which of the following statements is TRUE?

(A) Internal controls prevent asset theft.

(B) Internal controls always cost less than the money saved through cost prevention.

(C) Internal controls will prevent business owners from being arrested for crimes.

(D) Internal controls always make financial statements more accurate.

(E) Internal controls make people do what the owner wants them to do.

26. Which of the following is NOT a basic internal control?

(A) Preventing outsiders from auditing your records

(B) Preventing the accountants from handling cash

(C) Preventing the accountants from authorizing spending

(D) Using prenumbered sales receipts

(E) Providing physical security for easy-to-steal assets

27. The Sarbanes-Oxley Act (SOX)

(A) defines the code of ethics for accountants

(B) requires ethical violations to be disclosed on income tax returns

(C) defines all things lawful as ethical

(D) requires corporate conflicts of interest to be listed as liabilities on the balance sheet

(E) authorizes higher criminal penalties for managers if ethical policies are not enforced

28. Which statement below best explains why companies are willing to allow some theft of their store inventory?

(A) Collusion can always circumvent internal controls.

(B) Allowing some theft helps poor people in the community.

(C) The additional controls cost more than the dollar amount of theft it would prevent.

(D) Sophisticated managers can catch inventory theft without internal controls.

(E) It is better to design internal controls to catch thieves rather than to prevent the theft in the first place.

29. The bank statement shows a balance of $1,000. Your books show a cash balance of $810. There is a deposit not shown of $300 and outstanding checks of $500. The bank charged $20 in fees and paid $10 in interest. What is the correct balance in your cash account?

(A) $1,300   (D) $810

(B) $1,000   (E) $800

(C) $840

30. Company A set up a petty cash fund initially with a $200 debit to petty cash and a $200 credit to cash. When will Company A debit the petty cash account next?

(A) When Company A wants to increase the amount in the petty cash fund

(B) At the end of the month

(C) After a surprise inspection at a random time

(D) Whenever the petty cash fund is replenished

(E) When the petty cash fund runs out of money

31. On the books, you see an account called "unrealized gain/loss on marketable securities." In the account is a single transaction showing a $3,000 debit. Which statement could be TRUE?

    (A) Short-term investments in marketable securities have gone up $3,000, but the securities have not been sold.

    (B) The business sold equipment for a loss of $3,000.

    (C) Short-term investments in bonds were sold for a $3,000 loss.

    (D) Short-term investments in stock went down $3,000, but the stock was not sold.

    (E) The business sold its investments in marketable securities for a $3,000 gain.

32. Company A bought $5,000 of stock for a short-term investment. Two months later, it sold the stock for $6,000. The journal entry to record the sale includes

    (A) a $1,000 debit to realized gain/loss on sale of marketable securities

    (B) a credit to short-term investments for $5,000

    (C) a credit to cash for $6,000

    (D) a $1,000 credit to unrealized gain on sale of short-term investments

    (E) a $6,000 credit to realized gain on sale of short-term investments

33. In X-Corp's chart of accounts is a single account called "accounts receivable" and another called "allowance for uncollectible accounts." From this information alone, which statement below is TRUE?

    (A) X-Corp uses accrual accounting and does not use the direct write-off method.

    (B) X-Corp is a cash-basis taxpayer.

    (C) X-Corp uses accrual accounting and the direct write-off method.

    (D) X-Corp records sales revenues when it receives the money.

    (E) X-Corp has only one customer that owes money.

34. ABC Co. has $100,000 in accounts receivable and $4,000 in allowance for uncollectible accounts. Total sales on credit for June were $600,000. ABC's history indicates that 3% of accounts receivable will probably not be collected. In June, ABC gave up trying to collect JonesCo's $1,000 debt. What is the journal entry to write off the JonesCo account?

    (A) Debit bad debt expense $1,000; credit accounts receivable $1,000

    (B) Debit allowance for doubtful accounts $1,000; credit accounts receivable $1,000

    (C) Debit allowance for doubtful accounts $1,000; credit doubtful accounts expense $1,000

    (D) Credit accounts receivable $3,000; debit allowance for doubtful accounts $3,000

    (E) Debit doubtful accounts expense $3,000; credit accounts receivable $1,000; credit allowance for doubtful accounts $2,000

35. Which of the following is part of the journal entry to record billing a customer $1,000 for services, assuming you use cash-basis accounting?

    (A) Debit cash $1,000

    (B) Credit cash $1,000

    (C) There is no entry.

    (D) Debit accounts receivable $1,000

    (E) Credit deferred revenue $1,000

36. ABC Co. has $100,000 in accounts receivable and *no* allowance for uncollectible accounts. ABC's history indicates that 2% of accounts receivable will probably not be collected. In June, JonesCo notified ABC that it could not pay its $1,000 debt on time. ABC wishes to continue collecting on the JonesCo account. Which of the following is part of the journal entry to reflect these events, assuming that ABC uses the direct write-off method of handling bad debts?

    (A) Credit accounts receivable $1,000

    (B) Debit bad debt expense $2,000

    (C) Credit allowance for doubtful accounts $1,000

    (D) Credit allowance for doubtful accounts $2,000

    (E) There is no journal entry required for any of the above events.

37. X-Corp received a note to pay for $10,000 of sales. The note contains only these words: "ABC Co. promises to pay X-Corp $10,500 six months from now." Which statement below about this note is TRUE?

(A) X-Corp will NOT recognize any interest revenue on this note.

(B) $10,500 is the present value of this note.

(C) This is a non-interest-bearing note.

(D) If X-Corp took this note to the bank the same day it received the note, the bank would give X-Corp more than $10,500.

(E) There is a built-in but unstated 12% interest in this note.

38. SmithCo gave X-Corp a $10,000 12% note on December 31, 20x0. The bank where X-Corp discounts notes charges a 10% discount. If X-Corp maintains its books according to GAAP, which of the following is part of a journal entry that X-Corp should make on January 31, 20x1?

(A) Credit interest revenue $1,000

(B) Debit interest receivable $100

(C) Credit interest revenue $83.33

(D) Debit interest revenue $100

(E) X-Corp is a cash basis company that does not make a journal entry at this time.

39. X-Corp immediately discounted ABC Co.'s $10,000 non-interest-bearing 1-month note for $9,900. One month later, ABC Co. defaulted. The bank billed X-Corp $10,100, charging a $100 dishonored note fee. Which of the following is part of the journal entry on X-Corp's books as a result of the default?

(A) Debit dishonored note expense $100

(B) Debit note receivable $10,000; debit interest receivable $100

(C) Debit accounts receivable $10,100

(D) Credit accounts payable $10,100

(E) X-Corp does not owe the bank the $10,100. The bank must collect from ABC Co.

40. The following are all the asset accounts and liability accounts on the balance sheet.

- Cash $1,000
- Petty cash $100
- Short-term investments $8,900
- Inventories $10,000
- Total current liabilities $20,000
- Total long-term debt $80,000

Which of the following is the quick ratio?

(A) 50%
(D) 10%
(B) 5.5%
(E) 1.1%
(C) 100%

41. A grocery store buys lettuce every three days. Each day it puts the older lettuce in the front and the newer lettuce in the back, hoping that buyers will take the older lettuce first. Which inventory method does GAAP require this grocery store to use?

(A) First-in, first-out
(B) Last-in, first-out
(C) Weighted average
(D) Specific unit
(E) The grocery store may select any accurate inventory method.

42. The grocery store uses FIFO inventory. Three days ago, the store had no lettuce, so it bought 100 heads of lettuce at 10¢ per head. Two days ago it bought 200 heads of lettuce at 11¢ per head. Today it bought only 10 heads of lettuce at 12¢ per head. The store has 30 heads of lettuce in inventory. What is the value of the lettuce inventory?

(A) $3.60
(D) $3.20
(B) $3.40
(E) $3.00
(C) $3.30

43. A large retail giant has had a rapidly growing merchandise inventory for the past 20 years while prices consistently increased. It is looking for a quick one-time expense that it can use on its tax return. It is thinking of switching inventory methods. Which inventory method will result in the most tax savings, assuming the company is now using a different method?

    (A) FIFO

    (B) Weighted average

    (C) LIFO

    (D) Specific unit

    (E) Periodic

44. A manufacturer uses the weighted average system in inventory. At the beginning of this month, it has 80 units in inventory at a total cost of $3,920, for an average unit cost of $49. During this month, it manufactured 20 more units at $54 each (for a total cost of $1,080) and sold 10 units. Which of the following shows the cost of the units sold.

    (A) $515   (D) $520

    (B) $500   (E) $490

    (C) $540

45. X-Corp has a June 30 fiscal year and keeps its books according to GAAP. It paid $1,200 for a year's worth of insurance on June 1, 20x1. X-Corp makes all the correct journal entries. Considering only these events, which statement below is completely TRUE as of June 30, 20x1?

    (A) X-Corp will have $1,200 additional insurance expense.

    (B) X-Corp will have $1,200 additional prepaid insurance.

    (C) X-Corp will have $100 additional insurance expense and $1,100 additional prepaid insurance.

    (D) X-Corp will have $1,100 additional insurance expense and $100 prepaid insurance.

    (E) X-Corp will have $100 additional insurance expense and $1,100 additional insurance payable.

46. ABC, Inc. uses the consumption method of recording supplies. At the beginning of the year, it had supplies inventory of $100. During the year it purchased $1,000 of supplies. At the end of the year, the company determined that it had $120 of supplies in inventory. What is the journal entry to adjust inventory at year's end?

    (A) Debit supplies inventory $980; debit supplies expense $20; credit cash $1,000

    (B) Debit supplies expense $980; credit supplies inventory $980

    (C) Debit purchases $20; debit supplies expense $980; credit supplies inventory $1,000

    (D) Debit supplies inventory $20; credit supplies expense $20

    (E) Debit supplies expense $980; credit accounts payable $980

47. ABC Co., a very small machine shop, bought three machines for $19,000. According to a professional opinion, the values of the machines are: Machine A $12,000, Machine B $6,000, Machine C $2,000. When ABC recorded the purchase, at what price did it record the three machines?

	Machine A	Machine B	Machine C
(A)	11,400	5,700	1,900
(B)	12,000	6,000	1,000
(C)	11,000	6,000	2,000
(D)	12,000	6,000	2,000 with $1,000 of accumulated depreciation

    (E) As a single group of machines with a value of $19,000

48. Farmer Smith spent the following amounts for his farm business:

    - $500 to fix a broken motor on an existing combine

    - $600 to clear the land where a new barn would sit

    - $2,000 to buy a used tractor

    - $10,000 to renovate the old barn so it would last 10 more years

    Which of the following is part of the journal entry to record all four expenditures at the same time?

    (A) Debit barn account $10,600

    (B) Debit equipment $2,500

    (C) Debit repair expense $500

    (D) Debit repair expense $11,100

    (E) Debit land improvements $600

49. A professional self-employed violinist sold his violin for $100,000. He bought it 40 years ago for $10,000 and depreciated it over 30 years with a zero salvage value. Which is part of the journal entry to record the sale?

    (A) Debit cash $90,000

    (B) Debit gain on sale of violin $100,000

    (C) Debit violin account $10,000

    (D) Debit accumulated depreciation $10,000

    (E) Credit gain on sale of violin $90,000

50. ABC Co. recently bought a building, land with mineral rights, a patent good for five years, and goodwill when it bought a marketing firm. This year ABC profits have soared, especially from the marketing firm and from selling some of the minerals. Which is most likely completely TRUE about expenses this year from these items?

    (A) ABC will have some depreciation expense but no depletion expense.

    (B) ABC will have no land depreciation expense and no amortization from goodwill.

(C) ABC will depreciate the building and the land, and deplete the mineral rights.

(D) ABC will have some amortization expense from the patent and the goodwill.

(E) ABC will depreciate, deplete, or amortize all these items this year.

51. Which of the following is the best explanation of depreciation?

(A) Depreciation allocates the cost of an asset over its useful life.

(B) Depreciation measures the decline in value of an asset over its useful life.

(C) Depreciation allocates the cost of an asset to the period in which it was purchased.

(D) Depreciation calculates the savings fund contribution needed each year to replace the asset.

(E) Depreciation is the accounting profession's method of making the balance sheet as accurate as possible.

52. Which depreciation method below never uses a salvage value at any time?

(A) Straight-line method

(B) Double declining balance method

(C) Units of production method

(D) Accelerated depreciation method

(E) MACRS tax method

53. Farmer Brown bought an $11,000 tractor on April 10, 20x1. He estimated a $1,000 salvage value and a useful life of five years. He selected the straight-line method. In 20x1 he correctly reported $1,500 of depreciation on this tractor. Which depreciation *convention* did Farmer Brown select?

(A) Mid-year

(B) Mid-month

(C) Nearest month

(D) Nearest year

(E) Beginning of year

54. MegaCorp is a large retailer. Which item below would you NOT expect to find on MegaCorp's depreciation schedule?

    (A) Depreciation for a $1,000,000 building over its 40-year life

    (B) The date of purchase for all assets on the schedule

    (C) A column for the depreciation for each asset for the current year

    (D) Depreciation for a $100 electric drill with a useful life of 3 years

    (E) A column identifying the depreciation method used for each asset

55. Bob, a full-time self-employed farmer, spent cash for the following items:

    - Paved the drive to the barn: $11,000

    - Planted trees to protect his fields from wind: $1,000

    - Fence: $2,000

    - Mowing along the highway: $500

    Which of the following is part of the single journal entry to record all these transactions?

    (A) Debit land maintenance expense $1,500

    (B) Debit land $14,000

    (C) Credit land $1,000

    (D) Credit land maintenance expense $500

    (E) Debit land improvements $13,000

56. ABC Co. spent $15,000 to develop a working model of a new gadget and $5,000 for attorney fees to get a patent on the gadget. The estimated useful life of the gadget is 10 years. Which of the following is part of the journal entry to record a full year of amortization for the patent?

    (A) Credit accumulated amortization—patent $1,500

    (B) Credit accumulated amortization—patent $2,000

    (C) Credit patent expense $2,000

    (D) Credit patent $2,000

    (E) Debit patent $1,500

57. The method for calculating depletion for a natural resource is most similar to which depreciation method?

    (A) Units of production method

    (B) MACRS method

    (C) Straight-line method

    (D) Double declining balance method

    (E) Tax method

58. Which statement below best expresses the proper way to handle goodwill?

    (A) Goodwill, like land, does not get expensed over time.

    (B) Like short-term investments, raise goodwill when it increases in value and lower goodwill when it decreases in value.

    (C) Amortize goodwill using the straight-line method over 15 years.

    (D) Amortize goodwill using the straight-line method over the estimated useful life.

    (E) Write off goodwill when it goes down in value, but do not increase goodwill when it goes up in value.

59. Max, a self-employed computer programmer, contracted on December 3, 20x1, with an exterminator to kill termites in his office building. On December 22, 20x1, Max received a bill for termite services completed. Max paid the bill on January 5, 20x2. Max is wondering whether to use accrual accounting or cash basis accounting. Which statement correctly explains the difference between the two systems?

    (A) Accrual accounting shows the extermination expense on December 3; cash basis shows the expense on December 22.

    (B) Accrual accounting shows the extermination expense on December 22; cash basis shows the expense on January 5.

    (C) Accrual accounting shows the extermination expense on December 31; cash basis shows the expense on January 5.

    (D) Accrual accounting records the accounts payable on December 22; cash basis records accounts payable on January 5.

    (E) Accrual accounting never uses an accounts payable account; cash basis accounting does.

60. Which statement does NOT indicate a need for an adjusting entry?

    (A) Interest expense is owed on a note payable at the end of the year.

    (B) Interest expense was recorded from a loan payment made on the last day of the year.

    (C) Estimated warranty expense is owed from this period's warranties.

    (D) This month's depreciation expense has not yet been recorded.

    (E) A portion of prepaid rent was used up this month.

61. At the end of 20x1, ABC Co. owed $5,000 of wages to employees who were not paid until January 5, 20x2. ABC maintains its accounting books according to GAAP. Which statement below is TRUE?

    (A) ABC makes no entry until it pays the wages on January 5.

    (B) ABC should accrue cash out on December 31, 20x1.

    (C) ABC should debit wages expense $5,000 on January 5, 20x2.

    (D) ABC should credit wages payable $5,000 on January 5, 20x2.

    (E) ABC should credit wages payable $5,000 on December 31, 20x1.

62. X-Corp borrowed $10,000 on December 1, 20x1. It must pay off the loan with 10 monthly principal payments of $1,000 plus 12% interest on any unpaid balance. On January 1, 20x2, it paid $1,100. What journal entry should X-Corp make on December 31, 20x1?

    (A) Debit interest expense $1,100; credit interest payable $1,100

    (B) Debit interest payable $100; credit cash $100

    (C) Debit interest expense $100; credit interest payable $100

    (D) Debit principal payable $1,000; debit interest payable $100; credit loan payable $1,100

    (E) No entry is needed.

63. Which of the following is something you will find on the face of a bond?

    (A) The purchase price stated as a percent of present value

    (B) The present value of principal and interest payments

    (C) Market interest rate

(D) The dates of periodic payments

(E) A bond amortization schedule

64. Jones & Jones issued $100,000 of 6% bonds at a price of $95. The bond issuance cost was $3,000. Which of the following is part of the journal entry to record these bonds on Jones & Jones books?

(A) Debit cash $92,000

(B) Credit bonds payable $95,000

(C) Credit bond issuance expense $3,000

(D) Credit premium on bonds payable $5,000

(E) Debit interest expense $6,000

65. Which of the following is TRUE about the accounting books of a company that issued a $100,000 6% 10-year bond originally issued at 105?

(A) Over the life of this bond, the book value will approach $100,000.

(B) Over the life of this bond, the bond discount will shrink to zero.

(C) Over the life of this bond, the interest expense of each payment gets higher.

(D) Over the life of this bond, interest income decreases with each payment.

(E) Over the life of this bond, the premium will approach $5,000.

66. On December 1, 20x1, ABC Co. received $12,000 for 12 months of rent income paid in advance. ABC records this entry by: debit cash $12,000; credit deferred rent income $12,000. What type of account is deferred rent income?

(A) Asset   (D) Expense

(B) Contra-asset   (E) Liability

(C) Revenue

67. Partner B joined the ABC partnership by contributing $10,000 of cash, $20,000 of accounts receivable ($4,000 of which will very likely never be collected), and $3,000 of accounts payable. Which of the following is part of the journal entry to record this transaction on the partnership books?

    (A) Debit accounts receivable $13,000

    (B) Debit accounts receivable $16,000

    (C) Credit equity—partner B $23,000

    (D) Debit allowance for uncollectible accounts $4,000

    (E) Credit equity—partner B $30,000

68. Which of the following is NOT commonly one of the rights granted to common stockholders?

    (A) The right to vote in stockholders' meetings

    (B) The right to declare dividends

    (C) The right to share in dividends if declared

    (D) The right to a certain percentage of the corporation upon liquidation

    (E) The preemptive right

69. Mr. Clark incorporated his sole proprietorship. He contributed $5,000 of cash in addition to equipment with a historical cost of $16,000 and accumulated depreciation of $4,000. In exchange for these assets, Mr. Clark gets 100 shares of $10 par common stock. Which of the following is part of the journal entry to record this transaction on the corporate books?

    (A) Debit equipment $12,000

    (B) Debit accumulated depreciation $4,000

    (C) Credit cash $5,000

    (D) Credit common stock $1,000

    (E) Credit additional paid-in capital in excess of par $24,000

70. X-Corp has 1,000 shares of $100 par preferred stock outstanding, which originally sold at $130,000. Its board of directors voted a 10% dividend. Which of the following is part of the journal entry to record the vote?

    (A) Credit dividends $13,000

    (B) Credit dividends $10,000

    (C) Credit dividends payable $10,000

    (D) Credit cash $10,000

    (E) There is no journal entry to record at this time.

71. In a multi-step income statement, a tornado loss would come directly after

    (A) income before extraordinary items

    (B) income from continuing operations

    (C) foreign currency adjustments

    (D) gross profit

    (E) operating expenses

72. Which of the following would NOT appear on a statement of stockholders' equity?

    (A) New issuances of preferred stock

    (B) Purchases of treasury stock

    (C) Unrealized gains on hold-to-maturity investments

    (D) Foreign currency adjustments

    (E) Cash from the sale of land held for investment

73. On a balance sheet, which of the following is a contra-asset account?

    (A) Accounts receivable

    (B) Accounts payable

    (C) Equipment

    (D) Accumulated depletion

    (E) Trade name

74. Which of the following is a positive cash adjustment to the cash flows from financing activities section of the cash flow statement?

(A) Sale of equipment

(B) Employee repaid loan

(C) Sale of treasury stock

(D) Paid preferred stock dividends

(E) Depreciation expense

75. From the following corporate information, compute the return on common stockholders' equity.

Average common stock equity	$100,000
Net income	50,000
Preferred stock dividends	10,000
Number of common shares	20,000

(A) $2.00
(B) 40%
(C) $2.50

(D) 50%
(E) $3.00

CLEP FINANCIAL ACCOUNTING PRACTICE TEST 1

ANSWER KEY

1.	(C)	26.	(A)	51.	(A)
2.	(B)	27.	(E)	52.	(E)
3.	(D)	28.	(C)	53.	(C)
4.	(E)	29.	(E)	54.	(D)
5.	(B)	30.	(A)	55.	(E)
6.	(E)	31.	(D)	56.	(D)
7.	(C)	32.	(B)	57.	(A)
8.	(D)	33.	(A)	58.	(E)
9.	(D)	34.	(B)	59.	(B)
10.	(A)	35.	(C)	60.	(B)
11.	(D)	36.	(E)	61.	(E)
12.	(D)	37.	(C)	62.	(C)
13.	(D)	38.	(B)	63.	(D)
14.	(B)	39.	(C)	64.	(A)
15.	(E)	40.	(A)	65.	(A)
16.	(A)	41.	(E)	66.	(E)
17.	(C)	42.	(B)	67.	(C)
18.	(A)	43.	(C)	68.	(B)
19.	(E)	44.	(B)	69.	(D)
20.	(A)	45.	(C)	70.	(C)
21.	(E)	46.	(B)	71.	(A)
22.	(D)	47.	(A)	72.	(E)
23.	(A)	48.	(C)	73.	(D)
24.	(B)	49.	(D)	74.	(C)
25.	(D)	50.	(B)	75.	(B)

DETAILED EXPLANATIONS OF ANSWERS

PRACTICE TEST 1

(The **boldface, *italic*** numbers in the following paragraphs refer to the Chapters and Sections where review information can be found.)

1. **(C)** Double entry accounting means accountants record every transaction twice: once showing where the money came from and again showing where the money went. Not (A) or (E) because transactions get recorded elsewhere besides assets, equity, and debt sections. Not (B) because businesses record many non-cash transactions. Transactions do get recorded both in the ledger and journal, as (D) says, but that is not what is meant by double entry accounting. *(2.2)*

2. **(B)** Assets are economic resources that the business plans to use in the future to make money. Loans owed are not resources of the business but creditor claims on the business resources. *(2.3)*

3. **(D)** A balance sheet heading contains (1) the name of the business, (2) the title "Balance Sheet," and (3) a single date. The Business Entity Principle forbids combining the owner books with the business books, so the owner's name is not in the heading. All financial statements EXCEPT the balance sheet use a period of time. *(2.3)*

4. **(E)** The equity ratio formula is: Equity / Total assets = Equity ratio. Equity is $4,000 (10,000 assets – 6,000 liabilities). The equity ratio is 40% (4,000 / 10,000). *(2.4)*

5. **(B)** Although often expenses happen as a result of spending money, that is not always the case. Many adjustments, such as depreciation or adjustments to inventory, do not involve cash. *(3.2)* The other statements are true. (D) is true because the interest, not the borrowing, is an expense. *(3.1)*

6. **(E)** Depreciation expense explains how assets are used up over their estimated useful lives. *(3.1)* Not (A) because recognizing depreciation does not involve cash. Not (B) because depreciation is closer to measuring how much an asset goes down in value. Not (C) or (D) because depreciation expense happens over the estimated economic life of an asset. *(3.2)*

7. **(C)** Plugging the numbers into the income statement equation *(3.3)* produces:

$$\text{Sales} - \text{Cost of goods sold} = \text{Gross profit}$$

$$? - \$6,000 = \$3,000$$

$$\$9,000 - \$6,000 = \$3,000$$

8. **(D)** The equation for the statement of owner's equity *(3.4)* is:

$$\text{Equity—beginning} + \text{Net income} - \text{Withdrawal} = \text{Equity—end}$$

$$\$2,000 + \$10,000 - \$1,000 = \$11,000$$

9. **(D)** Owners commonly endanger their businesses by taking out too much money. Not (A) because the cash flow statement is the most difficult to create. Not (B) because net income includes non-cash items that must be adjusted out in order to compute cash flow from operations. Not (C) because cash flow statements will not help a banker see how quickly business assets depreciate. Not (E) because in order to create the cash flow statement, one must compute the *change* in balance sheet accounts. *(4.1)*

10. **(A)** Creating the cash flow statement requires creating a worksheet first. Not (B) because the worksheet does not consider changes in income statement accounts. Not (C) because the *change* in balance sheet accounts, not the amounts currently in the accounts, are used to create the cash flow statement. Not (D) because revenues and expenses are for the income statement. Not (E) because cash flow statement accounts do not exist. *(4.2)*

11. **(D)** The remaining four items are part of the cash flow statement. *(4.2)*

12. **(D)** Financing is the process of finding money for the business from sources other than normal operations. Not (A) or (B) because the $8,000 for the machine belongs in the "cash from investing activities" section *(4.3)*. Not (C) because interest expense is included in net income, the first number in the "cash from operations" section *(4.2 and 4.4)*. That leaves $7,500 (10,000 loan – 2,000 payment – 500 draw). *(4.4)*

13. **(D)** Employees rarely get to see business financial statements. Except for large publicly traded companies, owners keep their financial statements private, showing them only for some business purpose. The IRS requires your business income statement. *(5.1)*

14. **(B)** Given uncertainty, the Conservative Principle requires that financial statements be reported in the least favorable light. In this case, the larger liability is less favorable to the business. The Objectivity Principle (E) might have been a good answer if the problem had said that the evidence in favor of the larger liability is more objective than the evidence in favor of the smaller liability. *(5.2)*

15. **(E)** The Stable Monetary Unit Principle requires accountants to ignore inflation when presenting financial statements. All the other answers call for some restating of the amounts to adjust for inflation, and thus are wrong. *(5.2)*

16. **(A)** The Historical Cost Principle requires businesses to reflect assets at historical cost. Businesses may not increase the value of their assets to reflect the current market, so not (C) or (D). Depreciation is kept in a separate account called "accumulated depreciation—building." Not (E), which incorrectly reduces the building account for depreciation. Not (B) because the increase in value for the building comes not from inflation but an unusual increase in demand. *(5.2)*

17. **(C)** Only the temporary accounts get closed out. The income statement accounts (income and expense accounts) and the withdrawal account get closed to the owner's equity account at the end of the year. *(6.5)*

18. **(A)** The Business Entity Principle says owners do not mix personal books with their business books. *(2.3)* For the same reason, do not keep track of the personal groceries expense on the business books. When an owner spends business money for personal reasons, it is treated as a withdrawal. *(3.4)* The proper journal entry is a debit to withdrawal and a credit to cash. *(6.4)*

19. **(E)** When Bill made the mistake, he would have debited cash and credited plumbing income. Now that he must correct that mistake, his journal entry is just the opposite: debit plumbing income and credit cash. Correcting a mistake is one of the two times you would debit an income account. *(6.3)* The other time is when you make closing entries. (C) and (D) are theoretically possible, but nobody does it that way. *(6.6)*

20. **(A)** In the equation Assets = Liabilities + Owner's equity, the accounts on the left side of the equation (assets) normally have debit balances. However, because expenses are contra-equity accounts, they have balances

that normally are the opposite of equity accounts, so they also have normal debit balances. Income accounts, which explain why equity goes up, normally have credit balances. *(6.7)*

21. **(E)**   The general journal does not have any information on the current balances in the accounts. It is the general *ledger* that does. The information from the general journal gets posted to the general ledger. *(7.1)*

22. **(D)**   Since the question asks for what will be reported on the second-to-last day of the year, the closing entry for the year has not yet been posted. Closing entries are done on the last day of the year. It is significant that this is a new company. If the company were more than a year old, the closing entry from the previous year would show up on the ledger page. *(7.2)*

23. **(A)**   The journal entry to make a loan payment is: debit loans payable $600; debit interest expense $70; credit cash $670. Not (B) because of the word "credit." Not (C) because of the word "debit." Not (D) or (E) because the transaction has nothing to do with these two accounts. *(Chap 7 CLEP CRAM Sec. B)*

24. **(B)**   The journal entry to buy a $20,000 machine on $12,000 of credit is: debit machine $20,000; credit cash $8,000; credit loans payable $12,000. Not (A) or (C) because of the word "debit." Not (D) or (E) because on the day a company borrows money, it does not yet owe any interest expense. *(Chap 7 CLEP CRAM Sec. B)*

25. **(D)**   Internal controls always make financial statements more accurate, although they do not assure complete accuracy. The word "always" makes (B) incorrect. Not (A), (C), or (E) which are stated too strongly. Internal controls give some protection from theft and criminal prosecution, and they give people some incentive to do what the owner wants. *(8.1, 8.3, 8.4)*

26. **(A)**   The best, most neutral auditors are from outside. *(5.2)* Not (B) or (C) because both of these are standard separation of duty policies. (D) and (E) are standard internal control policies because they do not cost much but they protect much. *(8.2)*

27. **(E)**   Not (A) because the AICPA defines the code of ethics for accountants. Not (B) because SOX does not discuss income taxes. Not (C) because ethics goes beyond the law. Not (D) because ethical issues should

appear in notes to financial statements, not in the financial statements themselves. *(8.3)*

28. **(C)** Internal controls are imperfect. There comes a point at which additional controls cost more than the losses prevented. Not (A) because even though collusion can circumvent internal controls, that alone is not a reason to allow more theft. Still, (A) is not a bad answer because preventing collusion costs more and can be sidestepped by even more collusion. However, (C) is better because it explains why a company would always be willing to allow some theft. Not (B) because while this may or may not be true, it does not best explain why businesses are willing to allow some theft. Not (D) or (E), which are untrue statements. *(8.4)*

29. **(E)** Using Figure 9-1 as a guide, the bank adjusts as follows: bank balance + deposit not shown − outstanding checks = adjusted bank balance (1000 + 300 − 500 = 800). The books adjust as follows: book balance + interest − bank fee = adjusted book balance (810 + 10 − 20 = 800). *(9.1)*

30. **(A)** Debiting the petty cash fund raises its maximum amount. All other answers refer to replenishing petty cash. The journal entry to replenish petty cash does not involve the petty cash account. It includes a debit to various expense accounts for the amount of the receipts and a credit to the cash account. *(9.2)*

31. **(D)** Not (B), (C), or (E) because the word "unrealized" means the marketable securities were not sold. Not (B) because the words "marketable securities" refer to stocks, bonds, or other investments readily sold on public markets, not equipment. Not (A) or (E) because the words "single transaction" and "debit balance" means that the account recorded a single loss. *(9.3)*

32. **(B)** The journal entry to sell this stock includes a $6,000 debit to cash (increasing cash), a $5,000 credit to short-term investments (lowering the account to reflect the stock leaving the company), and a $1,000 credit to the gain account. Not (A) because of the word "debit." Not (C) because of the word "credit." Not (D) because of the word "unrealized" which is used only when investments go up or down, but have not been sold. Not (E) because the $6,000 amount is too large. *(9.3)*

33. **(A)** Having an accounts receivable account always means accrual—not cash—accounting, so not (B). Having the allowance for uncollectible ac-

counts always means allowance—not direct write-off—method, so not (C). *(10.3)* Not (D), which happens only in cash-basis accounting. The single accounts receivable does not mean only one customer because the accounts receivable account is a control account. Other accounts in a subsidiary record keep track of the many customers. *(10.1)*

34. **(B)**   When a business writes off an account, it removes the bad debt amount from *both* accounts receivable and the allowance for uncollectible accounts. The presence of an allowance for uncollectible accounts always means that a company does not use the direct write-off method. The allowance method records the expense earlier when the income was earned, so not (A), (C), or (E). Not (D) because the amount is wrong. *(10.1)*

35. **(C)**   Cash basis accounting records revenue when the cash is received, so at this time there is no entry. When the cash comes in, the journal entry will debit cash and credit sales. *(10.2)*

36. **(E)**   ABC's lack of an allowance for uncollectible accounts means that ABC uses the direct write-off method of accounting. However, since ABC wishes to continue the collection process, there is no write-off. If there were, it would debit bad debt expense $1,000 and credit accounts receivable $1,000. *(10.3)*

37. **(C)**   A non-interest-bearing note shows no interest rate on its face. Not (A) or (B) because X-Corp will recognize $500 as interest—the difference between the $10,500 face amount (the future value) and the $10,000 present value. Not (E) because the $500 of interest represents 10% interest over 6 months ($10,000 \times 10\% \times \frac{1}{2}$ year = $500), not 12% ($10,000 \times 12\% \times \frac{1}{2}$ year = $600). Not (D) because banks reduce the future value by a discount, so the proceeds must be less than $10,500. *(11.1)*

38. **(B)**   The journal entry is: debit interest receivable $100 ($10,000 \times 12\% \times 1/12$ year); credit interest revenue $100. Not (E) because X-Corp maintains its books according to GAAP, and cash basis violates GAAP. Not (C), which incorrectly uses the bank discount rate instead of the note interest rate. *(11.2)*

39. **(C)**   The journal entry upon a customer's default on a discounted note is debit accounts receivable—ABC Co. $10,100; credit cash $10,100. Not (A) because if ABC Co. pays the $10,100, then X-Corp will have suffered no expense; if ABC does not pay, the entire $10,100 is "doubtful accounts

expense." Not (B) because the extra $100 is not interest revenue. The word "payable" in (D) should be "receivable." Not (E) because all banks require the discounter of a note to guarantee payment by the note's maker. *(11.3)*

40. **(A)** Quick assets = Cash & cash equivalents + ST investments + Net accounts receivable. The quick ratio is Quick assets / Current liabilities. The calculation is: (1,000 + 100 + 8,900) / 20,000 = 50%. *(11.5)*

41. **(E)** Businesses may use any inventory system that does not distort the financial statements. The inventory system need not reflect the actual flow of inventory. Although the first lettuce in was the first lettuce out, the store owner need not use FIFO. *(12.1)*

42. **(B)** Under FIFO, the first lettuce in—the lettuce purchased at 10¢ and 11¢—was assumed to be the first sold. The latest lettuce purchased is still in inventory. So of the 30 heads of lettuce left, there are 10 @ 12¢ ($1.20) and 20 @ 11¢ ($2.20) for a total of $3.40 ($1.20 + $2.40 = $3.40). *(12.2)*

43. **(C)** In periods of rising prices, LIFO produces the lowest inventory and the highest cost of goods sold. *(12.7)* By switching to LIFO, the company will have a cumulative effect of a change in accounting method *(20.1)* that produces a large one-time transfer of debits from inventory to cost of goods sold. *(12.5)*

44. **(B)** After manufacturing 20 units at a total cost of $1,080, there were 100 units in inventory at a total cost of $5,000 (3,920 + 1,080) which averages to a cost of $50/unit. If the manufacturer sold 10 units, total cost of goods sold is $500 (50 × 10). If you chose (A), you incorrectly averaged the unit costs (49 + 54)/2 = 51.50 × 10 = $515. *(12.4)*

45. **(C)** When X-Corp bought the insurance, the journal entry would have been: debit prepaid insurance $1,200; credit cash $1,200. After one month—on June 30 at the end of the fiscal year—it would have made this adjustment: debit insurance expense $100; credit prepaid insurance $100. Not (A) or (D) which recognize too much insurance expense. Not (B) because prepaid insurance will lower by 1/12 to $1,100. Not (E) which incorrectly shows insurance payable instead of prepaid insurance. *(13.1)*

46. **(B)** The consumption method of recording supplies recognizes supplies expense when the supplies are consumed. That means they first go into

supplies inventory. If supplies inventory started at $100, buying supplies increased it to $1,100. A $980 credit reduces the inventory to a balance of $120. Not (A) because adjusting entries never involve cash. Not (C) because the purchases account is for merchandise inventory. Answer (D) would have been correct for the purchases method. Not (E) because if the problem says nothing about owing money, there is no need for accounts payable. *(13.2)*

47. **(A)** In a bulk purchase, the purchase price applies to the individual items purchased in proportion to their values.

	Value	Percent		Price		Cost
Machine A	$12,000	60%	×	$19,000 =	$11,400
Machine B	6,000	30%	×	19,000 =	5,700
Machine C	2,000	10%	×	19,000 =	1,900
TOTAL	$20,000	100%	×	19,000 =	$19,000

CLEP trick: Calculate only the cost of the machine with the simplest math. Machine C is worth 10% of all three combined. $19,000 × 10% = 1,900, so only (A) can be correct. (E) ignores the cost allocation, which would not be a bad answer in a very large company for which the cost of these machines would be immaterial. *(14.1)*

48. **(C)** The journal entry to record this spending is:

Repair expense (combine)	500
Land (land clearing)	600
Equipment (used tractor)	2,000
Accumulated depreciation—barn (renovation)	10,000
Cash	13,100

Answer (A) is close, because if there were no accumulated depreciation on the barn, the debit would go to the barn account. The $600, however, is not a cost of the barn (A) nor land improvements (E). Not (B) because repair cost is expensed not capitalized, unless it increases the life of the combine or is part of getting the combine operational for the first time. *(14.2)*

49. **(D)** The $10,000 violin has been depreciated down to zero. The journal entry is: debit cash $100,000; debit accumulated depreciation—violin $10,000; credit violin $10,000; credit gain on sale of violin $100,000. *(14.3)*

50. **(B)**   Not (A) because if ABC sold minerals, it will have depletion expense. *(16.3)* Not (C) because land does not depreciate. *(14.4)* Not (D) or (E) because the marketing firm goodwill will not amortize if the business is doing especially well. *(16.2)*

51. **(A)**   Not (B) because businesses still depreciate even when assets appreciate in value. Answer (C), which counts all the expense in the year purchased, violates the Matching Principle. Not (D) because depreciation is never a good estimate of the money needed to replace used-up assets. Not (E) because the accounting profession cares less about making the balance sheet accurate and more about making the income statement accurate. *(15.1)*

52. **(E)**   Not methods (A) or (C), which subtract salvage to compute depreciable cost. Not (B) because the double declining balance (DDB) method stops depreciating whenever book value reaches salvage value. Not (D) because both MACRS and DDB are accelerated methods. *(15.2)*

53. **(C)**   The formula for straight-line depreciation is:

   (Cost – Salvage) / Life = Depreciation

   (11,000 – 1,000) / 5 = $2,000 per year

If Farmer Brown only depreciated $1,500 the first year (meaning 9/12 of a year), then he must have started depreciating from April 1. Therefore he used the nearest month method. Mid-year convention (A) produces $1,000 (2,000 × ½) of depreciation, and mid-month convention (B) results in $1,417 (2,000 × 8.5/12). Both nearest year (D) and beginning of year (E) conventions produce $2,000 of depreciation. *(15.3)*

54. **(D)**   Since MegaCorp is a large retailer, it would likely not capitalize and depreciate a $100 drill. Its value is too small to be material. All the other items would be on a depreciation schedule. *(15.4)*

55. **(E)**   The journal entry to record all these expenditures is:

Land improvements (11,000 + 2,000)	13,000	
Land	1,000	
Maintenance expense	500	
Cash		14,500

Not (A), which mistakenly also expenses the wind row of trees. Not (B), which incorrectly debits land instead of land improvements. "Credit" makes (C) and (D) incorrect. *(16.1)*

56. **(D)** The $20,000 patent includes legal and prototype costs (5,000 + 15,000). It amortizes over its useful life of 10 years, or $2,000 per year. The accounting profession does not use an accumulated amortization account, but credits the intangible asset directly, so (A) and (B) are incorrect. "Credit" makes (C) wrong. Not (E), which ignores the $5,000 legal fees as part of the patent. *(16.2)*

57. **(A)** Like the units of production method, depletion estimates total volume of natural resources and computes depletion in proportion to the amount extracted. *(16.3)*

58. **(E)** Not (A) because goodwill is written off in a period when the value goes down. Not (B) because goodwill is not raised when it increases in value. Not (C) or (D) because goodwill is not amortized by any regular method. *(16.4 and 16.2)*

59. **(B)** Accrual accounting records the expense when incurred—12/22/x1. Cash basis shows the expense when paid—1/5/x2. Max has no expense on 12/3/x1 upon signing the contract because the exterminator had not yet performed any services. *(17.1)*

60. **(B)** Adjusting entries have no event except the passage of time to trigger them. Paying cash, such as when making a loan payment, is a triggering event that will record the interest expense. All the other answers have had no such triggering event, and so need adjusting entries. *(17.2)*

61. **(E)** If ABC Co. keeps its books according to GAAP, it uses accrual accounting. Accrual accounting requires this adjusting entry on 12/31/x1: debit wages expense $5,000; credit wages payable $5,000. (A) and (C) are true for cash basis accounting. Not (B) because cash is never accrued. The "credit" in (D) should be "debit" for it to be true. *(17.3)*

62. **(C)** X-Corp incurs one month of interest expense for the month of December, or $100 (10,000 $\times$ 12% $\times$ 1/12 year). This is confirmed by the $1,100 payment on January 1, 20x2. The $100 is an interest expense of 20x1, so X-Corp must make the journal entry shown in (C). *(17.6)*

63. **(D)** Not (A), (B), or (C), because the purchase price, present value of principal, interest payments, and market interest change regularly. *(18.1)*

64. **(A)** A bond price of 95 means Jones & Jones gets 95% of the face amount ($95,000) less the $3,000 issuance cost, to net $92,000. *(18.2)* The journal entry is:

Cash (100,000 × 95% – 3,000)	92,000	
Bond issuance cost expense	3,000	
Discount on bond payable (100,000 – 950,00)	5,000	
Bond payable		100,000

65. **(A)** The book value of any bond eventually equals the face value on the day the bond matures. The book value of a bond issued at a premium (as in this case) reduces until it reaches the face value, and the book value of a bond issued at a discount increases until it reaches the face value. Over time, both discounts and premiums shrink to zero. Answer (E) is the reverse. "Discount" in (B) should be "premium" for it to be true. Not (C) because the interest expense of these bonds will get lower over time. "Income" in (D) should be "expense" for it to be true. *(18.3)*

66. **(E)** Every account with the word "deferred" is a liability. *(18.4)*

67. **(C)** The journal entry to record B joining the partnership *(19.1)* is:

Cash	10,000	
Accounts receivable	20,000	
Allowance for uncollectible accounts		4,000
Accounts payable		3,000
Equity—Partner B		23,000
		(whatever balances)

68. **(B)** The board of directors, not the stockholders, votes to declare dividends. All of the other choices are basic rights of common stockholders. *(19.2)*

69. **(D)**   The journal entry to record incorporating Mr. Clark's business *(19.3)* is:

Cash	5,000	
Equipment	16,000	
Accumulated depreciation		4,000
Common stock (100 shares × $10 par)		1,000
Additional paid-in capital		16,000

(whatever balances)

70. **(C)**   After a vote for dividends, the corporation legally owes a liability to stockholders. The amount of a dividend is stated either as a dollar amount per share or as a percent of par. The dividend is $10,000 (1,000 shares × $100 par/share × 10% dividend). The journal entry is: debit dividends $10,000; credit dividends payable $10,000. Not (A) because the amount is too big. The "credit" in (B) should be "debit" for it to be true. Not (D) because the dividend is not paid until later. *(19.4)*

71. **(A)**   A tornado loss is an extraordinary item because it is unusual and infrequent. The top-to-bottom order of the items on the income statement would be (D), (E), (B), (A) (the tornado loss) and (C). *(20.1)*

72. **(E)**   All the other transactions affect the equity section. Unrealized gains on hold-to-maturity investments (C) and foreign currency adjustments (D) are two special income items that have their own cumulated earnings account in the equity section. *(20.2)*

73. **(D)**   All the others are asset accounts. *(20.3)*

74. **(C)**   Not (D) because paying dividends is a negative cash adjustment. (A) and (B) are found under "cash flow from investing activities." (E) appears under "cash flow from operations." *(20.4)*

75. **(B)**   The formula for return on common stockholders' equity *(20.5)* is:

$$\frac{\text{Net income} - \text{PS dividends}}{\text{Average common stock equity}} = \text{Return on CS equity}$$

$$\frac{50{,}000 - 10{,}000}{100{,}000} = 40\%$$

PRACTICE
TEST 2

CLEP FINANCIAL ACCOUNTING

PRACTICE TEST 2

(Answer sheets appear in the back of this book.)

TIME: 90 Minutes
75 Questions

DIRECTIONS: Each of the questions or incomplete statements below is followed by five possible answers or completions. Select the best choice in each case and fill in the corresponding oval on the answer sheet.

1. Which statement below regarding a business is TRUE?

    (A) Creditors have a claim on business assets equal to the amount in the liability section.

    (B) The business owner owns only as much of the business assets as the amount shown in owner's equity.

    (C) Financial statements are not for business owners but for creditors and potential investors.

    (D) Creditors get to share in business profit.

    (E) When business owners contribute to their business, owner's equity goes down.

2. Which of the following documents will NOT have a period of time in the heading?

    I.   Balance sheet

    II. Income statement

    III. Statement of owner's equity

    IV. Chart of accounts

(A) I and IV only

(B) I, III, and IV only

(C) II and III only

(D) IV only

(E) I, II, III, and IV

3. Which item below is one of the adjustments in the calculation of cash flow from operations?

(A) Cash out to pay back loans

(B) Depreciation expense

(C) Owner's contributions to the business

(D) Borrowing from creditors

(E) Buying machinery for use in the business

4. In what ways do auditors help give credibility to your business financial statements?

    I. Auditors guarantee the accuracy of your financial statements.

    II. Auditors attach their opinion about the fairness of your financial statements.

    III. Auditors do tests of accuracy on your accounting records.

    IV. Auditors prepare your income tax returns.

(A) I and III only

(B) II and IV only

(C) II and III only

(D) III and IV only

(E) I, II, and III

5. What is the balance of this T-account?

    (A) $300 credit balance

    (B) $300 debit balance

    (C) $400 credit balance

    (D) $700 debit balance

    (E) $700 credit balance

Cash	
500	100
	100
200	200
700	400

6. The journal entry to record $100 of cash sales includes

    (A) a debit to sales

    (B) a credit to income summary

    (C) a debit to cash

    (D) a debit to income summary

    (E) a closing entry to bring sales to zero

7. Which of the following is NOT a standard internal control for employees?

    (A) Hiring people who have their personal financial lives under control

    (B) Communicating to new employees, "I trust you."

    (C) Hiring bonded people if they are going to handle money

    (D) Checking personal references and prior employers before you hire any employee

    (E) Supervising employees

8. After reconciling the bank statement, which amounts will you include in your adjusting entry to correct your books?

    I.   Deposits not shown

    II. Bank fees

    III. Outstanding checks

    (A) I only

    (B) I and II only

    (C) II only

    (D) II and III only

    (E) I and III only

9. A sole proprietor must have a fiscal year that ends on

    (A) the date the sole proprietor selects

    (B) the last day of any month the sole proprietor selects

    (C) the date assigned by the state of incorporation

    (D) the date of the fiscal year-end defined on the incorporation papers

    (E) December 31

10. A current ratio of 55% definitely means that

    (A) current liabilities are less than current assets

    (B) the bills due today equal 55% of the amount of money the business currently has

    (C) if current liabilities total $10,000, the business has $5,500 of cash

    (D) the business has more debts due within one year than current assets to pay them

    (E) current assets equal 55% of total assets

11. When a business spends $300 of cash for this month's rent, the money is

    (A) capitalized

    (B) an explanation of why equity goes up

(C) prepaid

(D) expensed

(E) an explanation of why liabilities go up

12. Which statement below is TRUE about the T-account for cash?

   (A) The T-account is for keeping track of cash investments in short-term securities.

   (B) The right side of the T-account for cash records increases of cash.

   (C) There are separate T-accounts for increases and decreases of cash.

   (D) The T-account usually reveals the bank interest rate.

   (E) The T-account shows both the ups and downs of cash.

13. Which of the following is TRUE concerning the presentation of financial statements?

   (A) Negative numbers may be shown inside parentheses.

   (B) Start the main calculation in the left column and indent to the right for sub-calculations.

   (C) Report accumulated depreciation in the liability section.

   (D) All dollar amounts should contain a dollar sign.

   (E) Place a double underline under the answer of every calculation.

14. Which is TRUE about the statement of cash flows indirect method?

   (A) The statement of cash flows reports the ending balance in the balance sheet accounts.

   (B) The statement of cash flows is broken into four sections.

   (C) One of the sections of the statement of cash flows is cash flows from sales.

   (D) Buying a car will appear as a positive number on the statement of cash flows.

   (E) The statement of cash flows does not show the individual revenue and expense accounts.

15. X-Corp's income statement shows $50,000 of net income, even after a $30,000 loss on sale of short-term investments. Cash flow from operations has been positive for the last five years. Which fact about "cash flow from investing activities" would make the owner the happiest?

    (A) Cash from sale of equipment (which X-Corp bought last year for $20,000) is $5,000.

    (B) Cash from sale of short-term investments is $100,000.

    (C) Positive and negative numbers net together to be exactly zero.

    (D) Total cash flow from investing activities is a large negative number.

    (E) Total cash flow from investing activities is a large positive number.

16. Which statement is TRUE concerning the direct method of making the statement of cash flows?

    (A) The direct method does not start with net income.

    (B) The difference between the direct method and the indirect method involves only the cash flow from financing activities section.

    (C) The direct method reports all the cash-in from operations as a single number, "cash from continuing operations."

    (D) The cash flow from operations will normally be greater under the direct method than under the indirect method.

    (E) The direct method is easier to do than the indirect method.

17. The authoritative accounting standards a business must follow are known as

    (A) FASB   (D) SEC

    (B) GAAP   (E) IRS

    (C) GASB

18. Company X's building has gone up in value. The accountant does NOT record this increase because he assumes that the company will keep the building long into the future and then tear it down. The accountant's assumption

    (A) violates GASB

    (B) misapplies the Historical Cost Principle

(C) is not consistent with the facts

(D) correctly applies the Going Concern Principle

(E) applies the Future Consistency Principle

19. Which of the following statements is most likely one of the reasons X-Corp obtains an audit?

(A) The IRS requires an audit report along with the corporate tax return.

(B) Investors often want an opinion from someone who is not a CPA.

(C) Auditors guarantee the accuracy of the financial statements.

(D) Auditing is a free service provided by most states.

(E) The auditor's opinion will help X-Corp get a loan from a bank.

20. Owner Lauren looked at a journal entry and smiled happily. Which transaction listed below caused that smile when Lauren saw it?

(A) A debit to cash

(B) A credit to short-term investments

(C) A debit to equity

(D) A credit to accounts payable

(E) A debit to an expense

21. To start her new business, Lauren transferred $500 from her personal checking account to a new business account. Which item below is part of the business journal entry to record that transaction?

(A) Credit equity—Lauren

(B) Credit to cash—Lauren's personal bank account

(C) Credit to cash—business bank account

(D) Debit to start-up expense

(E) Debit to transfer account

22. Which answer below shows three types of accounts, all of which have normal credit balances?

    (A) Revenues, expenses, withdrawal

    (B) Liabilities, contra-liabilities, equity

    (C) Liabilities, revenues, contra-assets

    (D) Equity, withdrawal, revenues

    (E) Contra-assets, contra-equity, liabilities

23. A large-volume retail store wants a specialized journal as proof of each sale. What is the easiest way to make such a journal?

    (A) Handwriting general journal entries

    (B) Entering general journal entries into the computer

    (C) Typing individual sales into the sales subroutine on the computer

    (D) Using pre-numbered sales tickets and keeping the duplicate copy

    (E) Using the cash register tape

24. Which of the following would be missing in a computerized general journal entry that would be included with a handwritten general journal entry?

    (A) The date of the transaction

    (B) A checkmark to indicate the entry had been posted to the general ledger

    (C) The credits to the cash account

    (D) A short explanation of the entry

    (E) The account number

25. Which item listed below would NOT normally be found on the general ledger page for an inventory account?

    (A) A code showing the source of the entry

    (B) A short description of the entry

    (C) A running balance that was always a debit

    (D) Proof that the debits equal the credits

    (E) Both debit and credit entries

26. You make a surprise check of petty cash, which is under the control of a clerk. The clerk acts offended and cries, "What's the matter? Don't you trust me?" Which of the following responses is the best?

   (A) "Yes, I trust you, but I design controls as if I trust nobody."

   (B) "I'm just following the CPA's orders."

   (C) "I trust you. It is the person from last shift that I do not trust."

   (D) "I'm sorry. I have to do this."

   (E) "Complaining about internal controls is a sign that you are un-trustworthy."

27. Max, a business owner, took all of the following steps when hiring a new bookkeeper. Which step listed below was a mistake?

   (A) Max did a background check on the applicant he hired.

   (B) Max did not give the new bookkeeper the key to the cash register drawer.

   (C) Max asked another employee to open the mail and record the checks and cash that arrived.

   (D) Max rejected one applicant for being bonded.

   (E) Max gave the new bookkeeper no spending authority.

28. SmithCorp is getting ready to print its audited public financial statements, which show everything GAAP requires. Net income is $17 million. Smith, the president and major stockholder, is very ethical. Which item below will SmithCorp most likely include in the notes to the financial statements?

   (A) The average salaries by job description, but without employee names

   (B) A statement that SmithCorp follows the AICPA Code of Ethics

   (C) The fact that SmithCorp recently bought a large piece of property from Smith

   (D) The pending sexual harassment lawsuit asking for $25,000

   (E) The fact that Smith recently bought a $5 million personal residence

29. Below is X-Corp's bank reconciliation. Which answer correctly reflects the journal entry to record the bank reconciliation?

Balance per bank	$1,000	Balance per cash account	$ 800
+ Deposits not shown	100	+ Interest revenue	9
– Outstanding checks	–295	– Bank fees	–4
= Adjusted bank balance	$ 805	= Adjusted book balance	$ 805

(A) The journal entry will contain a credit to cash of $5.

(B) The journal entry will include a debit to cash of $100.

(C) The journal entry will include a credit of $4 to bank fees.

(D) The journal entry will reflect the $295 of extra checks written.

(E) The only credit in the journal entry will be a credit to interest revenue.

30. Owner Al started his petty cash with $200 and put Steve in charge of it. He set no spending limit. When he checked the petty cash box it had $80 in cash and only the following slips of paper: (1) $4 Tipped pizza man, (2) $60 Bought repair parts, and (3) $26 Hospital flowers. Which statement below is TRUE?

(A) All the money is accounted for.

(B) Steve has some explaining to do.

(C) The journal entry to replenish petty cash includes a credit to cash for $90.

(D) The journal entry to replenish petty cash includes a debit to petty cash for $90.

(E) The person in charge of petty cash should not have spent the $60 on repair parts.

31. X-Corp spent $10,000 of cash to buy some marketable securities as trading investments. Which statement below is TRUE?

(A) The transaction increased X-Corp's current ratio.

(B) The accumulated income from the increase of these investments will appear in a separate account in the equity section.

(C) These investments will appear on the balance sheet under "other long-term assets."

(D) The dividends from this investment are considered non-operating income.

(E) These investments are considered held-to-maturity investments.

32. Mr. Patel bought $10,000 of merchandise from X-Corp. He paid with a $1,000 note and promised to pay the rest in 30 days. Which of the following is part of the journal entry to record this transaction on X-Corp's books?

(A) Debit accounts receivable $9,000

(B) Credit notes payable $1,000

(C) Debit accounts receivable $10,000 and credit allowance for uncollectible accounts for $1,000

(D) Credit deferred sales $10,000

(E) Debit accounts receivable $10,000

33. ABC Co. has a $100,000 accounts receivable with a $2,000 allowance for doubtful accounts. ABC was not sure Newclient, Inc. would pay its $1,000 bill on time, but it did. Which of the following is part of the journal entry to record receiving Newclient's money?

(A) Debit the allowance for $1,000

(B) Credit cash for $1,000

(C) Credit the allowance for $1,000

(D) Credit accounts receivable $1,000

(E) Credit accounts receivable $1,000 and debit the allowance for $20

34. ABC Co. has $100,000 in accounts receivable and NO allowance for uncollectible accounts. ABC's history indicates that 1% of accounts receivable will probably not be collected. ABC uses the direct write-off method of handling bad debts. Which of the following is part of the journal entry to write off an $800 bad debt?

    (A) Credit allowance for uncollectible accounts $800

    (B) Debit accounts receivable $800

    (C) Debit allowance for uncollectible accounts $800

    (D) Debit uncollectible accounts expense $1,000

    (E) Debit uncollectible accounts expense $800

35. Which of the following is the journal entry to record receiving $1,000 from a customer for services you performed two months earlier, assuming you use cash basis accounting?

    (A) Debit cash $1,000; credit services revenue $1,000.

    (B) Debit cash $1,000; credit accounts receivable $1,000.

    (C) There is no journal entry at this time.

    (D) Debit accounts receivable $1,000; credit services revenue $1,000.

    (E) Debit accounts receivable $1,000; credit cash $1,000.

36. X-Corp received the following note to pay for $10,000 of goods sold: "ABC Co. promises to pay X-Corp $10,000 six months from now plus 10% interest." ABC Co. is a very profitable corporation. The day it got the note, X-Corp took it to a bank that charges a 5% discount. Which statement about this note is most likely TRUE?

    (A) X-Corp will recognize $600 of interest over the life of this note.

    (B) The present value of this note is $10,000.

    (C) This is a non-interest-bearing note.

    (D) The bank will give X-Corp less than $10,000.

    (E) The bank will probably not discount this note.

37. Mr. X gives Miss Y a $10,000 one-year non-interest-bearing note in exchange for $9,000 of merchandise. Six months later, Miss Y discounts the note at a bank that charges a 6% discount. How much will the bank give Miss Y?

    (A) $10,600

    (B) $10,300

    (C) $10,000

    (D) $9,730

    (E) $9,700

38. Which of the following is NOT part of quick assets?

    (A) Cash

    (B) Petty cash

    (C) Inventories

    (D) Short-term investments

    (E) Net accounts receivable

39. The following are from X-Corp's financial statements.

    Total sales on account for the year: $365,000

    Net accounts receivable at the beginning of the year: $37,500

    Net accounts receivable at the end of the year: $36,500

    Which of the following is the correct days' sales in accounts receivable?

    (A) 100 days

    (B) 36.5 days

    (C) 10 days

    (D) 37 days

    (E) 1,000 days

40. A coal company uses the LIFO system. In 20y2 the company purchased 101 tons of coal @ $51 per ton ($5,151), and sold 100 tons. Using the inventory record below, what is the coal company's 20y2 cost of goods sold (CGS) and ending inventory (EI)?

    - 20x1 10 tons @ $20 = $200
    - 20x2 15 tons @ $22 = $330
    - 20x8 5 tons @ $40 = $200
    - 20y1 20 tons @ $50 = $1,000
    - Total inventory 50 tons and $1,730

    (A) CGS = $5,151 and EI is $1,730

    (B) CGS = $4,280 and EI is $2,601

    (C) CGS = $4,300 and EI is $2,581

    (D) CGS = $4,441 and EI is $2,440

    (E) CGS = $5,100 and EI is $1,781

41. Speedy Used Cars uses the specific unit method of keeping track of its inventory. Today Speedy sold one car for $5,000 that it originally purchased for $3,000. By mistake, Speedy's accountant debited cost of goods sold $300 and credited cars inventory $300. How will this error affect Speedy's trial balance, cost of goods sold, and ending inventory?

	Trial Balance	Cost of goods sold	Ending Inventory
(A)	In balance	Understated	Overstated
(B)	Off by $2,700	Understated	Overstated
(C)	In balance	Overstated	Understated
(D)	Off by $300	Understated	Understated
(E)	In balance	Overstated	Overstated

42. Using the following information, estimate ABC Co.'s ending inventory using the gross profit method.

Beginning merchandise inventory:	$80,000
Purchases:	$220,000
Gross profit:	(unknown but usually 50% of sales)
Sales:	$400,000

(A) $120,000

(B) $100,000

(C) $80,000

(D) $60,000

(E) $40,000

43. Using the following information, and rounding to the nearest day, compute the number of days in inventory.

Cost of goods sold:	$200,000
Beginning inventory:	$ 30,000
Ending inventory:	$ 50,000

(A) 82 days

(B) 73 days

(C) 140 days

(D) 110 days

(E) 91 days

44. X-Corp, which has a June 30 fiscal year-end, keeps its books according to GAAP. It paid $1,200 for a year's worth of insurance on June 1, 20x1. Assume X-Corp makes all the correct journal entries at the end of the fiscal year. What is the correct adjusting entry on July 31, 20x1, concerning this insurance?

(A) Credit cash $100; debit insurance expense $100.

(B) Debit insurance expense $1,100, credit insurance payable $1,100.

(C) Debit insurance expense $100; credit prepaid insurance $100.

(D) Debit prepaid insurance $100; credit cash $100.

(E) Debit insurance expense $1,100; credit prepaid insurance $1,100.

45. ABC, Inc. uses the purchases method of recording its supplies. At the beginning of the year, it had supplies inventory of $100. During the year it purchased $1,000 of supplies. At the end of the year, the company determined that it had $120 of supplies in inventory. Which of the following is the journal entry to adjust inventory at year-end?

   (A) Debit supplies expense $980; credit supplies inventory $980

   (B) Debit supplies inventory $980; debit supplies expense $20; credit cash $1,000

   (C) Debit purchases $20; debit supplies expense $980; credit supplies inventory $1,000

   (D) Debit supplies inventory $20; credit supplies expense $20

   (E) Debit supplies expense $980; credit accounts payable $980

46. The Machine Shop, Inc. bought three machines for $17,000 and spent $3,000 shipping them to the shop. When they got to the shop, Machine A was found to be almost worthless, and was sold for $1,000 scrap. Machine B was worth $6,000 and Machine C was worth $3,000. When The Machine Shop, Inc. recorded the purchase, at what price were the three machines recorded?

	Machine A	Machine B	Machine C
(A)	2,000	12,000	6,000
(B)	1,700	10,200	5,100
(C)	0	7,000	2,000
(D)	1,000	8,000	4,000

   (E) As a single group of machines with a value of $17,000 and $3,000 shipping expense

47. On January 1, 20x1, X-Corp bought a building for $400,000. It depreciated the building using straight-line depreciation over 40 years. On January 1, 20z1 (exactly 20 years later), it sold the building for $250,000 in exchange for a $100,000 3-month note and the rest cash. Which of the following is part of the journal entry to record this transaction?

   (A) Debit cash $100,000

   (B) Credit accumulated depreciation—building $200,000

(C) Debit cash from sale of building $250,000

(D) Credit building $200,000

(E) Credit gain on sale of building $50,000

48. Miguel, a sole proprietor, bought a safe for his business, but it was located 100 miles from his business. He paid $200 for the safe, spent $80 to rent a truck, hired two movers to help for a total of $100, bought lunch for the trip $20, and paid $2,000 to repair the axel of the rental truck, which broke due to the weight of the safe. Which of the following is part of the journal entry to record all of the above spending?

(A) Debit truck rental expense $2,080

(B) Debit furniture and equipment $400

(C) Debit furniture and equipment $2,400

(D) Debit loss on furniture and equipment $400

(E) Debit furniture and equipment $2,380

49. Which of the following is TRUE about reflecting the sale of land on the cash flow statement?

(A) The cash received from the sale of land will appear under cash flow from operations.

(B) The cash received from the sale of land will be a positive adjustment under cash flow from investing activities.

(C) The gain on the sale of the land will appear separately in cash flow from operations.

(D) The gain on the sale of the land will already be included in the net income number at the beginning of the cash flow from operations section.

(E) The cash received from the sale of the land will be a negative adjustment under cash flow from financing activities.

50. ABC Co. bought a $30,000 pickup truck. ABC estimates that the truck has a 3-year or 100,000-mile life and a residual value of $3,000. ABC drives the truck 40,000 miles the first year and 30,000 miles the second year. ABC selects the double declining balance method, full-year convention. What is the depreciation expense in the second year?

(A) $6,667

(D) $6,000

(B) $10,000

(E) $18,000

(C) $12,000

51. ABC Co. bought a $30,000 pickup truck. ABC estimates that the truck has a 3-year or 100,000-mile life and a residual value of $3,000. ABC drives the truck 40,000 miles the first year and 30,000 miles the second year. ABC selects the units of production method, full-year convention. What is the depreciation expense in the second year?

(A) $12,000

(D) $9,000

(B) $8,100

(E) $15,400

(C) $10,800

52. ABC Co. bought an $11,000 machine with an estimated salvage value of $1,000 and an estimated life of 7 years. The IRS considers the machine 5-year property. ABC uses the half-year convention. Consult the IRS table below and calculate ABC's tax depreciation expense for the asset's first year.

MACRS Depreciation Method (Partial)

Year	5-year property	7-year property	10-year property
1	0.2	0.1429	0.1
2	0.32	0.2449	0.18
3	0.192	0.1749	0.144

(A) $1,100

(D) $2,000

(B) $1,000

(E) $1,429

(C) $2,200

53. X-Corp bought a building 20 years ago for $200,000. It estimated the useful life at 50 years and the salvage value at $20,000. Now, it is apparent that the building can last only 5 more years, and will be worth $30,000 as scrap. How should X-Corp handle this new information?

    (A) X-Corp should continue depreciating the building as it always has.

    (B) X-Corp may change the salvage value of the building in calculating depreciation, but not the estimated useful life.

    (C) X-Corp should take any remaining book value on the building, subtract the $30,000 scrap value and depreciate the difference over 5 years.

    (D) X-Corp may change both the estimated useful life and salvage value by recalculating what the depreciation should have been over the last 20 years and showing the cumulated effect of the change as a large loss this year.

    (E) X-Corp should write off the remaining book value of the building this year.

54. ABC Co. did a large landscaping program around its corporate headquarters that cost $30,000. What is the proper way to handle this cost?

    (A) Expense the $30,000 as grounds maintenance expense.

    (B) Capitalize the $30,000 as land and never depreciate it.

    (C) Debit accumulated depreciation—building $30,000.

    (D) Capitalize as a land improvement and depreciate over the remaining life of the building.

    (E) Capitalize as a land improvement and never depreciate it.

55. Which item below is NOT an intangible asset?

    (A) Gold coins with historic value

    (B) A patent on a machine developed in-house

    (C) Pieces of paper representing stock in a corporation

    (D) $40,000 spent to get a restaurant franchise

    (E) A famous trade name

56. Which of the following statements is TRUE about a very famous trade name that cost $50,000 and a copyright worth $100,000 on a book about presidential candidates in an election two years from now?

    (A) Amortize the book over the estimated life of the author plus 70 years.

    (B) Amortize the trade name over 15 years.

    (C) Neither the trade name nor the book copyright should be amortized.

    (D) Amortize the $100,000 value of the book copyright over the useful life.

    (E) The trade name may never amortize, but amortize the cost of the copyright over no more than 3 years.

57. A gravel company paid $600,000 for a hillside with an estimated 200,000 tons of gravel inside it. The company estimates it will completely dig out the hillside in 6 years. In the first year of operation, the company extracted and sold 50,000 tons of gravel for $10 per ton. Which of the following is part of the journal entry to record the cost of the gravel sold?

    (A) Debit amortization expense $150,000

    (B) Debit depletion expense $150,000

    (C) Debit depreciation expense $100,000

    (D) Credit mineral rights for $100,000

    (E) Credit accumulated depletion—Gravel Hill for $500,000

58. The following diagram shows how Smith and Company delays paying wages at their plant. It pays wages every Friday for wages earned the previous week. Employees work five days per week.

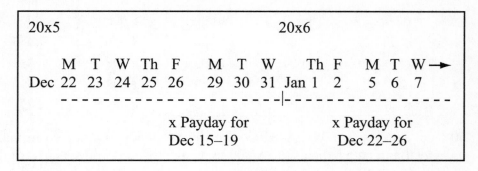

Assuming that each day plant employees earn a total of $1,000 of wages, which of the following is part of the journal entry on December 31, 20x5, to accrue the cost of unpaid wages?

(A) Debit wages expense $3,000; credit wages payable $3,000

(B) Debit wages expense $3,000; credit cash $3,000

(C) Debit wages payable $3,000; credit wages expense $3,000

(D) Debit wages expense $8,000; credit wages payable $8,000

(E) Debit wages payable $13,000; credit wages expense $13,000

59. Smokey Barbecue Grills offers a 100% money-back one-year guarantee on their grills. Smokey estimates that it will have to return 1% of 20x1 sales. During 20x1, Smokey sold $700,000 of barbecue grills. During 20x1, it already returned $2,000 on 20x1 sales, recording it as warranty expense. Assuming Smokey made no other entries for warranties, which of the following is part of the journal entry that Smokey should make on December 31, 20x1?

(A) Debit warranties expense $2,000

(B) Credit warranties expense $2,000

(C) Credit warranties payable $5,000

(D) Debit deferred warranty income, $5,000

(E) Credit deferred warranty income, $2,000

Questions 60 and 61 use the following loan amortization schedule:

Pmt Date	Payment	Principal	10% Interest	Balance
				100,000
6/30/x1	6,000	1,000	5,000	99,000
12/31/x1	6,000	1,050	4,950	97,950
6/30/x2	6,000	1,103	4,898	96,848
12/31/x2	6,000	1,158	4,842	95,690
6/30/x3	6,000	1,216	4,784	94,474

60. On January 1, 20x1, ABC Co. borrowed money and agreed to make *semi*-annual payments of $6,000 to repay the loan. Above is part of the loan amortization schedule for that loan. What is the current portion of the loan on December 31, 20x1?

   (A) $12,000

   (B) $9,740

   (C) $6,000

   (D) $2,153

   (E) $2,261

61. Referencing the same loan amortization schedule as used in Question #60, which of the following is part of the adjusting entry to accrue interest expense on this loan on December 31, 20x1?

   (A) Debit interest expense $4,898

   (B) Debit interest expense $9,740

   (C) Credit interest payable $6,000

   (D) Credit interest payable $1,103

   (E) No adjusting entry is necessary.

62. At the end of the fiscal year, Smith & Co. made the following journal entry:

   Wages expense $1,000
        Wages payable $1,000
   (To accrue wages expense owed employees on 12/31/20x1)

   On January 1, 20x2, Smith & Co.'s accountant made a reversing entry. On the next payday, Smith & Co. paid $6,000 of wages—the $1,000 of wages incurred in 20x1 and $5,000 of wages from 20x2. Which of the following is part of the journal entry to record the $6,000 payroll?

(A) Debit wages expense $6,000

(B) Debit wages expense $5,000

(C) Debit prepaid wages, $1,000

(D) Debit wages payable $1,000

(E) Credit cash $5,000

63. X-Corp issued $1,000,000 of bonds at a price of 100. On which financial statement(s) will this transaction show up?

(A) Balance sheet

(B) Cash flow statement

(C) Balance sheet and cash flow statement

(D) Income statement

(E) Income statement and balance sheet

64. Jones & Jones issued $100,000 of 6% bonds at a price of 105. The bond issuance cost was $3,000. Which of the following is part of the journal entry to record these bonds on Jones & Jones's books?

(A) Debit cash $3,105

(B) Credit bonds payable $105,000

(C) Credit cash $102,000

(D) Credit premium on bonds payable $5,000

(E) Debit interest expense $6,000

65. Mega Manufacturing, Inc. has on its books a $100,000 bond payable and a credit to premium on bonds payable of $10,000. The bonds were issued when the market interest was 8%. The bonds have a face interest rate of 9% and make semi-annual periodic payments. Which of the following is part of the journal entry to make the next periodic payment required by the bond?

(A) Debit premium on bonds payable $400

(B) Debit interest expense $4,400

(C) Credit cash $4,400

(D) Debit interest expense $4,500

(E) Credit premium on bonds payable $100

66. Holliday Tool Magazine had $120,000 of deferred subscriptions revenue on its books on May 31, 20x1. During the next month, 1/12 of those subscriptions are earned. Which of the following is part of the journal entry at the end of June as a result of these facts?

    (A) Credit prepaid subscriptions $12,000

    (B) Credit subscriptions revenue $10,000

    (C) Credit prepaid subscriptions $10,000

    (D) Debit subscriptions expense $10,000

    (E) No journal entry is required by these facts.

67. The ABC partnership agreement says that partners split the profits 20% to A, 30% to B, and 50% to C after paying guaranteed payments of $30,000 to A, $20,000 to B, and $10,000 to C. The partnership earned $50,000. How much is partner A's share?

    (A) $32,000   (D) $26,000

    (B) $30,000   (E) $24,000

    (C) $28,000

68. X-Corp sold 100,000 shares of $2 par common stock to investors. According to its articles of incorporation, it may issue 100,000,000 shares. It purchased 10,000 shares of treasury stock. On the balance sheet, how will X-Corp report the common stock account?

    (A) Common stock (100,000,000 authorized, 100,000 issued, 90,000 outstanding)

    (B) Common stock (100,000 authorized, 100,000,000 issued, 10,000 outstanding)

    (C) Common stock (200,000 authorized, 100,000,000 issued, 999,990,000 outstanding)

    (D) Common stock (100,000,000 authorized, 200,000 issued, 190,000 outstanding)

    (E) Common stock (200,000,000 authorized, 200,000 issued, 380,000 outstanding)

69. X-Corp has a December 31 year end. Mr. X is the sole officer/ stockholder, and owns all 40,000 shares outstanding. Late in December 20x1, Mr. X determined that X-Corp earned $300,000 of net income for 20x1 even after paying Mr. X's $100,000 salary. Mr. X determined that he could take out $200,000 additional cash for himself. What is the best way to give Mr. X the additional $200,000?

    (A) Let Mr. X take a $200,000 draw.

    (B) Give Mr. X a $200,000 cash dividend.

    (C) Give Mr. X a $200,000 stock dividend.

    (D) Give Mr. X a $200,000 salary bonus.

    (E) Split the stock 5-for-1.

70. ABC Co. owned $10,000 of $1 par treasury stock. It sold the stock for $14,000. Which of the following is part of the journal entry to record the sale of the treasury stock?

    (A) Credit additional paid-in capital $14,000

    (B) Credit common stock $10,000

    (C) Debit treasury stock $10,000

    (D) Credit gain on sale of treasury stock $4,000

    (E) Credit additional paid-in capital $4,000

71. Which of the following is part of the closing entries for a corporation?

    (A) Credit revenues

    (B) Credit dividends

    (C) Debit expenses

    (D) Credit assets

    (E) Debit assets

72. On the multi-step corporate income statement, which item below comes before "Income from continuing operations before provision for income tax"?

   (A) Income taxes on continuing operations

   (B) Extraordinary gain

   (C) Cumulative effect of a change in accounting method

   (D) Gain on sale of short-term investments

   (E) Discontinued operations

73. On the indirect method of calculating cash flow from operations, depreciation, amortization, and depletion are all positive adjustments. Which of the following is the best reason explaining why that is so?

   (A) These items all increase net income.

   (B) These items represent cash received during the period.

   (C) These items represent cash from sales of fixed assets.

   (D) These items represent cash saved for new investments in fixed assets.

   (E) These items lowered net income this period but did not involve any cash.

74. X-Corp has 100,000 shares outstanding. Its net income was $200,000. It paid $10,000 of common stock dividends and $20,000 of preferred stock dividends. Calculate the earnings per share of common stock.

   (A) $2.20   (D) $1.70

   (B) $2.00   (E) $0.50

   (C) $1.80

75. X-Corp has $800,000 of total assets and $100,000 of total liabilities. The preferred stock account has a credit balance of $100,000. The corporation issued 60,000 shares of common stock and it holds 10,000 shares of treasury stock. Calculate book value per share of common stock.

   (A) $14.00/share   (D) $11.67/share

   (B) $13.33/share   (E) $10.00/share

   (C) $12.00/share

CLEP FINANCIAL ACCOUNTING
PRACTICE TEST 2

ANSWER KEY

1.	(A)	26.	(A)	51.	(B)
2.	(A)	27.	(D)	52.	(C)
3.	(B)	28.	(C)	53.	(C)
4.	(C)	29.	(E)	54.	(D)
5.	(B)	30.	(B)	55.	(A)
6.	(C)	31.	(D)	56.	(E)
7.	(B)	32.	(A)	57.	(B)
8.	(C)	33.	(D)	58.	(D)
9.	(E)	34.	(E)	59.	(C)
10.	(D)	35.	(A)	60.	(E)
11.	(D)	36.	(B)	61.	(E)
12.	(E)	37.	(E)	62.	(A)
13.	(A)	38.	(C)	63.	(C)
14.	(E)	39.	(D)	64.	(D)
15.	(D)	40.	(E)	65.	(B)
16.	(A)	41.	(A)	66.	(B)
17.	(B)	42.	(B)	67.	(C)
18.	(D)	43.	(B)	68.	(A)
19.	(E)	44.	(C)	69.	(D)
20.	(A)	45.	(D)	70.	(E)
21.	(A)	46.	(A)	71.	(B)
22.	(C)	47.	(E)	72.	(D)
23.	(E)	48.	(C)	73.	(E)
24.	(B)	49.	(B)	74.	(C)
25.	(D)	50.	(A)	75.	(C)

DETAILED EXPLANATIONS OF ANSWERS

PRACTICE TEST 2

(The **boldface, *italic*** numbers in the following paragraphs refer to the Chapters and Sections where review information can be found.)

1. **(A)**   Creditors do not own the business; they have a claim on business assets. If the owner does not pay as promised, creditors can ask a court to make the owner pay. (B) is close, but the owner truly owns everything. Not (C) because financial statements are also for the owner. Not (D) because only owners get to keep business profit. Creditors are content with their interest. Not (E) because contributions make equity go up. *(2.3)*

2. **(A)**   The balance sheet has a date in the heading, not a period of time. *(2.3)* The chart of accounts is not a financial statement, so it has no date or period of time. *(3.5)* The income statement and the statement of owner's equity *(3.3)* both report for a period of time.

3. **(B)**   Depreciation is a non-cash expense that reduces net income. It must be backed out to calculate cash flow from operations. Not (A), (C), or (D), which appear under cash from financing activities. Not (E), which appears under cash from investing activities. *(4.2)*

4. **(C)**   Auditors test your books for accuracy, then attach an opinion about the fair presentation of your financial statements. Although CPAs commonly do income taxes, CPAs who do auditing do not. Auditors do not guarantee accuracy. *(5.2)*

5. **(B)**   The left side of T-accounts is the debit side; the right side is the credit side. If there are sums on both sides, the two numbers net together. "Net together" means subtract and place the remainder on the side with the larger number. (700 debit – 400 credit = 300 debit) *(6.4)*

6. **(C)**   The journal entry is: debit cash $100; credit sales income $100. The "debit" in (A) should be "credit" for it to be true. Not (B) or (D) because income summary appears only on the last day of the year during closing entries. Not (E) because this is not the time for closing entries. *(Chap 7 CLEP CRAM Sec. B)*

7.   **(B)**   "I trust you" is not a standard internal control. Internal controls say, "Our job is to trust no one." All the other answers are good internal controls. *(8.1)* People with healthy economic lives are less tempted to steal, bonding ensures that you hire trustworthy people, and checking and supervising employees helps discover potential problems. *(8.2)*

8.   **(C)**   A business must correct its books only for items not already recorded on the books. Both deposits not shown and outstanding checks already appear in the company's books. *(9.1)*

9.   **(E)**   Tax law requires sole proprietors to have a fiscal year ending December 31. A sole proprietorship does not register with the state like a corporation does, so (C) and (D) are wrong. (B) is correct for a corporation, not a sole proprietorship. *(2.5)*

10.   **(D)**   The current ratio = current assets / current liabilities. Current assets are available to pay current liabilities. Current liabilities are debts due within one year. Not (A) because if the ratio is 55%, then current assets are less than current liabilities. (C) would be true only if cash is a business's only current asset. *(2.4)*

11.   **(D)**   Amounts are "expensed" when the money is gone forever, such as paying rent. *(3.1)* Not (A) because spending is capitalized when money buys a valuable asset. *(2.2)* Prepaid rent would have been capitalized if it were for a longer period than "this month's rent," so not (C). Not (B) or (E) because expenses explain why equity (not liabilities) goes down, not up.

12.   **(E)**   The cash T-account has cash increasing on the left side and decreasing on the right side, so (B) and (C) are wrong. (A) and (D) are just untrue statements. *(3.6)*

13.   **(A)**   Report negative numbers either with a minus sign in front or in parentheses. (B) incorrectly switched the words "right" and "left." Not (C) because accumulated depreciation is a contra-asset, not a liability. Not (D) because only the first number and the calculation result get a dollar sign. Not (E) because the double underline is for the final key number of each report only. *(3.7)*

14.   **(E)**   The statement of cash flows does not use the income and expense accounts. "Ending balance" in (A) should be "change" for it to be true. The cash flow statement has three, not four, sections (B), and no sec-

tion is called "cash flows from sales" (C). Buying a car (D) will appear as a negative number. *(4.2, 4.3)*

15. **(D)** Owners like a negative number under cash flow from investing activities because it means the business is buying income-producing property. This is especially true if cash flow from operations has been positive for the past five years. A break-even (C) or a positive number (E) means no increase in income-producing investments. Not (A), because if the company bought equipment for $20,000 last year and sold it for $5,000 this year, it would incur a loss. Not (B), because even though $100,000 of cash came in from selling short-term investments, the problem states that the company experienced a $30,000 loss on the sale. *(4.3)*

16. **(A)** The *indirect* method starts with net income. Not (B), because the only section involved is cash flow from operating activities. Not (C) because the direct method shows several categories of cash in and cash out. Not (D) because both methods will produce the same amount for cash flow from operations. Not (E) because the direct method is actually more difficult. *(4.5)*

17. **(B)** GAAP stands for Generally Accepted Accounting Principles. The Financial Accounting Standards Board (FASB) and Government Accounting Standards Board (GASB) are agencies that determine GAAP. The Internal Revenue Service (IRS) and the Securities Exchange Commission (SEC) are two government agencies that also make accounting rules. *(5.2)*

18. **(D)** Accountants assume every business is a going concern that will continue indefinitely. Not (A) because GASB makes accounting rules for governments. Not (B) because keeping the building at its historical cost also properly applies the Historical Cost Principle. Not (C) because accountants assume all businesses are going concerns despite the facts. Not (E) because there is no Future Consistency Principle. *(5.2)*

19. **(E)** Not (A) because the IRS requires no audit. Not (B) because all auditors are CPAs. Not (C) because auditors do not guarantee accuracy; they merely render an opinion. Not (D) because businesses must pay CPAs to perform audits. *(5.2)*

20. **(A)** Debits increase cash, and all owners like that. The other answers reveal problems: Crediting a short-term investment means the value went down (B). Debiting equity (C) and expenses (E) means the owner's share decreased. A credit to accounts payable (D) increases debts. *(6.1)*

21. **(A)** The journal entry would be debit to cash, credit to equity—Lauren. Not (B) because Lauren's personal account will not appear on the business books. Not (C) because of the word "credit." Not (D) because there was no expense; the $500 is not gone and not (E) because businesses do not use a transfer account. *(6.2)*

22. **(C)** The accounts with normal credit balances are: contra-assets, contra-expenses, liabilities, equity, and revenues. The accounts with debit balances, which make the other answers false are: expenses and withdrawal, contra-liabilities, withdrawal, and contra-equity (such as withdrawal). *(6.7)*

23. **(E)** The cash register tape is a written record of all sales transactions. For a large-volume retail store, all the other hand-entry methods would be slower. *(7.3)*

24. **(B)** In manual systems, bookkeepers must manually post each number from the general journal to the proper account in the general ledger. The checkmark means the posting was done. Because computers automatically post general journal entries to the ledger, there is no need for checkmarks. All other items are in both computerized and manual general ledger systems. *(7.1)*

25. **(D)** The debits equal the credits in the general journal, but not on each account page of the general ledger. *(7.2)* A trial balance of all the accounts in the general ledger proves that the debits equal the credits. *(6.4)* Not (A) or (B) because both the code and the description would be on the page. Not (C) because the running balance column for an inventory account would always have a debit balance. *(6.7)* Not (E) because inventory accounts go up (debits) and down (credits).

26. **(A)** Not (B) because internal controls are your responsibility, even if you use input from your CPA. Not (C) because petty cash should be under the control of only one person. *(9.2)* Not (D) because internal controls make for good relationships and there is no need to apologize. Although the statement in (E) is true, don't be accusatory. *(8.1)*

27. **(D)** Bonding is good. It means an insurance company is willing to pay Max if the employee steals. Max should not have rejected an applicant for being bonded. Not (A) because background checks are good. Not (B), (C) or (E) because Max *should* separate the bookkeeping duties from custody over assets. *(8.2)*

28. **(C)** The problem states that President Smith is only a "major stock-holder," so there must be other stockholders. A potential conflict of interest that other stockholders should know about exists in the land deal between SmithCorp and Smith. *(8.3)* Not (A) because there is no need to report salaries. Not (B) because the AICPA Code of Ethics is for accountants, not businesses. Not (D) because the sexual harassment suit is too small to be material. *(8.4)* Not (E) because personal information does not go on the business books. *(2.3)*

29. **(E)** The journal entry will be: debit cash $5; debit bank fees (or miscellaneous) $4; and credit interest revenue $9. "Credit" in (A) and (C) should be "debit" for them to be correct. Not (B) or (D), which come from the left side, because only the adjustments on the right side of the bank reconciliation reflect items not yet on the company books. *(9.1)*

30. **(B)** The petty cash is $30 short, so (A) is not true. Cash plus receipts must equal the original total of $200. Here they total $170 (80 + 4 + 60 + 26 = 170). Steve must explain the shortage. Since there is no spending limit, Steve should not be in trouble for spending $60 (E). Not (C) or (D) because the journal entry to replenish petty cash will credit cash $120 to bring the account back up to $200. *(9.2)*

31. **(D)** Since X-Corp is not in the business of earning money from short-term investments, dividend and interest income from investments are non-operating. Not (A) because buying short-term investments lowers one current asset (cash) and raises another (investments) by the same amount. The current ratio will not change. *(20.5)* Not (B), which is true only of available-for-sale investments, not trade investments. *(9.3 and 20.1, note 13)* Not (C) because these investments are short-term. *(9.3)* Not (E) because by definition trade investments are not held-to-maturity investments.

32. **(A)** The journal entry is: debit accounts receivable $9,000; debit notes receivable $1,000; credit sales $10,000. Not (B) because a business would credit notes payable when it *gave* a note, not when it *received* one. Not (D) because the word "deferred" indicates a liability account. *(10.1)*

33. **(D)** The journal entry is: debit cash; credit accounts receivable. The allowance for doubtful accounts is not involved, so not (A), (C), or (E). "Credit" in (B) should be "debit" for it to be right. The "not sure" language is a red herring. The allowance is an estimate about accounts receivable as a whole and is not adjusted for doubts about individual accounts. *(10.1)*

34. **(E)** The words "direct write-off method" eliminates (A) and (C), which have allowance for doubtful accounts in them. "Debit" in (B) should be "credit" for it to be right. The amount in (D) is wrong because it uses the estimated total bad debts (1% of $100,000) instead of the actual amount written off. *(10.3)*

35. **(A)** Under the cash basis of accounting, record revenue when the money comes in. The words "cash basis" eliminate (B), (D), and (E), which contain the words "accounts receivable." Not (C) because cash always triggers a journal entry. *(10.2)*

36. **(B)** Not (C) because there is a 10% interest rate stated on the note. Not (A) because 6 months of interest is $500 (10,000 × 10% × ½ year). The future value is $10,500. Not (D) because the discount will be $262.50 (10,500 × 5% × ½ year) and the proceeds will be $10,237.50. Not (E) because since ABC is very profitable and X-Corp is guaranteeing payment, any bank would discount this note. *(11.1)*

37. **(E)** The formulas are:

$$\text{Future value} - \text{Discount} = \text{Proceeds} \ (10,000 - 300 = 9,700)$$

$$\text{Discount} = \text{Future value} \times \text{discount\%} \times \text{years} =$$
$$10,000 \times 6\% \times \tfrac{1}{2} \text{ year} = 300$$

The discount period is 6 months because it was a 1-year note and Miss Y discounted it 6 months after receiving it. *(11.2)*

38. **(C)** All the other types of assets are quick assets. *(11.5)*

39. **(D)**

$$\text{Average net accounts receivable} = (\text{BOY} + \text{EOY})/2 =$$
$$(37,500 + 36,500)/2 = 37,000$$

$$\text{One day's sales} = \text{Total sales on account} / 365 \text{ days} =$$
$$36,500 / 365 = \$1,000/\text{day}$$

$$\text{Days' sales in A/R} = \text{Average net accounts receivable} / \text{One day's sales} =$$
$$37,000 / 1,000 = 37 \text{ days.}$$

(11.5)

40. **(E)** LIFO means last-in, first-out. That means the 100 tons sold came from the last purchase at $51/ton, for a total of $5,100 (100 × 51). In 20y2, the company bought one more ton than it sold, meaning one ton at $51 was added to inventory to equal $1,781 (1,730 + 51 = 1781). *(12.3)*

41. **(A)** Speedy took $300 out of inventory instead of $3,000 *(12.4)*, meaning inventory will be overstated and cost of goods sold will be understated by $2,700. *(12.5)* The trial balance will be in balance as long as the journal entry had equal debts and credits. *(6.4)*

42. **(B)** The formula for gross profit is:

Sales –	Cost of goods sold	= Gross profit
Sales – (Beginning inventory + Purchases – Ending inventory)		= (Sales × 50%)
400,000 – (80,000 + 220,000 – ?)		= (400,000 × 50%)
400,000 – (300,000 – ?)		= 200,000
400,000 – (300,000 – **100,000**)		= 200,000 *(12.6)*

43. **(B)** The formula for days in inventory is:

365 /	Inventory turnover	= Days in inventory
365 / (Cost of goods sold /	Average Inventory	) = Days in inventory
365 / (Cost of goods sold / (Beg. inventory + End inventory) / 2) = Days in inventory		
365 / (200,000 / (30,000 + 50,000) / 2) = Days in inventory		
365 / (200,000 / 40,000		) = Days in inventory

365 / 5 = 73 Days in inventory   *(12.8)*

44. **(C)** X-Corp would recognize one month of insurance expense. Not (A) or (D) because all the cash was paid on June 1. Not (B) or (E) because $1,100 would recognize 11 months of insurance expense in the month of June. *(13.1)*

45. **(D)** Under the purchases method of recording supplies, a business recognizes supplies expense when it purchases supplies. Therefore, during the year, ABC would have debited supplies expense for the $1,000 of supplies purchased and inventory would still be $100. (D) is the only answer to increase inventory the necessary $20. *(13.2)*

46. **(A)** In a bulk purchase, the total purchase price is allocated to each item in proportion to its value. The total purchase price of assets is every-

thing necessary to make them operational, including shipping. The purchase price is $20,000 (17,000 + 3,000).

	Value	Percent	Price	Cost
Machine A	$ 1,000	10% ×	$20,000 =	$ 2,000
Machine B	6,000	60% ×	20,000 =	12,000
Machine C	3,000	30% ×	20,000 =	6,000
TOTAL	$10,000	100% ×	20,000 =	$20,000

If you chose (B) or (E), you forgot to add the shipping as part of the machine. (C) and (D) do not add up to what was paid. *(14.2)*

47. **(E)**   The general journal entry is:

Cash	150,000	
Notes receivable	100,000	
Accumulated depreciation—building	200,000	
[(400,000 bldg / 40 yrs) × 20 yrs]		
Building		400,000
Gain on sale of building		50,000

Not (A) or (C) because the cash amount is wrong. "Credit" in (B) should be "debit" for it to be right. Not (D) because when a building is sold, the entire amount (400,000) is removed. You might have picked (D) thinking that depreciation over 20 years lowered the building account. Instead, depreciation goes into the contra-asset account called "accumulated depreciation—building." *(11.1 and 14.3)*

48. **(C)**   All costs are part of getting Miguel's asset operational, and thus are part of the cost of the asset, so (B) and (E) are wrong. There is no rental expense (A) or loss (D). *(14.4)*

49. **(B)**   Answers (A) and (E) report the sale in the wrong section of the cash flow statement. The net income from operations amount, which starts the Cash Flow Statement (indirect method) does not contain the gain on the sale (D), nor is the gain found under cash flow from operations (C). Instead the gain gets added to the book value of the asset sold to calculate cash flow from the sale. *(14.5)*

50. **(A)** Double declining balance method does not use salvage value in calculating the depreciable amount. The formula is:

[Book value at the beginning of the year / Life] $\times$ 2 = Depreciation

Year 1: [$30,000 / 3] $\times$ 2 = $20,000

Year 2: [($30,000 – $20,000 first yr depr) / 3] $\times$ 2 = $6,667 *(15.2)*

51. **(B)** The formula for units of production depreciation is:

(Cost – Salvage) / Total estimated units $\times$ Units this year = Depreciation expense

($30,000 – $3,000) / 100,000 $\times$ 30,000 (2nd year) = $8,100 *(15.2)*

52. **(C)** Look up the first-year decimal under 5-year property and multiply it by the cost ($11,000 \times .2 = 2,200$). Tax depreciation does not use salvage value, so (D) is wrong. The table automatically builds in the half-year convention, so no need to divide your answer by 2, making answers (A) and (B) wrong. Do not use the estimated useful life as in answer (E); use the IRS-defined life. *(15.2)*

53. **(C)** Not (A) or (B) because businesses may change accounting estimates at any time without making any retroactive adjustment. (D) is correct for changes in accounting methods, but not for changes in accounting estimates. Answer (E) violates the Matching Principle. *(15.5)*

54. **(D)** Landscaping close to a building has a life equal to that of the building. Not (A) because assets with a life longer than one year are not expensed. Not (B) or (E) because land improvements are depreciated. Debiting accumulated depreciation (C) happens only when renovation of an existing asset extends its life. *(16.1)*

55. **(A)** Intangible assets cannot be touched and must be represented by documents. The gold coins are touchable. All the other assets are not. *(16.2)*

56. **(E)** If an intangible asset has an indefinite life—such as the trade name—it is not amortized, so not (B). The book copyright should be amortized, however, so not (C). If the economic life is shorter than the legal life—such as the election book—use the economic life, so not (A). Not (D) because what gets amortized is the historical cost, not the market value. *(16.2)*

57. **(B)** The formula to compute depletion is:

(Hist. cost of minerals / Est. total units of minerals) $\times$ Units mined = Depletion

($600,000   /   200,000   ) $\times$ 50,000   = $150,000

The journal entry is: debit depletion expense $150,000; credit accumulated depletion $150,000. The words "amortization" and "depreciation" make (A) and (C) wrong. The amount in (E) is wrong. Crediting the asset itself (D) would be correct for an intangible asset, but natural resources use an accumulated depletion account. *(16.3)*

58. **(D)** This company has eight days of unpaid wages on 12/31/x5. At $1,000/day, that equals $8,000 of wages expense not yet recorded. Not (A), (B), or (C) because they accrue only three days of wages expense. Answer (E) accrues too much. Answers (C) and (E) are wrong also because they reverse the debits and credits. *(17.2)*

59. **(C)** On 20x1 sales, there is an estimated warranty liability of $7,000 (700,000 $\times$ 1%). If $2,000 has already been paid out, Smokey should estimate another $5,000 of warranty expense. The journal entry will be: debit warranty expense $5,000; credit warranties payable $5,000. Not (D) or (E) because Smokey did not get any warranty income by charging extra for the warranty. Answers (A) and (B) are the wrong amount, and (B) also incorrectly credits an expense. *(17.4)*

60. **(E)** The current portion of a loan is the principal that is due within the coming year. Because the loan payments are semi-annual, consider only the next two payments. Add both numbers in the circle on the following schedule: *(17.5)*

Pmt Date	Payment	Principal	10% Interest	Balance
				100,000
6/30/x1	6,000	1,000	5,000	99,000
12/31/x1	6,000	1,050	4,950	97,950
6/30/x2	6,000	1,103	4,898	96,848
12/31/x2	6,000	1,158	4,842	95,690
6/30/x3	6,000	1,216	4,784	94,474

61. **(E)** Because the loan payment is on the last day of the year, all interest expense owed for the year will be completely paid. If the loan payment were on January 1, 20x2, Smokey would owe $4,950 of interest on 12/31/20x1. *(17.6)*

62. **(A)** Below are the VJEs. Column 2 accrues the wages expense and liability. The wages expense will close to zero at the end of the year as shown in Column 3. The reversing entry in Column 5 allows Smith & Co.'s accountant to record payroll as always. The balance in Column 7 shows that wages expense includes only the $5,000 of 20x2 wages. *(17.7)*

1	2	3	4	5	6	7
Partial list of accounts	12/31/x1	Closing entry	Balance	Reverse 1/1/x2	Payday	Balance
Cash					(6,000)	(6,000)
Retained earnings		1,000	1,000			1,000
Wages payable	(1,000)		(1,000)	1,000		—
Wages expense	1,000	(1,000)	—	(1,000)	6,000	5,000

63. **(C)** Bonds are long-term debts, so they will show up on the balance sheet. *(18.1)* The $1 million of cash in will appear in the cash flow statement. *(20.4)* The transaction issuing the bonds does not appear on the income statement, although the interest expense later will show up there. The bonds never appear on the retained earnings statement.

64. **(D)** A price of 105 means Jones & Jones gets 105% of the face amount (100,000) of the bonds, or $105,000 less the $3,000 issuance cost, for a net amount of $102,000. The journal entry to issue these bonds is:

Cash	102,000	
Bonds issuance cost expense	3,000	
Bonds payable		100,000
Premium on bonds payable (amount over face)		5,000

(18.2)

65. **(B)** Calculate the bond interest expense by multiplying the book value of the bonds × market interest [(100,000 + 10,000) × 8% × ½ year = $4,400]. Calculate the $4,500 periodic payment by multiplying the face

amount by the face rate (100,000 × 9% × ½ year [semi-annual payment] = $4,500). The journal entry to make the periodic payment is:

Bond interest expense (110,000 × 8% × ½)	4,400	
Premium on bond payable (whatever balances)	100	
Cash (100,000 × 9% × ½)		4,500
		(18.3)

66. **(B)** The deferred revenue account is a liability reflecting the future duty to publish magazines. Holliday Tool Magazine must recognize the $120,000 as revenue over the 12 months of the subscription. The journal entry to record one month of revenue *(18.4)* is:

Deferred subscriptions revenue	$10,000
Subscriptions revenue	10,000

This is revenue to the magazine, not an expense, so (D) is wrong.

67. **(C)** After allocating $60,000 (30,000 + 20,000 + 10,000) of guaranteed payments, there remains a $10,000 loss in the partnership (50,000 earnings − 60,000 guaranteed payments). Partner A's share of that loss is $2,000 (10,000 × 20%). Partner A's share of profits is her guaranteed payment less her share of the loss for a net of $28,000 (30,000 − 2,000). *(19.1)*

68. **(A)** Selling shares to investors is "issuing." Issued stock is outstanding unless the company buys back some of its own stock as treasury stock. The articles of incorporation "authorize" the maximum number of shares. Outstanding shares are 90,000 (100,000 − 10,000 treasury stock), so only answer (A) is correct. *(19.2)*

69. **(D)** If X-Corp gives Mr. X a bonus, X-Corp would lower net income by $200,000, thus saving corporate income tax. None of the other choices have that result. Dividends are nondeductible. The stock dividend (C) and the stock split (E) do not result in removing any cash from the corporation. *(19.3)*

70. **(E)** The treasury stock account is a contra-equity account with a debit balance. It contains the total amount paid for the treasury stock. The journal entry to sell this treasury stock is: debit cash $14,000; credit treasury stock $10,000; credit additional paid-in capital $4,000. Not (B) because no new stock is issued. "Debit" in (C) should be "credit" for it to be true. Not (D)

because GAAP does not allow recognizing a gain on the sale of a company's own stock. *(19.5)*

71. **(B)** Only revenues, expenses, and dividends close out, so not (D) or (E). Close revenues with debits, and close expenses and dividends with credits. *(19.6)*

72. **(D)** The order is (D), (A), (E), (B), and (C). *(20.1)*

73. **(E)** Depreciation expense lowers net income. Because it is a non-cash expense, depreciation gets added back as a positive adjustment to net income on the cash flow statement. All the other answers are false statements. *(20.4)*

74. **(C)** The formula for earnings per share is:

(Net income – PS dividends) / Number of CS outstanding = EPS

(200,000 – 20,000) /   100,000   = $1.80

(20.5)

75. **(C)** The formula for book value per share of common stock is:

(Total equity   – PS equity) /Number of CS outstanding = BVPS

([800,000 assets – 100,000 liab] – 100,000) / (60,000 CS – 10,000 TS) = $12.00

(20.5)

ANSWER
SHEETS

CLEP FINANCIAL ACCOUNTING

PRACTICE TEST 1

1. Ⓐ Ⓑ Ⓒ Ⓓ Ⓔ	26. Ⓐ Ⓑ Ⓒ Ⓓ Ⓔ	51. Ⓐ Ⓑ Ⓒ Ⓓ Ⓔ
2. Ⓐ Ⓑ Ⓒ Ⓓ Ⓔ	27. Ⓐ Ⓑ Ⓒ Ⓓ Ⓔ	52. Ⓐ Ⓑ Ⓒ Ⓓ Ⓔ
3. Ⓐ Ⓑ Ⓒ Ⓓ Ⓔ	28. Ⓐ Ⓑ Ⓒ Ⓓ Ⓔ	53. Ⓐ Ⓑ Ⓒ Ⓓ Ⓔ
4. Ⓐ Ⓑ Ⓒ Ⓓ Ⓔ	29. Ⓐ Ⓑ Ⓒ Ⓓ Ⓔ	54. Ⓐ Ⓑ Ⓒ Ⓓ Ⓔ
5. Ⓐ Ⓑ Ⓒ Ⓓ Ⓔ	30. Ⓐ Ⓑ Ⓒ Ⓓ Ⓔ	55. Ⓐ Ⓑ Ⓒ Ⓓ Ⓔ
6. Ⓐ Ⓑ Ⓒ Ⓓ Ⓔ	31. Ⓐ Ⓑ Ⓒ Ⓓ Ⓔ	56. Ⓐ Ⓑ Ⓒ Ⓓ Ⓔ
7. Ⓐ Ⓑ Ⓒ Ⓓ Ⓔ	32. Ⓐ Ⓑ Ⓒ Ⓓ Ⓔ	57. Ⓐ Ⓑ Ⓒ Ⓓ Ⓔ
8. Ⓐ Ⓑ Ⓒ Ⓓ Ⓔ	33. Ⓐ Ⓑ Ⓒ Ⓓ Ⓔ	58. Ⓐ Ⓑ Ⓒ Ⓓ Ⓔ
9. Ⓐ Ⓑ Ⓒ Ⓓ Ⓔ	34. Ⓐ Ⓑ Ⓒ Ⓓ Ⓔ	59. Ⓐ Ⓑ Ⓒ Ⓓ Ⓔ
10. Ⓐ Ⓑ Ⓒ Ⓓ Ⓔ	35. Ⓐ Ⓑ Ⓒ Ⓓ Ⓔ	60. Ⓐ Ⓑ Ⓒ Ⓓ Ⓔ
11. Ⓐ Ⓑ Ⓒ Ⓓ Ⓔ	36. Ⓐ Ⓑ Ⓒ Ⓓ Ⓔ	61. Ⓐ Ⓑ Ⓒ Ⓓ Ⓔ
12. Ⓐ Ⓑ Ⓒ Ⓓ Ⓔ	37. Ⓐ Ⓑ Ⓒ Ⓓ Ⓔ	62. Ⓐ Ⓑ Ⓒ Ⓓ Ⓔ
13. Ⓐ Ⓑ Ⓒ Ⓓ Ⓔ	38. Ⓐ Ⓑ Ⓒ Ⓓ Ⓔ	63. Ⓐ Ⓑ Ⓒ Ⓓ Ⓔ
14. Ⓐ Ⓑ Ⓒ Ⓓ Ⓔ	39. Ⓐ Ⓑ Ⓒ Ⓓ Ⓔ	64. Ⓐ Ⓑ Ⓒ Ⓓ Ⓔ
15. Ⓐ Ⓑ Ⓒ Ⓓ Ⓔ	40. Ⓐ Ⓑ Ⓒ Ⓓ Ⓔ	65. Ⓐ Ⓑ Ⓒ Ⓓ Ⓔ
16. Ⓐ Ⓑ Ⓒ Ⓓ Ⓔ	41. Ⓐ Ⓑ Ⓒ Ⓓ Ⓔ	66. Ⓐ Ⓑ Ⓒ Ⓓ Ⓔ
17. Ⓐ Ⓑ Ⓒ Ⓓ Ⓔ	42. Ⓐ Ⓑ Ⓒ Ⓓ Ⓔ	67. Ⓐ Ⓑ Ⓒ Ⓓ Ⓔ
18. Ⓐ Ⓑ Ⓒ Ⓓ Ⓔ	43. Ⓐ Ⓑ Ⓒ Ⓓ Ⓔ	68. Ⓐ Ⓑ Ⓒ Ⓓ Ⓔ
19. Ⓐ Ⓑ Ⓒ Ⓓ Ⓔ	44. Ⓐ Ⓑ Ⓒ Ⓓ Ⓔ	69. Ⓐ Ⓑ Ⓒ Ⓓ Ⓔ
20. Ⓐ Ⓑ Ⓒ Ⓓ Ⓔ	45. Ⓐ Ⓑ Ⓒ Ⓓ Ⓔ	70. Ⓐ Ⓑ Ⓒ Ⓓ Ⓔ
21. Ⓐ Ⓑ Ⓒ Ⓓ Ⓔ	46. Ⓐ Ⓑ Ⓒ Ⓓ Ⓔ	71. Ⓐ Ⓑ Ⓒ Ⓓ Ⓔ
22. Ⓐ Ⓑ Ⓒ Ⓓ Ⓔ	47. Ⓐ Ⓑ Ⓒ Ⓓ Ⓔ	72. Ⓐ Ⓑ Ⓒ Ⓓ Ⓔ
23. Ⓐ Ⓑ Ⓒ Ⓓ Ⓔ	48. Ⓐ Ⓑ Ⓒ Ⓓ Ⓔ	73. Ⓐ Ⓑ Ⓒ Ⓓ Ⓔ
24. Ⓐ Ⓑ Ⓒ Ⓓ Ⓔ	49. Ⓐ Ⓑ Ⓒ Ⓓ Ⓔ	74. Ⓐ Ⓑ Ⓒ Ⓓ Ⓔ
25. Ⓐ Ⓑ Ⓒ Ⓓ Ⓔ	50. Ⓐ Ⓑ Ⓒ Ⓓ Ⓔ	75. Ⓐ Ⓑ Ⓒ Ⓓ Ⓔ

CLEP FINANCIAL ACCOUNTING

PRACTICE TEST 2

1. (A) (B) (C) (D) (E)
2. (A) (B) (C) (D) (E)
3. (A) (B) (C) (D) (E)
4. (A) (B) (C) (D) (E)
5. (A) (B) (C) (D) (E)
6. (A) (B) (C) (D) (E)
7. (A) (B) (C) (D) (E)
8. (A) (B) (C) (D) (E)
9. (A) (B) (C) (D) (E)
10. (A) (B) (C) (D) (E)
11. (A) (B) (C) (D) (E)
12. (A) (B) (C) (D) (E)
13. (A) (B) (C) (D) (E)
14. (A) (B) (C) (D) (E)
15. (A) (B) (C) (D) (E)
16. (A) (B) (C) (D) (E)
17. (A) (B) (C) (D) (E)
18. (A) (B) (C) (D) (E)
19. (A) (B) (C) (D) (E)
20. (A) (B) (C) (D) (E)
21. (A) (B) (C) (D) (E)
22. (A) (B) (C) (D) (E)
23. (A) (B) (C) (D) (E)
24. (A) (B) (C) (D) (E)
25. (A) (B) (C) (D) (E)

26. (A) (B) (C) (D) (E)
27. (A) (B) (C) (D) (E)
28. (A) (B) (C) (D) (E)
29. (A) (B) (C) (D) (E)
30. (A) (B) (C) (D) (E)
31. (A) (B) (C) (D) (E)
32. (A) (B) (C) (D) (E)
33. (A) (B) (C) (D) (E)
34. (A) (B) (C) (D) (E)
35. (A) (B) (C) (D) (E)
36. (A) (B) (C) (D) (E)
37. (A) (B) (C) (D) (E)
38. (A) (B) (C) (D) (E)
39. (A) (B) (C) (D) (E)
40. (A) (B) (C) (D) (E)
41. (A) (B) (C) (D) (E)
42. (A) (B) (C) (D) (E)
43. (A) (B) (C) (D) (E)
44. (A) (B) (C) (D) (E)
45. (A) (B) (C) (D) (E)
46. (A) (B) (C) (D) (E)
47. (A) (B) (C) (D) (E)
48. (A) (B) (C) (D) (E)
49. (A) (B) (C) (D) (E)
50. (A) (B) (C) (D) (E)

51. (A) (B) (C) (D) (E)
52. (A) (B) (C) (D) (E)
53. (A) (B) (C) (D) (E)
54. (A) (B) (C) (D) (E)
55. (A) (B) (C) (D) (E)
56. (A) (B) (C) (D) (E)
57. (A) (B) (C) (D) (E)
58. (A) (B) (C) (D) (E)
59. (A) (B) (C) (D) (E)
60. (A) (B) (C) (D) (E)
61. (A) (B) (C) (D) (E)
62. (A) (B) (C) (D) (E)
63. (A) (B) (C) (D) (E)
64. (A) (B) (C) (D) (E)
65. (A) (B) (C) (D) (E)
66. (A) (B) (C) (D) (E)
67. (A) (B) (C) (D) (E)
68. (A) (B) (C) (D) (E)
69. (A) (B) (C) (D) (E)
70. (A) (B) (C) (D) (E)
71. (A) (B) (C) (D) (E)
72. (A) (B) (C) (D) (E)
73. (A) (B) (C) (D) (E)
74. (A) (B) (C) (D) (E)
75. (A) (B) (C) (D) (E)

Index

Index

REA's Test Preps
The Best in Test Preparation

- REA "Test Preps" are **far more** comprehensive than any other test preparation series
- Each book contains up to **eight** full-length practice tests based on the most recent exams
- **Every** type of question likely to be given on the exams is included
- Answers are accompanied by **full** and **detailed** explanations

REA publishes over 70 Test Preparation volumes in several series. They include:

Advanced Placement Exams (APs)
Art History
Biology
Calculus AB & BC
Chemistry
Economics
English Language & Composition
English Literature & Composition
European History
French Language
Government & Politics
Latin
Physics B & C
Psychology
Spanish Language
Statistics
United States History
World History

College-Level Examination Program (CLEP)
Analyzing and Interpreting Literature
College Algebra
Freshman College Composition
General Examinations
General Examinations Review
History of the United States I
History of the United States II
Introduction to Educational Psychology
Human Growth and Development
Introductory Psychology
Introductory Sociology
Principles of Management
Principles of Marketing
Spanish
Western Civilization I
Western Civilization II

SAT Subject Tests
Biology E/M
Chemistry
French
German
Literature
Mathematics Level 1, 2
Physics
Spanish
United States History

Graduate Record Exams (GREs)
Biology
Chemistry
Computer Science
General
Literature in English
Mathematics
Physics
Psychology

ACT - ACT Assessment

ASVAB - Armed Services Vocational Aptitude Battery

CBEST - California Basic Educational Skills Test

CDL - Commercial Driver License Exam

CLAST - College Level Academic Skills Test

COOP & HSPT - Catholic High School Admission Tests

ELM - California State University Entry Level Mathematics Exam

FE (EIT) - Fundamentals of Engineering Exams - For Both AM & PM Exams

FTCE - Florida Teacher Certification Examinations

GED - (U.S. Edition)

GMAT - Graduate Management Admission Test

LSAT - Law School Admission Test

MAT - Miller Analogies Test

MCAT - Medical College Admission Test

MTEL - Massachusetts Tests for Educator Licensure

NJ HSPA - New Jersey High School Proficiency Assessment

NYSTCE - New York State Teacher Certification Examinations

PRAXIS PLT - Principles of Learning & Teaching Tests

PRAXIS PPST - Pre-Professional Skills Tests

PSAT/NMSQT

SAT

TExES - Texas Examinations of Educator Standards

THEA - Texas Higher Education Assessment

TOEFL - Test of English as a Foreign Language

TOEIC - Test of English for International Communication

USMLE Steps 1,2,3 - U.S. Medical Licensing Exams

Research & Education Association
61 Ethel Road W., Piscataway, NJ 08854
Phone: (732) 819-8880   **website: www.rea.com**

Please send me more information about your Test Prep books.

Name _____

Address _____

City _____ State _____ Zip _____